RICHARDSON

T0016083

Big Book of General Knowledge Crosswords

150 challenging quiz crossword puzzles

Book 1

Published by Richardson Publishing Limited.
www.richardsonpublishing.com

10 9 8 7 6 5 4 3 2 1

© 2023 Richardson Publishing Limited.
Puzzles © 2023 H Bauer Publishing.

Typeset by Clarity Media Ltd.

Cover design by Junior London Ltd.

ISBN 978-1-913602-36-9

Printed and bound by CPI Group (UK) Ltd, Croydon CR0 4YY.

The contents of this publication are believed correct at the time of printing. Nevertheless the publisher can accept no responsibility for errors, omissions, or changes in the detail given, or for any expense or loss thereby caused.

A catalogue record for this book is available from the British Library.

If you would like to comment on any aspect of this book, please contact us at:

E-mail: puzzles@richardsonpublishing.com

Follow us on Twitter @puzzlesandgames
instagram.com/richardsonpuzzlesandgames
facebook.com/richardsonpuzzlesandgames

MIX
Paper | Supporting
responsible forestry
FSC
www.fsc.org
FSC® C171272

Contents

Crosswords   6

Solutions   308

Instructions

Write the answers to each of the questions
in the grid to complete the crossword puzzle.
Answers may run across two or more entries and
in those instances it is detailed in the question.

Crosswords

Across

3 Frances ___, Best Actress in a Leading Role Oscar winner for Three Billboards Outside Ebbing, Missouri (9)

8 2006 fantasy novel by Sherwood Smith (4)

9 1987 novel by Robin Cook (8)

10 City in Ventura County, California, US, associated with the strawberry industry (6)

13 Gareth ___, rugby union wing; 1977 Wales Test debutant against France (5)

14 2014 romcom starring Cameron Diaz and Jason Segel (3,4)

15 **and 21** 1976 Swedish Rally winner in the World Rally Championships (3,6)

16 Winged sandals such as those worn by Hermes in Greek mythology (7)

17 1966 Grand National winner ridden by Tim Norman (5)

21 **See 15 Across**

22 Place also called Calvary outside the walls of Jerusalem where Jesus was crucified (8)

23 Vikram ___, author of novels The Golden Gate and An Equal Music (4)

24 In philately, a joined pair of stamps printed with one inverted in relation to the other (4-5)

Down

1 1851 opera by Giuseppe Verdi whose title character is a court jester (9)

2 **and 18** 2011 thriller by Gerald Seymour (1,8,5)

4 Charles ___, US golfer; 1971 Masters Tournament winner (5)

5 Tenth month of the year in the Gregorian calendar (7)

6 **and 19** Warship of Henry VIII that sank in the Solent in 1545 and was raised in 1982 (4,4)

7 Yannick ___, 1983 French Open singles tennis championship winner (4)

11 2010 film comedy starring Will Forte in the title role (9)

12 **and 14 Down** 2004 biopic about the life of Bobby Darin (6,3,3)

14 **See 12 Down**

15 Currency of French Indochina between 1885 and 1952 (7)

18 **See 2 Down**

19 **See 6 Down**

20 James ___, author of 1957 autobiographical novel A Death in the Family (4)

Across

1 and 8 Pirate flag consisting of a white skull and crossbones on a black background (5,5)

7 John ___, 1987, 1994 and 1995 British Fashion Awards Designer of the Year (8)

8 See 1 Across

10 2009 sci-fi film starring Bruce Willis and Radha Mitchell (10)

12 James McNeill ___, US artist whose works include Arrangement in Grey and Black, No 1: The Artist's Mother (8)

14 and 18 Down Actor who played Jason Grimshaw in ITV soap Coronation Street from 2000-16 (4,6)

16 Anne-Marie ___, actress who portrayed Julia Lennon in 2009 biopic Nowhere Boy (4)

17 Stork of southeast Asia and India such as the greater ___ or lesser ___ (8)

20 The ___, 1978 debut novel by Timothy Mo (6,4)

23 Digital system used in British television for the reception of stereo sound signals (5)

24 and 22 Down 1981 romcom starring Gordon John Sinclair and Dee Hepburn (8,4)

25 1981 novel by Peter Carey (5)

Down

1 Town on the River Tyne; home of the Venerable Bede (6)

2 Paris ___, LGBT campaigner and journalist (4)

3 1918 debut novel by Wyndham Lewis (4)

4 William ___, commander of the HMS Bounty who died in 1817 (5)

5 Inlet of the Atlantic Ocean in Cork, Republic of Ireland, housing Whiddy Island (6,3)

6 Valerie ___, actress who played the title role in 1948 film drama Blanche Fury (6)

9 Evans ___, 2004 London Marathon and Chicago Marathon men's race winner (5)

11 Black-skinned wine grape of California (9)

13 The ___, 2006 children's novel by Lemony Snicket (3)

15 Anthony ___, Best Actor in a Supporting Role Oscar winner for Viva Zapata! (5)

16 1992 film drama starring Jeremy Irons and Juliette Binoche (6)

18 See 14 Across

19 Daniel ___, author of Moll Flanders (5)

21 Madison ___, 2017 US Open singles tennis championship runner-up (4)

22 See 24 Across

Across

1 Golf links that hosted The Open Championship in 2018 (10)

8 European republic; capital Reykjavik (7)

9 Lucy ___, actress who played Amy Squirrel in 2011 film comedy Bad Teacher (5)

10 **and 22 Down** Forward section of a missile, aircraft or rocket (4,4)

11 Number opposite sixteen on a dartboard (4)

12 Josef ___, Czech composer of symphony Asrael and tone poem A Summer's Tale (3)

14 1996 novel by Patrick McGrath (6)

15 John ___, English scientist born in 1766 noted for his research into colour blindness (6)

18 Ornamental sphere surmounted by a cross; part of the Crown Jewels (3)

20 Edmund ___, English tragic actor who played Shylock at Drury Lane in 1814 (4)

21 **and 2 Down** 1998 novel by Maeve Binchy (4,4)

23 Name by which the Autodromo Internazionale Enzo e Dino Ferrari is better known (5)

24 City in central Sudan; scene of the defeat of a British and Egyptian army by the Mahdi in 1883 (2,5)

25 The ___, 1889 Savoy Opera by Gilbert and Sullivan subtitled The King of Barataria (10)

Down

1 John ___, author of novels Go Away Death and The Executioners (7)

2 **See 21 Across**

3 Character played by Harold Sakata in 1964 action film Goldfinger (6)

4 Comic book character whose alter ego is Clark Kent (8)

5 Neil ___, musician and comedian who played Ron Nasty in 1978 TV film The Rutles: All You Need Is Cash (5)

6 Largest city in Minnesota, US, west of state capital Saint Paul (11)

7 1956 film musical starring Deborah Kerr and Yul Brynner (3,4,3,1)

13 Seaport on North Island, New Zealand; capital of the country from 1841-65 (8)

16 P L ___, author of 1934 children's book Mary Poppins (7)

17 Francis ___, Scottish painter whose works include 1921's Roses at Cassis (6)

19 Island of Equatorial Guinea formerly known as Fernando Po (5)

22 **See 10 Across**

No. 3

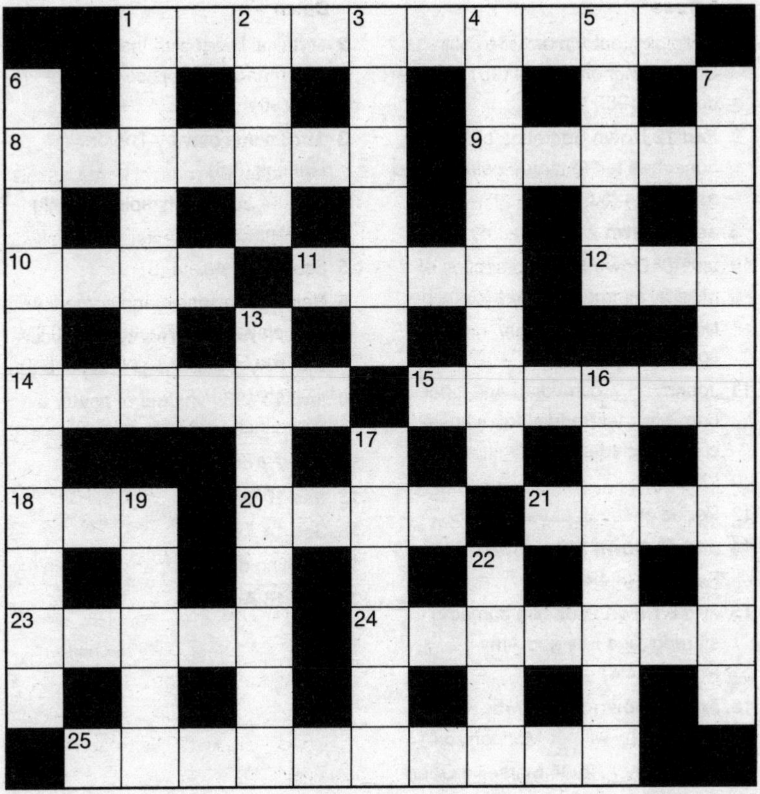

Across

1 Yves ___, actor married to actress Simone Signoret from 1951 until her death in 1985 (7)

7 **and 12 Down** Secretion of the honeybee fed to larvae being raised as queens (5,5)

8 **and 5 Down** 2011 novel by Lisa Gardner (4,3,4)

9 Musical instruction that a piece be performed smoothly and connectedly (6)

11 Johnny ___, comedian and actor born Michael Pennington whose credits include BBC TV sitcom Ideal (5)

13 Period of seven days (4)

14 **and 18 Down** 2011 novel by A L Kennedy (3,4,4)

15 **and 6 Down** 2008 film comedy starring Tina Fey and Amy Poehler (4,4)

16 **and 20 Down** Jockey who rode 1973 Derby winner Morston (5,4)

17 Dominik ___, 2004 Marseille Open singles tennis tournament winner (6)

21 1985 film drama starring Harrison Ford and Kelly McGillis (7)

22 **See 9 Down**

23 Doris ___, Iran-born winner of the 2007 Nobel Prize in Literature (7)

Down

2 Mythical beast with the upper body of a man and the lower body of an ass (10)

3 1973 stage play by Trevor Griffiths (3,5)

4 Erki ___, 2000 Olympic decathlon gold medallist (4)

5 **See 8 Across**

6 **See 15 Across**

9 **and 22 Across** Variety of lettuce with frilly reddish-pink leaves (5,5)

10 **and 13** 1964 volume of poetry by Philip Larkin (3,7,8)

12 **See 7 Across**

13 **See 10 Down**

18 **See 14 Across**

19 Fighting dog of Japanese origin (4)

20 **See 16 Across**

Across

1 In Greek mythology, the fluid said to flow in the veins of the gods (5)

4 and 7 Down 1859 novel by Charles Dickens featuring characters Charles Darnay and Sydney Carton (1,4,2,3,6)

10 Rudolf ___, composer of 1925 operetta The Vagabond King (5)

11 Town in Cornwall northeast of Camborne once associated with the copper mining industry (7)

12 See 22 Down

13 and 23 1960 Olympic 1,500m gold medallist (4,7)

15 Gordon ___, 1983-90 England midfielder; 1982 Aston Villa European Cup Final winner (6)

17 Alyssa ___, actress who played Phoebe Halliwell in US television series Charmed from 1998-2006 (6)

19 Common ___, silvery-grey and white bird nicknamed the sea-swallow (4)

20 2012 novel by Lynda La Plante (8)

23 See 13 Across

24 2019 film thriller starring Joaquin Phoenix and Robert De Niro (5)

25 Long-legged doglike mammal of south Asia and Africa (5)

26 John ___, 1976 Olympic figure skating gold medallist (5)

Down

2 Capital of Egypt (5)

3 Alfred ___, author of 1898 novel Owd Bob: The Grey Dog of Kenmuir (8)

5 and 18 Actor who played the title role in 1980s BBC TV drama series Tucker's Luck (4,5)

6 German singer who recorded 1999 UK no 1 single Mambo No 5 (A Little Bit of) (3,4)

7 See 4 Across

8 Large long-necked long-legged wading bird such as the common ___ or whooping ___ (5)

9 1970s BBC TV drama series about road haulage firm Hammond Transport Services (3,8)

14 Nocturnal mammal also known as a honey bear (8)

16 Joe ___, former Wasps back-rower; 1999 England Test debutant against Tonga (7)

18 See 5 Down

21 Amy ___, US actress who played Beatrice in 2012 comedy-drama film Much Ado About Nothing (5)

22 and 12 Across English actor who starred as Chief Supt John Kingdom in 1970s ITV drama series New Scotland Yard (4,8)

No. 6

Across

6 Best Actor in a Supporting Role Oscar winner for Iris (3,9)

8 and 22 1908 children's book by Kenneth Grahame (3,4,2,3,7)

9 Standard unit of currency of India (5)

10 Martin ___, Astronomer Royal from 1972-82 (4)

12 Heading or initial letter in a manuscript printed or painted in red ink (6)

14 Samuel ___, 1990 Commonwealth Games 800m gold medallist (5)

15 See 12 Down

16 Curve with an S-shaped profile used in coving (4)

19 Sixth largest of the Hawaiian Islands; nickname the Pineapple Isle (5)

21 Italian painter whose works include 1503 oil St Jerome Punishing the Heretic Sabinian (7)

22 See 8 Across

Down

1 West Sussex village housing a 12th-century castle and a manor house (8)

2 Fragrant rootstock of various irises used in perfumery (5)

3 City in Central Province, Sri Lanka, designated a UNESCO World Heritage site in 1988 (5)

4 Women's badminton world team championship (4,3)

5 Belinda Bauer novel longlisted for the Booker Prize in 2018 (4)

6 English agriculturist born in 1674 who developed the seed drill (6,4)

7 Republic in the Indian Ocean, capital Victoria, whose largest island is Mahe (10)

11 Russian space station launched in February 1986 (3)

12 and 15 Across Australian actor who portrayed Winston Churchill in 2009 action film Inglourious Basterds (3,6)

13 Ultimate battle in Scandinavian mythology between the gods and forces of evil (8)

14 1957-65 BBC TV current affairs programme presented by Cliff Michelmore (7)

17 Swimming stroke in which feet are kicked like paddles and arms reach forward and pull back through the water (5)

18 Timothy ___, 2014 Cannes Film Festival Best Actor winner for Mr Turner (5)

20 The ___, one of three ships commanded by Christopher Columbus in 1492 (4)

No. 6

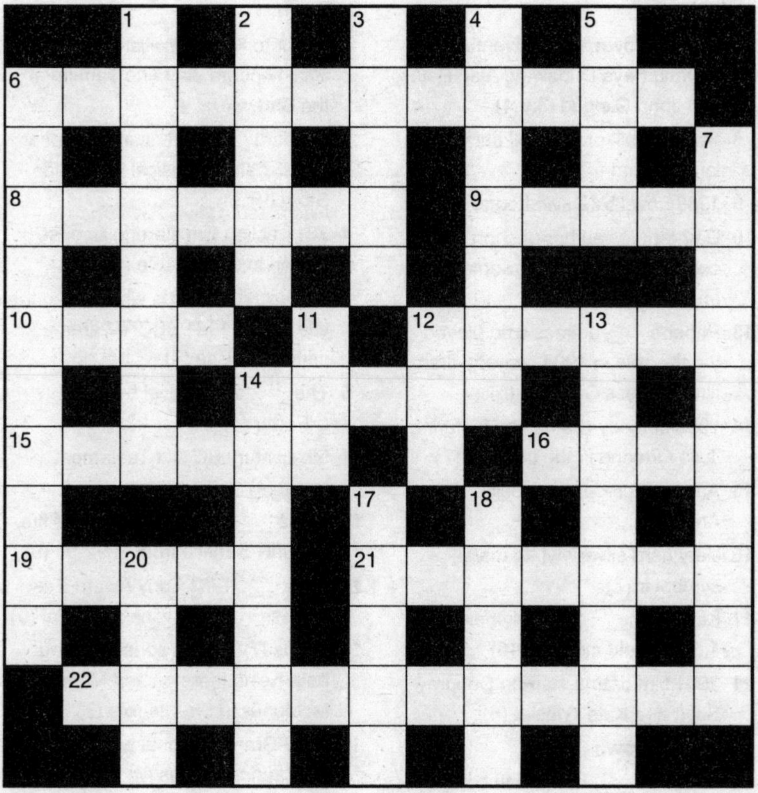

Across

3 and 19 Down 1983 adventure film starring Faye Dunaway, Alan Bates and John Gielgud (3,6,4)

8 Sword similar to the foil but with a larger guard (4)

9 1988 novel by David Lodge (4,4)

10 Damon ___, author of short story collections More Than Somewhat and Take It Easy (6)

13 Phoebe ___, actress who played the title role in 1994 comedy-drama film Princess Caraboo (5)

14 1995 comedy-drama film featuring Julia Ormond in the title role (7)

15 Animal representing zodiac sign Aries (3)

16 Very hard silvery-white metal; symbol Ir (7)

17 Kipchoge ___, 1968 Olympic 1,500m gold medallist (5)

21 2001 film drama starring Dougray Scott and Kate Winslet (6)

22 See 20 Down

23 Emanuel ___, Hungarian composer born in 1863; inventor of a two-keyboard piano (4)

24 Device invented by Leon Foucault consisting of a spinning wheel on an axle (9)

Down

1 Suitor to Kate in William Shakespeare play The Taming of the Shrew (9)

2 Leonard ___, American composer of 1957 stage musical West Side Story (9)

4 2011 action film starring Saoirse Ronan in the title role (5)

5 Saskia ___, actress who played the title role in 1991 BBC TV drama series Clarissa (7)

6 The ___, 2017 novel by Dawn O'Porter (4)

7 5th-century BC Old Testament priest (4)

11 Stella ___, Director General of the Security Service from 1992-96 (9)

12 Jane ___, 1981 Tony Award Best Actress in a Play winner for Piaf (9)

14 1970s ITV drama series starring both Kevin Moreton and Mark McManus in the title role (3)

15 1979 Grand National winner ridden by Maurice Barnes (7)

18 Greek author of fables (5)

19 See 3 Across

20 and 22 Across Cyprus-born chairman of Millwall FC from 1997-2005; entrepreneur on BBC TV show Dragons' Den from 2005-12 (4,8)

No. 8

Across

1 John Francis ___, US automobile manufacturing pioneer who died in 1920 (5)

7 Francis ___, British rear admiral who devised a scale of wind velocities in 1805 (8)

8 Secret criminal organisation originating in Sicily that spread to mainland Italy and the US (5)

10 Cured ham from Italy usually served as an hors d'oeuvre (10)

12 **and 16 Down** 1951 novel by Daphne du Maurier (2,6,6)

14 Mixture of smoke, fog and chemical fumes (4)

16 Chessman also called a castle (4)

17 Ricardo ___, Argentine golfer; 2009 SAS Masters tournament winner (8)

20 Inactive stratovolcano; highest mountain in Ecuador (10)

23 Old Testament Hittite officer married to Bathsheba (5)

24 Agent for Silvia, in her escape, in William Shakespeare play The Two Gentlemen of Verona (8)

25 Nick ___, presenter of Channel 4 game show Countdown from 2012-2021 (5)

Down

1 Chinese appetiser of steamed dumplings containing fillings (3,3)

2 Raven in 1841 Charles Dickens novel Barnaby Rudge (4)

3 Supreme god of the ancient Greeks (4)

4 Roman god of love (5)

5 Joop ___, Dutch cyclist; 1980 Tour de France winner (9)

6 Shirley ___, 1982 Commonwealth 100m hurdles gold medallist (6)

9 Builder of the ship Argo in Greek mythology (5)

11 Garry ___, 1987-96 Leeds rugby league centre; 1991 Man of Steel Award winner (9)

13 Boxing sanctioning organisation run by Edward S Levine (1,1,1)

15 University city; capital of Northern Region, Malawi (5)

16 **See 12 Across**

18 String instrument common in Central European folk music placed horizontally and plucked (6)

19 Barack ___, US president from 2009-17 (5)

21 Stanley ___, FIFA president from 1961-74 (4)

22 Small slender European freshwater fish also called an ide (4)

No. 8

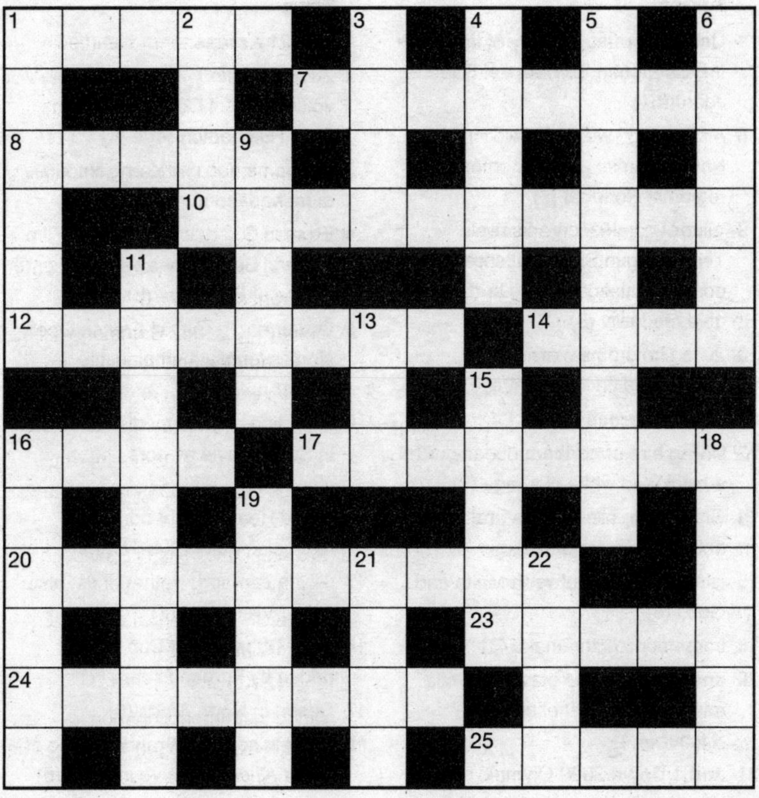

No. 9

Across

1 Unincorporated territory of the US in the Caribbean Sea; capital San Juan (6,4)

8 Archipelago west of Morocco in the North Atlantic; an autonomous region of Portugal (7)

9 Viktor ___, 1935 World Table Tennis Championships singles, doubles, mixed doubles and team gold medallist (5)

10 2015 film drama starring Brie Larson and Jacob Tremblay (4)

11 **See 20 Across**

12 Diving bird of northern oceans with a black and white plumage (3)

14 Greek god; son of Zeus and Leto and twin brother of Artemis (6)

15 Island that lies between Malta and Gozo (6)

18 Large constrictor snake (3)

20 **and 11** Actor who played the title role in 2007 film thriller The Hitcher (4,4)

21 **and 1 Down** 2000 Olympic men's long jump gold medallist (4,7)

23 Swiss grated potato pancake sometimes flavoured with bacon (5)

24 Ludovico ___, Italian author of epic poem Orlando Furioso and play I Suppositi (7)

25 D B ___, India Test cricketer who made an unbeaten 164 against Australia in Mumbai in 1986 (10)

Down

1 **See 21 Across**

2 2013 animated film featuring the voice talent of Colin Farrell and Josh Hutcherson (4)

3 Seaport in County Kerry, Republic of Ireland, on the River Lee (6)

4 Edward G ___, 1949 Cannes Film Festival Best Actor award winner for House of Strangers (8)

5 Guillermo ___, 2004 French Open singles tennis championship runner-up (5)

6 Selection of savoury dishes served in Scandinavia as hors d'oeuvres (11)

7 World Heavyweight boxing champion from 1908-15 (4,7)

13 City in Zeeland, Netherlands, also called Vlissingen (8)

16 2007 Dubai World Cup winner ridden by Fernando Jara (7)

17 Desert in North Africa (6)

19 River in northern France; scene of a major Allied offensive in 1918 (5)

22 Town in Highland, northeast Scotland, due south of John O'Groats (4)

Across

1 Natalya ___, 2012 Olympic 400m hurdles gold medallist (7)

7 P ___, India Test cricketer who took 5-106 against England at Lord's in 2011 (5)

8 Anthony ___, Best Actor in a Leading Role Oscar winner for The Silence of the Lambs (7)

9 **and 17** 1947 novel by Compton Mackenzie (6,6)

11 **See 18 Down**

13 Male of a red deer aged five years old or more (4)

14 1988 children's novel by Roald Dahl (7)

15 Lake ___, largest natural lake in Wales (4)

16 Woollen fabric resembling felt used for the tops of billiard tables (5)

17 **See 9 Across**

21 Disease of children caused by a deficiency of vitamin D (7)

22 The ___, Test cricket series between England and Australia (5)

23 **and 4 Down** 2005 Cheltenham Gold Cup winner ridden by Barry Geraghty (7,4)

Down

2 2019 Australian Open women's singles tennis championship winner (5,5)

3 Seaport and capital of Kanagawa Prefecture, Honshu, Japan (8)

4 **See 23 Across**

5 Eric ___, rugby union wing; 1995 New Zealand Test debutant against Wales (4)

6 Willie ___, MLB player nicknamed The Say Hey Kid; New York Giants 1954 World Series winner (4)

9 Marine gastropod mollusc such as the waved ___ (5)

10 Country of Central Asia; capital Bishkek (10)

12 Madeleine ___, actress who played Julie Moore in 2002 film drama We Were Soldiers (5)

13 7th-century BC Hebrew minor prophet (8)

18 **and 11 Across** 2003 novel by Michael Connelly (4,5)

19 Basic monetary unit of Cambodia (4)

20 Limestone mountain in central Switzerland between Lakes Lucerne, Lauerz and Zug (4)

No. 10

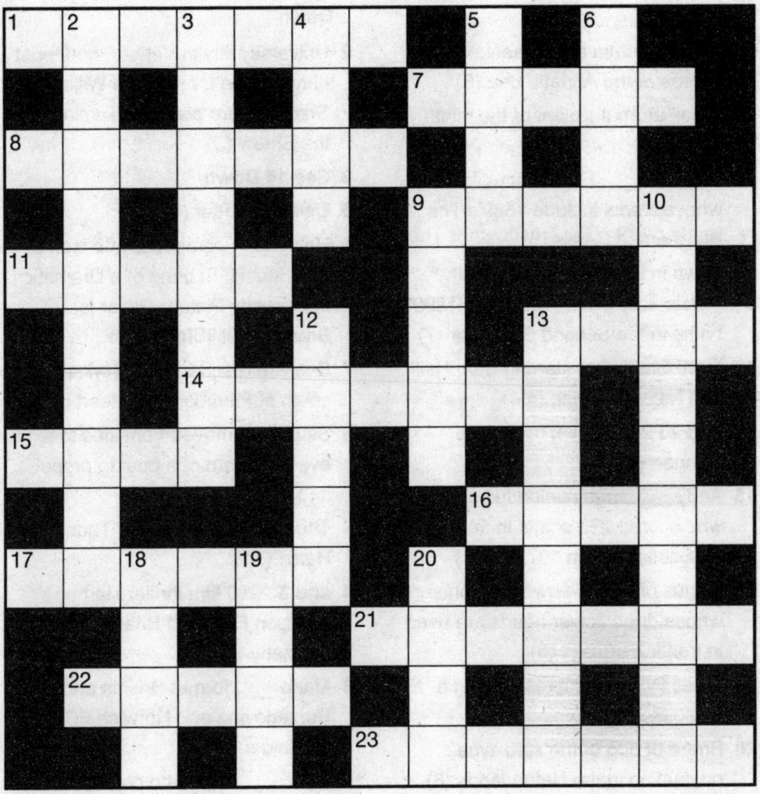

Across

1 City in Croatia on the eastern shores of the Adriatic Sea (5)

4 Small aromatic plant of the mint family (5)

10 Auguste ___, French sculptor whose works include 1889's The Burghers of Calais (5)

11 Town in KwaZulu-Natal, South Africa; scene of a December 1899 battle in the Second Boer War (7)

12 1989 film thriller starring Sam Neill and Nicole Kidman (4,4)

13 and 23 2012 novel by Sophie Hannah (4,2,5)

15 Andy ___, rugby union full-back who scored 273 points in 51 Tests for Scotland from 1972-82 (6)

17 Genus of yellow-flowered plants whose dried flower heads are used in treating bruises (6)

19 Small flying insect resembling a mosquito (4)

20 Breed of dog of the spitz type originating in the Netherlands (8)

23 See 13 Across

24 Device for amplifying microwaves that works on the same principle as a laser (5)

25 George C ___, Best Actor in a Leading Role Oscar winner for Patton (5)

26 City in Friuli-Venezia Giulia, Italy, partially damaged by a 1976 earthquake (5)

Down

2 University city in Veneto, northeast Italy; setting for much of William Shakespeare play The Taming of the Shrew (5)

3 See 14 Down

5 Den of an otter (4)

6 Henry ___, composer who won a Best Music, Scoring of a Dramatic or Comedy Picture Oscar for Breakfast at Tiffany's (7)

7 Seaside resort in East Yorkshire south of Flamborough Head (11)

8 Single oar moved from side to side over the stern of a boat to propel it (5)

9 The ___, 1887 novel by Thomas Hardy (11)

14 and 3 1990 film thriller starring Harrison Ford and Brian Dennehy (8,8)

16 Mario ___, former Bosnia and Herzegovina and Norwich FC midfielder (7)

18 Sam ___, actor who played Bunny Warren in BBC TV sitcom Porridge (5)

21 Ole ___, vaudeville comedy partner of Chic Johnson with whom he starred in 1941 film Hellzapoppin' (5)

22 Rex ___, former Governor of the Falkland Islands who died in 2012 (4)

Across

6 Capital of Free State, South Africa (12)

8 D S ___, Australia Test cricketer who made 177 against Bangladesh in Cairns in 2003 (7)

9 City in Hokkaido, Japan, on Ishikari Bay northwest of Sapporo (5)

10 Ninth letter of the Greek alphabet (4)

12 The Adventures of ___, 1940 novel by Alison Uttley (3,3)

14 Richard ___, US president from 1969-74 (5)

15 Ruth ___, Best Actress in a Supporting Role Oscar winner for Rosemary's Baby (6)

16 Long-haired sheepdog also called a Hungarian Water Dog (4)

19 Garlic mayonnaise (5)

21 Jack ___, actor who played Otto Witt in 1964 film drama Zulu (7)

22 One of the fairies in William Shakespeare stage play A Midsummer Night's Dream (12)

Down

1 1956 novel by Ed McBain (3,5)

2 Capital of Jordan (5)

3 1996 crime film starring Jennifer Tilly and Gina Gershon (5)

4 ___ Empire, name by which the former Turkish dynasty in Europe, Africa and Asia was also known (7)

5 1871 opera by Giuseppe Verdi (4)

6 Town in the unitary authority of Stockton-on-Tees associated with the chemical industry (10)

7 USAF test pilot portrayed by Fred Ward in 1983 film drama The Right Stuff (3,7)

11 Alcoholic drink flavoured with juniper berries (3)

12 Female adult pig (3)

13 Fifth month of the French Republican Calendar bridging January and February (8)

14 Industrial city in Krasnoyarsk Krai, Russia, at the foot of the Putorana Plateau (7)

17 Ancient kingdom of the Sabeans (5)

18 Small town in Flintshire, Wales, noted for its 13th-century ruined castle (5)

20 Organization formed in 1961 to administer a common policy for the sale of petroleum (4)

No. 12

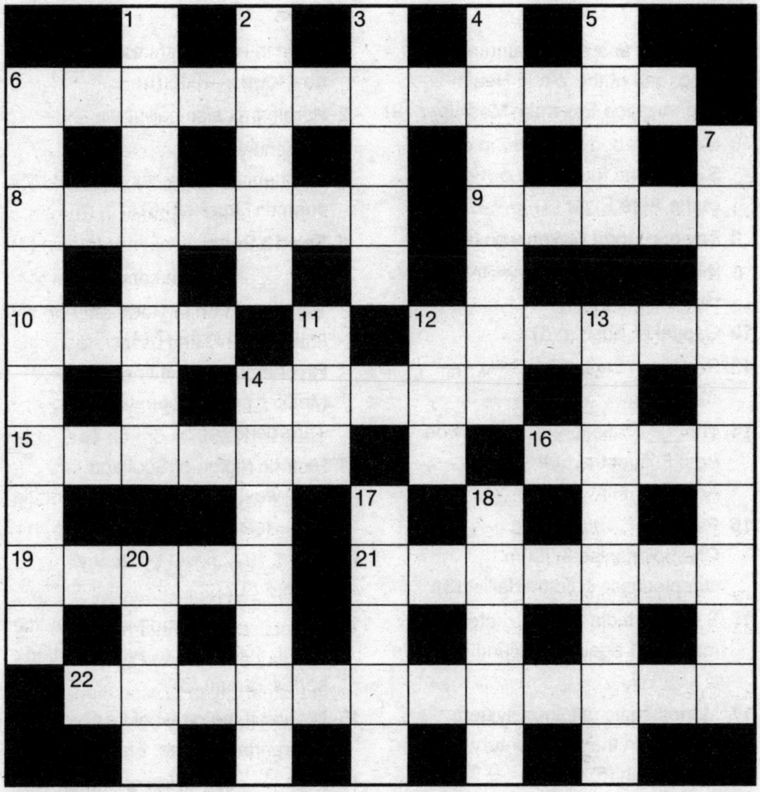

Across

3 Painkiller and anti-inflammatory drug; one of the World Health Organization Essential Medicines (9)

8 Lake ___, body of water in central Switzerland formed by a widening of the Aare River (4)

9 Town in North Devon whose 24-arch Long Bridge spans the River Torridge (8)

10 Capital of Austria (6)

13 River with the largest delta in Africa (5)

14 The ___ Patient, epic which won Best Film at the 50th British Academy Film Awards (7)

15 Patriz ___, 1983 World Championships 3,000m steeplechase gold medallist (3)

16 S C ___, India Test cricketer who made 131 against England at Lord's in 1996 (7)

17 Monotheistic religious system founded in the 19th century by Bahá'u'lláh (5)

21 Capital of Tasmania, Australia (6)

22 Musical horn also called a lepatata (8)

23 Prose ___ or Younger ___, guide to Icelandic poetry by historian Snorri Sturluson (4)

24 2011 film comedy starring Kevin James and Rosario Dawson (9)

Down

1 Town in Hertfordshire designated a new town in 1946 (9)

2 Purple fruit also called an eggplant (9)

4 Elephant in stories for children by Jean de Brunhoff (5)

5 **See 12 Down**

6 Carl ___, German composer whose scenic cantata Carmina Burana was first staged in 1937 (4)

7 River in Spain that flows to the Mediterranean southwest of Tarragona (4)

11 Historic region of Scotland northwest of the great fault running from Helensburgh to Stonehaven (9)

12 **and 5** 1932 novel by Nancy Mitford (9,7)

14 Ron ___, actor who played the title role in 1960s US television action series Tarzan (3)

15 Island off the coast of La Rochelle, Charente-Maritime, France (3,2,2)

18 Paul ___, comedian and actor who played Ted Bovis in BBC TV sitcom Hi-de-Hi! (5)

19 1981 novel by Stephen King (4)

20 Score of nothing by a cricketer (4)

No. 13

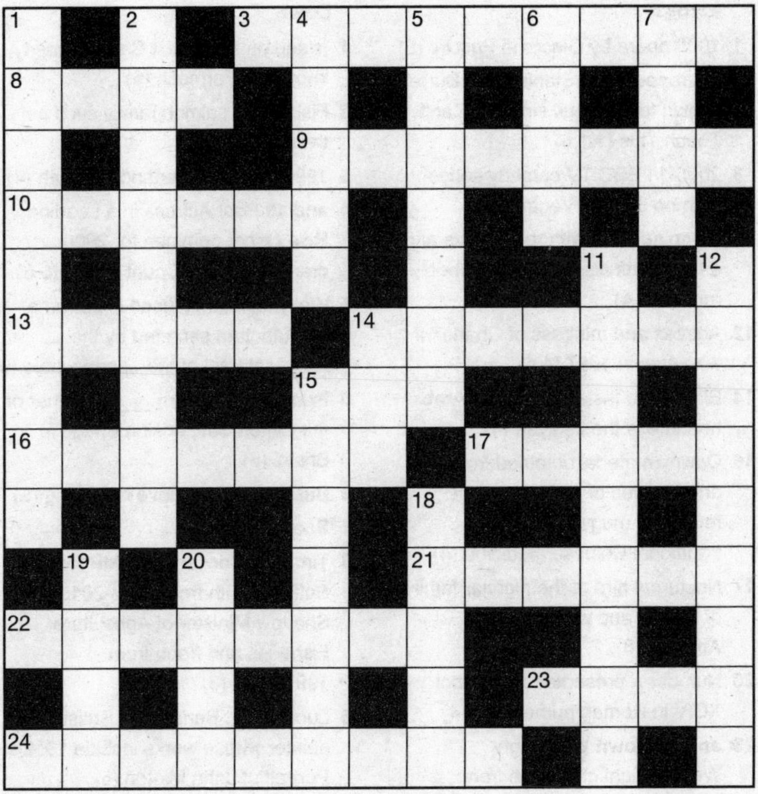

No. 14

Across

1 1900 opera by Giacomo Puccini (5)

7 US rapper born Stanley Kirk Burrell known for 1990 hit single U Can't Touch This (1,1,6)

8 2005-11 BBC TV comedy series starring Johnny Vegas (5)

10 Climbing plant with red flowers and edible pods also called a scarlet runner (6,4)

12 Actress and mistress of Charles II who died in 1687 (4,4)

14 Black cord fastened around Arab headdress the keffiyeh (4)

16 Downy material obtained from the dried leaves of an Asian plant related to mugwort used in traditional Chinese medicine (4)

17 Nocturnal bird of the nightjar family of central and western North America (8)

20 Number represented by symbol XCIV in Roman numerals (6-4)

23 **and 11 Down** WBC Light Welterweight champion from 2009-11 (5,9)

24 Thick soft tufty silk or worsted velvet cord used in embroidery (8)

25 Small swift falcon such as the Eurasian ___ or African ___ (5)

Down

1 Island off southeast China formerly known as Formosa (6)

2 Fish of the salmon family such as the lake ___ (4)

3 1996 novel by Frederick Forsyth (4)

4 **and 18** Best Actress in a Leading Role Oscar nominee for 2000 drama You Can Count on Me (5,6)

5 Waxy substance used in perfume manufacture secreted by the intestinal tract of the sperm whale (9)

6 Isambard Kingdom ___, designer of the Clifton Suspension Bridge in Bristol (6)

9 Basic attacking move in fencing (5)

11 **See 23 Across**

13 Tim ___, Conservative MP for Suffolk South from 1983-2015; Shadow Minister of Agriculture, Fisheries and Food from 1997-2001 (3)

15 Lucian ___, Berlin-born British painter whose works include 1952's Portrait of John Minton (5)

16 Principality in southwest Europe that includes the resort of Monte Carlo (6)

18 **See 4 Down**

19 Gertrude ___, author of 1933 book The Autobiography of Alice B Toklas (5)

21 Type of flaky pastry produced in very thin sheets (4)

22 City in Nevada, US, noted as a gambling and divorce centre (4)

Across

1 and 6 Down 1850 William Makepeace Thackeray novel whose characters include Emily Fotheringay and Captain Costigan (3,7,2,9)

8 Hard durable plastic laminate invented by Daniel J O'Conor and Herbert A Faber (7)

9 Fruit such as a Granny Smith or Golden Delicious (5)

10 and 11 2008 film thriller starring Kelly Reilly and Michael Fassbender (4,4)

11 See 10 Across

12 A ___, South Africa Test cricketer who took 6-32 against the West Indies in Bridgetown in 2005 (3)

14 Town in Saxony-Anhalt, Germany, at the confluence of the Elbe and Mulde Rivers (6)

15 and 20 Actor who played the title role in 1967 sci-fi film Quatermass and the Pit (6,4)

18 Ridge at the upper end of the fingerboard of a violin (3)

20 See 15 Across

21 2004 debut novel by Martin Sixsmith (4)

23 Ancient British tribe that rebelled against the Romans under Queen Boudicca (5)

24 and 25 2000 novel by Alexander McCall Smith (5,2,3,7)

25 See 24 Across

Down

1 1968 film thriller starring Tim O'Kelly and Boris Karloff (7)

2 Lake ___, southernmost of the Great Lakes of North America (4)

3 University city in southwest Nigeria (6)

4 Thomas ___, author of 1673 literary work Roman Forgeries (8)

5 Cathedral city in North Yorkshire on the River Ure (5)

6 See 1 Across

7 Capital of the Northwest Territories, Canada (11)

13 English snooker player; 2016 Northern Ireland Open tournament winner (4,4)

16 Fencing counter attack following a successful parry (7)

17 Alex ___, actor who plays Bill S Preston, Esq in the Bill and Ted comedy film series (6)

19 2007 comedy and horror film starring Jess Weixler and John Hensley (5)

22 River that flows to the Bristol Channel at Cardiff (4)

Across

1 See 22 Across

7 and 10 Down 2017 action film starring Scarlett Johansson and Pilou Asbaek (5,2,3,5)

8 Dumplings made of pieces of semolina pasta (7)

9 See 17 Across

11 and 15 Flat round cake, usually served hot, said to be named after a young woman of Bath who first sold them (5,4)

13 Mike ___, songwriter and composer of 1984 musical The Hunting of the Snark (4)

14 18th-century development in London WC2 by the Adam brothers (7)

15 See 11 Across

16 Former German security force which is the focus of the 2007 Oscar-winning film The Lives of Others (5)

17 and 9 1991 film drama starring Christopher Eccleston as Derek Bentley (3,3,4,2)

21 Ava ___, Best Actress in a Leading Role Oscar nominee for Mogambo (7)

22 and 1 2002 comedy-drama film starring Jack Nicholson, Kathy Bates and Hope Davis (5,7)

23 Two-wheeled vehicle such as a penny-farthing (7)

Down

2 Cultivated variety of muskmelon with warty rind and orange flesh (10)

3 Liz ___, 1990 Commonwealth 10,000m gold medallist (8)

4 Capital and chief port of Qatar (4)

5 Tropical African tree whose oily seeds yield a fat used in soap manufacture (4)

6 Noble family of Italy that governed Modena and Reggio from the 13th- to the 18th-century (4)

9 and 13 2011 novel by Danielle Steel (5,8)

10 See 7 Across

12 Port in Para, Brazil, on the Para River (5)

13 See 9 Down

18 Dog in a traditional Punch and Judy Show (4)

19 Takashi ___, Japanese footballer who has played for clubs including Eibar, Betis and Cerezo Osaka (4)

20 Filbert ___, 1974 Commonwealth 1,500m gold medallist (4)

Across

1 Rafael ___, former world no 1 tennis player nicknamed 'El Pelon' (The Bald) (5)

4 **and 3 Down** Dystopian novel by Aldous Huxley first published in 1932 (5,3,5)

10 Constable in William Shakespeare play Measure for Measure (5)

11 Daughter of Polonius in William Shakespeare play Hamlet (7)

12 Federal republic in northeast Africa; capital Addis Ababa (8)

13 Katarina ___, 1988 Olympic figure skating gold medallist (4)

15 **and 17** 1955 debut novel by Alan Hunter (6,4,2)

17 **See 15 Across**

19 Collective noun for a group of quails (4)

20 1974 film drama starring David Essex as Jim MacLaine (8)

23 Jim ___, poet and musician who authored 1978 memoir The Basketball Diaries (7)

24 Sixth sign of the zodiac (5)

25 Charles Strouse and Martin Charnin show; 1977 Tony Award winner for Best Musical and Best Original Score (5)

26 Coniferous tree with egg-shaped cones and needle-like leaves (5)

Down

2 State of Malaysia occupying northern Borneo (5)

3 **See 4 Across**

5 Jon ___, Spanish golfer; 2018 CareerBuilder Challenge tournament winner (4)

6 Capital of Lithuania (7)

7 2013 novel by Lee Child (5,2,4)

8 Another name for a googly in cricket (5)

9 The ___, 2009 biographical drama film starring Helen Mirren and Christopher Plummer (4,7)

14 Capital of Liberia (8)

16 French stew of mutton or lamb with vegetables (7)

18 European republic; capital Rome (5)

21 Lenore ___, US actress who played Olympe in 1936 film drama Camille (5)

22 God of mischief and destruction in Norse mythology (4)

Across

6 Singer and actor who portrayed Richard Wagner in 1975 biopic Lisztomania (4,8)

8 1972 film musical starring Liza Minnelli as Sally Bowles (7)

9 and 22 1813 novel by Jane Austen (5,3,9)

10 and 16 Author of novels Angel Time, Violin and Merrick (4,4)

12 Small nocturnal burrowing rodent of dry regions of Asia and north Africa (6)

14 Damson ___, London-born actor who stars as Franklin Saint in US TV series Snowfall (5)

15 D J ___, England Test cricketer who made an unbeaten 110 against South Africa in Durban in 1957 (6)

16 See 10 Across

19 Domesticated South American cud-chewing animal (5)

21 University friend of Hamlet in the William Shakespeare play of that name (7)

22 See 9 Across

Down

1 1970 comedy-drama film co-starring, written and directed by John Cassavetes (8)

2 John ___, British Army officer hanged as a spy in 1780 during the American War of Independence (5)

3 In mathematics, an angle of less than 90° (5)

4 Fred ___, US golfer; 1992 Masters Tournament winner (7)

5 2004 action and comedy film starring Queen Latifah and Jimmy Fallon (4)

6 and 12 1917 novel by P G Wodehouse (10,3)

7 One of a group of water-dwelling animals of the order Actinaria (3,7)

11 Freshwater fish also known as an orfe (3)

12 See 6 Down

13 Vera ___, author of 1933 memoir Testament of Youth (8)

14 Andean mountain in west Bolivia east of Lake Titicaca (7)

17 Small mouse-like long-snouted mammal such as the common ___ (5)

18 Freshwater game fish such as the brown ___ or rainbow ___ (5)

20 River that flows through Florence, Italy (4)

No. 18

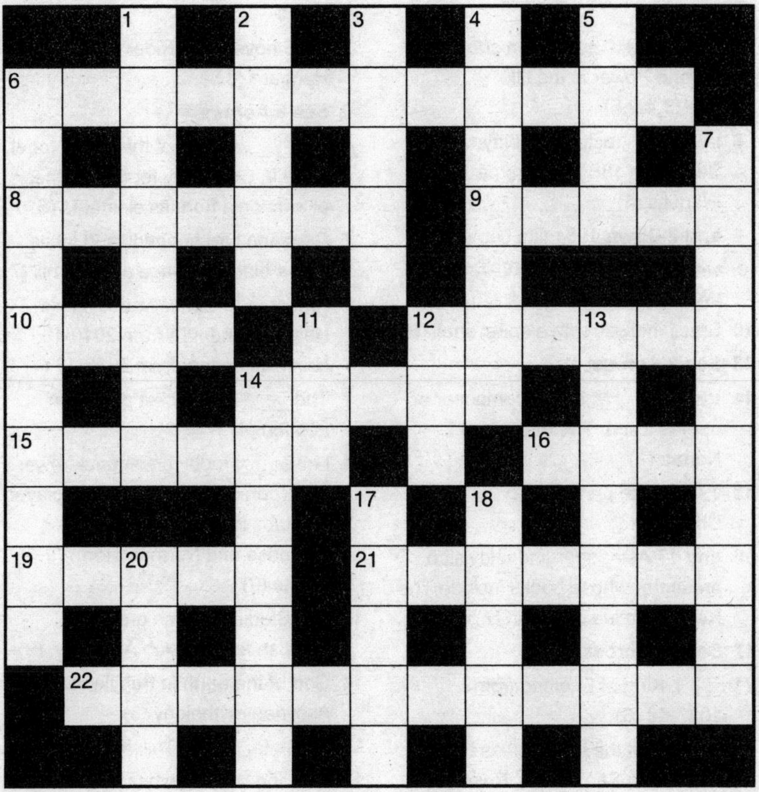

Across

3 and 13 1940 action film starring Tyrone Power in the title role (3,4,2,5)

8 Lukas ___, actor who played Samuel in 1985 film drama Witness (4)

9 and 2 Down 1984 film comedy starring, written and directed by Woody Allen (8,5,4)

10 Small mollusc with a spiral shell (6)

13 See 3 Across

14 Vincenzo ___, Italian composer of operas Zaira, The Pirate and Norma (7)

15 1983 stage play by Caryl Churchill (3)

16 and 17 Astrologer and television presenter whose books include The Real Counties of Britain (7,5)

17 See 16 Across

21 ___ I, King of England from 1037-40 (6)

22 Country of the West Indies in the Caribbean Sea; capital Roseau (8)

23 Legendary creature also called an abominable snowman (4)

24 City in Alaska, US, founded by E T Barnette in 1901 (9)

Down

1 1896 novel by H Rider Haggard (3,6)

2 See 9 Across

4 Fritz ___, winner of the 1918 Nobel Prize in Chemistry for the synthesis of ammonia from its elements (5)

5 Common bird of ponds and lakes with a black plumage and red bill (7)

6 Amber ___, Conservative MP for Hastings and Rye from 2010-19; Home Secretary from 2016-18 (4)

7 The ___, Test cricket ground in London (4)

11 Louis ___, rugby union back-rower who represented France and played for clubs including Montpellier, Toulouse and Northampton Saints (9)

12 ___ Stadium, home ground of Scottish football club Aberdeen (9)

14 God of the earth in Babylonian and Assyrian mythology (3)

15 US state; capital Tallahassee (7)

18 Soft fine-grained white sedimentary rock consisting of almost pure calcium carbonate (5)

19 Capital of the Belgian Congo until 1926 when it was replaced by Léopoldville (now Kinshasa) (4)

20 Standard unit of currency of Ethiopia (4)

43

Across

1 S'busiso ___, former Sharks wing; South Africa 2019 Rugby World Cup squad member (5)

7 See 18 Down

8 Gore ___, US author of novels Julian and Creation (5)

10 1999 film drama starring Shirley Henderson and Gina McKee (10)

12 Maiden in Greek mythology who agreed to marry any man who could defeat her in a running race (8)

14 and 4 Down English poet who authored volumes The Rural Muse and The Village Minstrel (4,5)

16 Rich ___, 2002 PGA Championship winner (4)

17 Strong white metallic element; symbol Ti (8)

20 Akbar Hashemi ___, president of Iran from 1989-97 (10)

23 and 21 Down 1923 stage play by George Bernard Shaw (5,4)

24 The ___, British weekly newspaper published from 1990-98 (8)

25 The ___, 1984 autobiographical novel by Marguerite Duras (5)

Down

1 US state; capital Carson City (6)

2 Percy ___, inventor of the Catseye road stud (4)

3 Play without words by Samuel Beckett first performed on television in 1981 (4)

4 See 14 Across

5 State capital of Maryland, US (9)

6 Bernard ___, presenter of BBC TV and ITV consumer affairs programmes who married actress Barbara Kelly in 1942 (6)

9 Alan ___, American musicologist whose books include Mister Jelly Roll (5)

11 Seaport in Munster, southeast Republic of Ireland, on the River Suir (9)

13 New Zealand bird of the honeyeater family with a bluish-green plumage and white tuft under the throat (3)

15 Claude ___, Best Actor in a Supporting Role Oscar nominee for Mr Skeffington (5)

16 Peter ___, author of stage plays Red Noses and The Ruling Class (6)

18 and 7 Across 1927 story collection by P G Wodehouse (4,2,8)

19 Creature in Greek mythology with the head and trunk of a woman and wings of a bird (5)

21 See 23 Across

22 Villainous ensign in William Shakespeare play Othello (4)

No. 21

Across

1 Setting of 1878 Thomas Hardy novel The Return of the Native (5,5)
8 Hebrew prophet of the 6th century BC (7)
9 Card game for four; a forerunner of bridge (5)
10 Trading group established in Europe in 1960 whose members now include Iceland and Norway (4)
11 Christian ___, French fashion designer (4)
12 In tonic sol-fa, the fourth degree of any major scale (3)
14 Genus of plants that includes the wood sorrel (6)
15 **and 5 Down** 2007 novel by Douglas Coupland (3,3,5)
18 Tall tree affected by fungal disease DED (3)
20 Archaic or poetic name for Ireland (4)
21 Argonaut in Greek mythology; husband of Marpessa (4)
23 **and 7 Down** 2006 action-comedy film starring Ben Stiller and Carla Gugino (5,2,3,6)
24 Mat ___, New Zealand-born rugby union Number 8 at Harlequins from 2015-19 (7)
25 Royal Air Force officer of three-star rank equivalent to a Royal Navy vice-admiral (3,7)

Down

1 1909 opera by Richard Strauss (7)
2 River rising in North Macedonia that flows through Albania to the Adriatic (4)
3 ___ the Elephant, children's song written in 1956 (6)
4 S ___, South Africa cricketer; 1998 Test debutant against England in Nottingham (8)
5 **See 15 Across**
6 **and 17** Actress who portrayed Edna Purviance in 1992 biopic Chaplin (8,3,6)
7 **See 23 Across**
13 British comic character, leader of The Bruin Boys, created by Julius Stafford Baker (5,3)
16 Grey-coloured dabbling duck (7)
17 **See 6 Down**
19 Charlie ___, WBC Flyweight champion from March-September 1983 (5)
22 1999 Derby winner ridden by Kieren Fallon (4)

Across

1 Bird with a crested head also called a green plover (7)

7 and 17 Site in California, US, that hosted the 1960 Winter Olympics (5,6)

8 Neil ___, manager of Cardiff City FC from 2016-19 (7)

9 Root vegetable of the cabbage family eaten raw in salads (6)

11 and 23 World chess champion from 1969-72 (5,7)

13 1997 film thriller starring Nicole de Boer and Nicky Guadagni (4)

14 Hard rubber also called vulcanite used for electrical insulators (7)

15 and 22 1946 novel by Robert Graves (4,5)

16 See 19 Down

17 See 7 Across

21 Standard monetary unit of Guatemala (7)

22 See 15 Across

23 See 11 Across

Down

2 Brownish resinous material obtained from the roots of some plants of the parsley family (10)

3 Capital of Manitoba, Canada (8)

4 City in Alpes-Maritimes, France, on the Mediterranean Sea (4)

5 and 9 Yellow corrosive mixture of nitric and hydrochloric acid used to dissolve metals (4,5)

6 Gete ___, 2006 and 2007 Berlin Marathon women's race winner (4)

9 See 5 Down

10 West Indies Test cricket ground in Kingston, Jamaica (6,4)

12 Seabird of the gannet family such as the red-footed ___ or blue-footed ___ (5)

13 Genus of vipers named after a horned serpent in Greek mythology (8)

18 Plant related to the onion; a national emblem of Wales (4)

19 and 16 Across Prime minister of Israel from 1999-2001 (4,5)

20 1972 comedy and drama film starring Michael Caine and Mickey Rooney (4)

Across

1 and 17 1974 film musical starring Richie Havens as Othello (5,2,4)

4 and 15 Actor who played Colonel Sherman T Potter in US television sitcom M*A*S*H (5,6)

10 Toni ___, Spanish rider; winner of the 2006 Portuguese motorcycle Grand Prix MotoGP (5)

11 US state; capital Phoenix (7)

12 1965 novel by Maj Sjöwall and Per Wahlöö; first to feature detective Martin Beck (8)

13 See 19 Across

15 See 4 Across

17 See 1 Across

19 and 13 1998 action film starring Jackie Chan and Chris Tucker (4,4)

20 Charles ___, director of films The Titfield Thunderbolt and The Lavender Hill Mob (8)

23 University city; capital of North Denmark Region, Denmark (7)

24 Igor ___, USSR defender/midfielder; 1960 UEFA European Nations' Cup Final winner (5)

25 and 26 2009-13 Castleford Tigers stand-off; 2011 Man of Steel award winner (5,5)

26 See 25 Across

Down

2 First sign of the zodiac (5)

3 2000 film drama starring Tom Hanks and Helen Hunt (4,4)

5 Martin ___, author of novels Yellow Dog and Other People (4)

6 1970 Western film starring John Wayne and Jorge Rivero (3,4)

7 Gebregziabher ___, 2009 IAAF World Cross Country Championships senior men's event winner (11)

8 Jessica ___, actress who played Jane Rochford in 2015 BBC TV drama series Wolf Hall (5)

9 1975 drama film starring Ryan O'Neal in the title role (5,6)

14 Liliaceous plant of the Mediterranean with a thick flower stalk (8)

16 Broad-tailed Australian parrot of the genus Platycercus such as the pale-headed ___ (7)

18 The ___, play by Aristophanes in which Dionysus descends to Hades in order to bring back Euripides (5)

21 1999 film drama starring Anthony Hopkins in the title role (5)

22 Robert ___, pioneer of synthesised sound born in New York in 1934 (4)

Across

6 Small antelope of eastern and southern Africa (12)

8 Kele ___, rugby union lock; 2002 Fiji Test debutant against Scotland (7)

9 Alchemical name for the element mercury (5)

10 Daughter of King Eurytus in Greek mythology loved by Heracles (4)

12 Saša ___, 1991-98 SFR and FR Yugoslavia midfield footballer whose clubs included Bolton Wanderers, Aston Villa and Crystal Palace (6)

14 River that flows to the Atlantic at Lisbon, Portugal (5)

15 2016 biopic starring Colin Firth and Jude Law (6)

16 1979 film drama starring Ray Winstone and Mick Ford (4)

19 Courtier in William Shakespeare stage play Hamlet (5)

21 City in the Czech Republic; administrative centre of the Moravo-Silesian Region (7)

22 2010 comedy and drama film starring Rachel McAdams, Harrison Ford and Diane Keaton (7,5)

Down

1 US comedian who played Scott Calvin in 1994 family film The Santa Clause (3,5)

2 Eighth son of Jacob in the Bible; ancestor of one of the 12 tribes of Israel (5)

3 and 20 2015 film thriller starring Anton Yelchin and Imogen Poots (5,4)

4 Son of Poseidon and Gaea in Greek mythology noted for his strength (7)

5 Jay ___, US comedian who hosted NBC's The Tonight Show from 1992-2009 and again from 2010-2014 (4)

6 and 7 2011 novel by Chris Ryan (7,3,3,7)

7 See 6 Down

11 2012 winner of the Oaks ridden by Seamie Heffernan (3)

12 Long tapered rod used to strike a ball in the game of snooker (3)

13 Bird with an erectile crest, such as the sulphur-crested ___ or umbrella ___ (8)

14 Region of central Italy; capital Florence (7)

17 Department of France; capital Auxerre (5)

18 Council region of South Island, New Zealand, founded by Scottish settlers (5)

20 See 3 Down

No. 25

Across

3 1961 stage play by Samuel Beckett whose characters are Winnie and Willie (5,4)

8 Back part of a golf club head where it bends to join the shaft (4)

9 Dry brown brandy distilled in the French district of Gers (8)

10 See 11 Down

13 1979-81 ITV sitcom starring Maureen Lipman and Simon Williams (5)

14 ___ 10, US spacecraft launched in 1972 that made the first fly-by of Jupiter (7)

15 Canine companion of Stimpy created by Canadian animator John Kricfalusi (3)

16 Peter ___, US golfer; 2013 Madeira Islands Open tournament winner (7)

17 Capital of Japan from 794-1868 (5)

21 English title of a 1989 novel by Banana Yoshimoto (6)

22 See 12 Down

23 **and 24** Norwegian anthropologist who sailed from Peru to the Pacific Islands in 1947 (4,9)

24 See 23 Across

Down

1 **and 6** 1977 novel by Richard Adams featuring characters Rowf and Snitter (3,6,4)

2 Lord Frederick ___, character in Charles Dickens novel Nicholas Nickleby killed by Sir Mulberry Hawk in a duel (9)

4 Former name of Hagatna, capital of the Pacific island of Guam (5)

5 Squash plant with a large rounded orange-yellow fruit associated with Halloween (7)

6 See 1 Down

7 Imperial dynasty of China from 1271-1368 (4)

11 **and 10 Across** 2011 novel by Peter Robinson (6,3,6)

12 **and 22 Across** 2011 film comedy starring Jim Carrey and Carla Gugino (2,7,8)

14 Female swan (3)

15 Malcolm ___, 1974-97 Conservative MP for Edinburgh Pentlands; 1995-97 Foreign Secretary (7)

18 Niclas ___, golfer; 2006 Mallorca Classic tournament winner (5)

19 Collective noun for a group of badgers (4)

20 Brett ___, 1990 Australian PGA Championship winner (4)

Across

1 and 15 Down 1988 Olympic men's 400m gold medallist (5,5)

7 Hampshire home of the National Motor Museum (8)

8 Roberto ___, cyclist; 2000, 2003, 2004 and 2005 Vuelta a España winner (5)

10 Tournament for professional women golfers contested by teams representing Europe and the US (7,3)

12 Suburb of Birkenhead on the Wirral Peninsula noted for 2000 League Cup Final runners-up ___ Rovers FC (8)

14 River in Scotland that flows through the Grampian Mountains to the Moray Firth (4)

16 National style of wrestling of Japan (4)

17 Musical chord whose notes are played in rapid succession rather than simultaneously (8)

20 Rocky island in south Ayrshire, Scotland, housing a gannetry (5,5)

23 and 16 Down Fellow recruit of Mouldy, Wart, Feeble and Bullcalf in William Shakespeare play Henry IV Pt 2 (5,6)

24 1979 novel by Arthur Hailey (8)

25 G A ___, boys' adventure story writer whose works include 1884's With Clive in India (5)

Down

1 Metamorphic rock that can be split into thin layers (6)

2 W P U J C ___, Sri Lanka Test cricketer who took 6-22 against West Indies in Kandy in 2005 (4)

3 First wife of Jacob in the Old Testament (4)

4 and 6 Decorated US soldier and actor who played the title role in 1952 Western film The Cimarron Kid (5,6)

5 1996 stage play by Enda Walsh (5,4)

6 See 4 Down

9 River in north France; scene of heavy fighting in World War One (5)

11 Comedian known as The Cheeky Chappie born Thomas Henry Sargent in Brighton in 1894 (3,6)

13 Karel Capek play premiered in 1921 which introduced the word robot to the English language (1,1,1)

15 See 1 Across

16 See 23 Across

18 Pen name of William Sydney Porter, author of short story collections Roads of Destiny and The Four Million (1,5)

19 Musical instrument of India consisting of a pair of drums of variable pitch (5)

21 Standard monetary unit of Iran (4)

22 André ___, French author of 1909 novel Strait is the Gate (4)

Across

1 Name, until 1966, of African country Lesotho (10)

8 Market town in Worcestershire situated within a meander of the River Avon (7)

9 Derek ___, actor who starred as Dominic in BBC TV sitcoms Oh Brother! and Oh Father! (5)

10 Alcoholic drink often served with seafood in Turkey (4)

11 Paul ___, actor who starred as Frankie Wilde in 2004 comedy-drama film It's All Gone Pete Tong (4)

12 Standard monetary unit of Japan (3)

14 Romain ___, 2010 European Championships decathlon gold medallist (6)

15 See 18 Across

18 and 15 Brother of actor George Sanders who played Dr Louis Judd in 1942 horror film Cat People (3,6)

20 1982 action film starring Jeff Bridges and Bruce Boxleitner (4)

21 Paul ___, Swiss artist whose works include 1922's Red Balloon (4)

23 1977 film comedy starring John Denver and George Burns (2,3)

24 Hanna-Barbera cartoon superhero who fought villains including Ferocious Flea (4,3)

25 Folk-blues musician whose albums with Brownie McGhee include 1960's Down Home Blues (5,5)

Down

1 and 17 1980 film drama starring Edward Woodward in the title role (7,6)

2 District in the City of Westminster, London, known for its restaurants (4)

3 and 16 Mostly nocturnal marsupial of south Australia (6,7)

4 Knight of the Round Table and lover of Queen Guinevere in Arthurian legend (8)

5 Leonard ___, actor who played Spock in 1960s US television series Star Trek (5)

6 The ___, 2011 novel by Val McDermid (11)

7 Former Sale Sharks centre; Samoa 2015 Rugby World Cup squad member (6,5)

13 Large extinct elephant-like mammal (8)

16 See 3 Down

17 See 1 Down

19 Andrea ___, 2017 Italian motorcycle Grand Prix Moto3 series race winner (5)

22 Uncastrated male pig (4)

No. 27

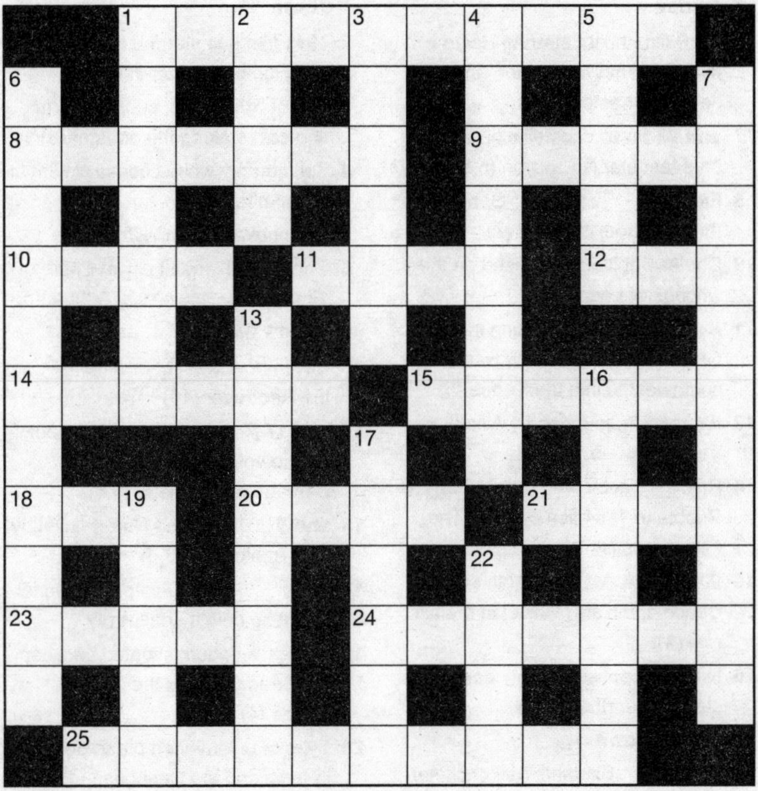

Across

1 2010 film thriller starring Helen Mirren, Sam Worthington and Jessica Chastain (3,4)

7 **and 22** Small constellation whose brightest star is Procyon (5,5)

8 Frederick ___, Director-General of the BBC from 1938-42 (7)

9 Chinese philosophy based on the writings of Laozi (6)

11 River in SE France, rising in the Graian Alps and flowing west and southwest to join the Rhone (5)

13 Aircraft firm founded by Alliott Verdon Roe in 1910 (4)

14 Rick ___, actor who played Barney Rubble in 1994 film comedy The Flintstones (7)

15 2001 biopic featuring both Judi Dench and Kate Winslet in the title role (4)

16 Number opposite twenty on a standard dartboard (5)

17 **See 12 Down**

21 N R D ___, England Test cricketer who made 117 against New Zealand in Dunedin in 2013 (7)

22 **See 7 Across**

23 Orde ___, British Army brigadier, creator of the Chindits in Burma in World War II (7)

Down

2 1941 film noir starring Ida Lupino and Humphrey Bogart (4,6)

3 Belt of light winds, sudden storms and calms along the equator (8)

4 Soft creamy white cheese similar to Camembert (4)

5 1880 novel by Emile Zola (4)

6 Capital and largest city of East Timor (4)

9 **See 13 Down**

10 City in northwest Louisiana, US, on the Red River (10)

12 **and 17 Across** Liverpudlian poet whose volumes include Storm Damage and Armada (5,6)

13 **and 9** 2011 Agatha Raisin novel by M C Beaton (2,3,3,5)

18 Blyth ___, 1996 Olympic Individual Eventing gold medallist (4)

19 Ancient kingdom situated between the Dead Sea and the Gulf of Aqaba (4)

20 Type of unleavened bread popular in India and the Caribbean (4)

Across

1 Bob ___, Best Director Oscar winner for Cabaret (5)

4 Tuft of small stiff feathers on the first digit of a bird also called a bastard wing (5)

10 Capital of Ghana (5)

11 Region of Greece in the central Peloponnese; capital Tripoli (7)

12 1993 novel by Sebastian Faulks (8)

13 Gregory ___, Best Actor in a Leading Role Oscar winner for To Kill a Mockingbird (4)

15 Muse of comedy and pastoral poetry in Greek mythology (6)

17 See 25 Across

19 **and 6 Down** 1924 Olympic 400m gold medallist (4,7)

20 Province of northeast China; capital Shenyang (8)

23 ___ I, King of Italy assassinated by Gaetano Bresci in Monza in 1900 (7)

24 City in Tamil Nadu, India, on the bank of the River Cauvery (5)

25 **and 17** Actor who married Barbra Streisand in 1998 (5,6)

26 Sam ___, actor who plays Chesney Brown in ITV soap Coronation Street (5)

Down

2 Word representing the letter O in the NATO phonetic alphabet (5)

3 **and 14** 1997 action film starring Casper Van Dien and Dina Meyer (8,8)

5 1982 novel by Shirley Conran (4)

6 **See 19 Across**

7 1971 novel by John Updike (6,5)

8 Judy ___, regular cast member on US television series Rowan and Martin's Laugh-In, married to Burt Reynolds from 1963-65 (5)

9 ___ International, New York motor racing circuit that hosted the F1 United States GP from 1961-80 (7,4)

14 **See 3 Down**

16 John ___, 1972 Olympic 400m hurdles gold medallist (4-3)

18 Jeremiah ___, 18th-century English surveyor best known for his work with Charles Mason on resolving a boundary dispute between Maryland and Pennsylvania (5)

21 Hardwood of tropical Africa used as a substitute for teak (5)

22 River in Scotland upon which Newton Stewart, Dumfries and Galloway, stands (4)

No. 29

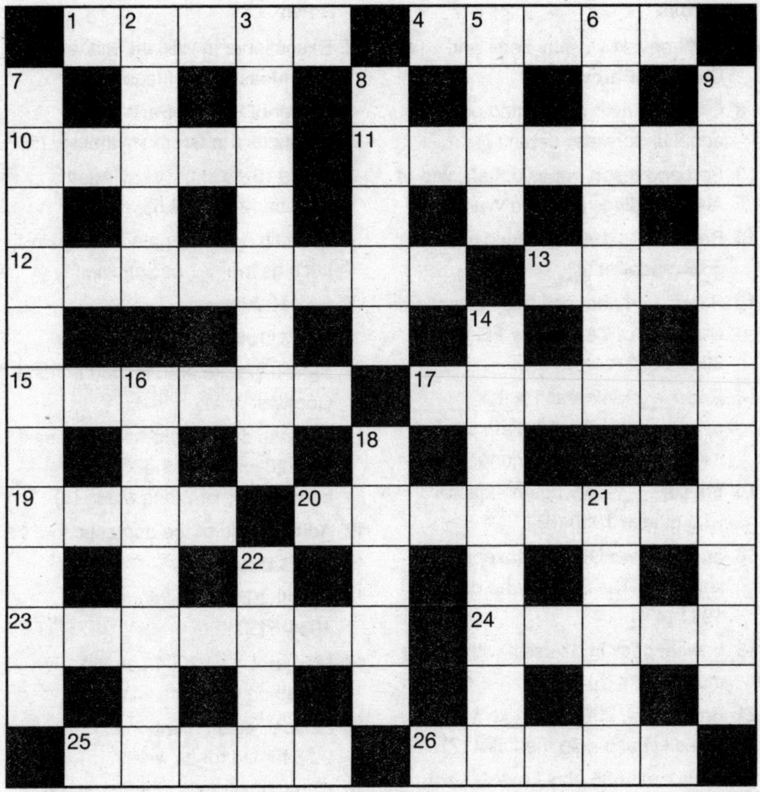

Across

6 1979 novel by Kathy Lette and Gabrielle Carey (7,5)

8 Line on a map connecting points of equal underwater depth (7)

9 Port and resort in Lazio, Italy; site of Allied landings in World War II (5)

10 Balázs ___, 1996 Olympic hammer gold medallist (4)

12 Sam ___, Lebanese businessman; chairman of Cardiff City FC from 2000-06 (6)

14 Rod ___, 1962 and 1969 calendar-year Grand Slam singles tennis championship winner (5)

15 Fridtjof ___, Norwegian explorer who died in 1930 (6)

16 and 5 Down US jazz saxophonist known as The Sound who died in 1991 (4,4)

19 Lowest deck in a vessel with four or more decks (5)

21 Brimin ___, 2008 Olympic 3,000m steeplechase gold medallist (7)

22 Author of 1696 play Loves's Last Shift; Poet Laureate from 1730-57 (6,6)

Down

1 Executioner in William Shakespeare play Measure for Measure (8)

2 Father of Hector, Paris and Cassandra in Greek mythology (5)

3 6 and 13 1968 novel by Agatha Christie (2,3,8,2,2,6)

4 Moorish castle or palace in Spain such as the ___ of Segovia (7)

5 See 16 Across

6 See 3 Down

7 Barren granite area of land in north Cornwall (6,4)

11 Chinese dynasty from 206 BC until AD 220 including the Xin interregnum of Wang Mang (3)

12 Adult female of the domestic fowl (3)

13 See 3 Down

14 ___ III, King of Belgium from 1934-51 (7)

17 Margaret ___, 2004 London Marathon elite race winner (5)

18 Biblical region mentioned in 1 Kings 9:28 famed for its wealth (5)

20 Commonest basic pattern of the human fingerprint (4)

No. 30

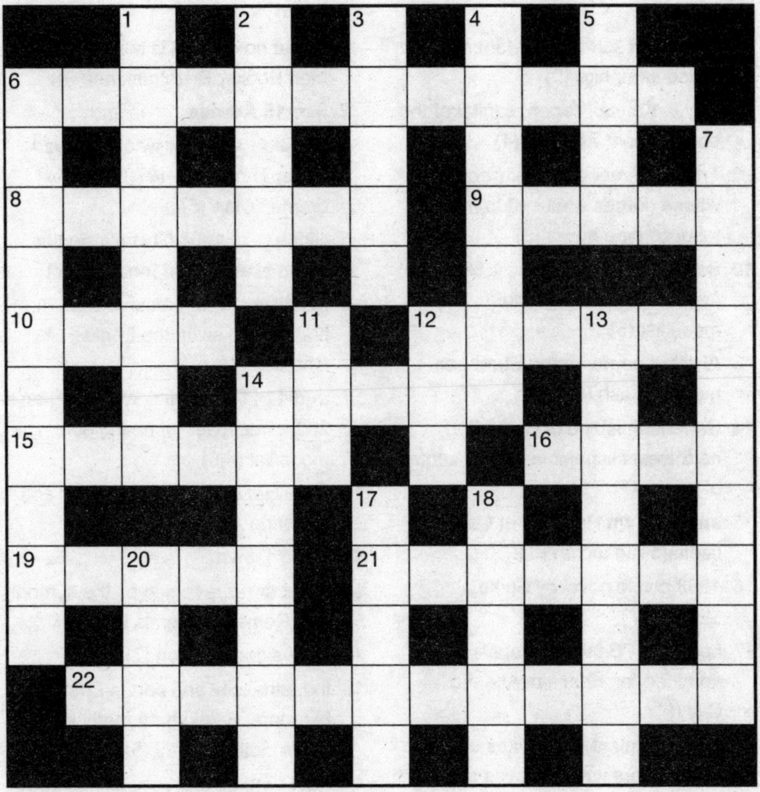

Across

3 Succulent salt-marsh plant also called samphire (9)

8 City in Kansai, Japan; capital of the country from 710-784 (4)

9 Tropical American evergreen tree whose gourds are used to make tobacco pipe bowls (8)

10 Bob ___, 1964 Olympic 1,500m freestyle swimming gold medallist (6)

13 Another name for the European mountain ash (5)

14 Caribbean island of Haiti off northwest Hispaniola once a centre of piracy (7)

15 **and 2 Down** Province of Canada; capital Fredericton (3,9)

16 1963 comic novel by Spike Milligan (7)

17 Louis ___, Best Director Oscar nominee for 1980 film Atlantic City (5)

21 Aromatic plant with spikes of small blue flowers whose leaves are used in cooking (6)

22 English name of the seat of government of the Netherlands (3,5)

23 Raymond ___, Canadian actor who played Perry Mason and Robert Ironside on television (4)

24 Black to steel-grey manganese oxide-hydroxide ore (9)

Down

1 Debut novel by A D Miller; 2011 Man Booker Prize nominee (9)

2 **See 15 Across**

4 Ronald ___, actor who portrayed Dylan Thomas in 1978 BBC TV drama Dylan (5)

5 Ulrich ___, 1908 Olympic singles figure skating gold medallist (7)

6 Matthew ___, steamship captain; first man to swim the English Channel (4)

7 **and 12** 2006 Commonwealth men's 200m freestyle swimming gold medallist (4,9)

11 2010 film drama starring Cher and Christina Aguilera (9)

12 **See 7 Down**

14 Number represented by the symbol X in Roman numerals (3)

15 Nine-sided polygon (7)

18 Industrial city and port in East Flanders, Belgium, formerly known for its cloth industry (5)

19 Fast-running flightless bird of South America (4)

20 Dark long-necked bird similar to the cormorant (4)

Across

1 **and 18 Down** Dog with a silky dark red coat and a long feathered tail (5,6)

7 Freddie ___, actor who played the title role in 2005 family film Charlie and the Chocolate Factory (8)

8 Sidney ___, prolific filmmaker whose movies include Serpico and Network (5)

10 See 11 Down

12 Greek Cynic philosopher born in Sinope who advocated self-sufficiency (8)

14 Supreme creator god in Norse mythology (4)

16 Main port and commercial capital of Yemen (4)

17 See 11 Down

20 Danny ___, author of 2007 novel Random Acts of Heroic Love (10)

23 Number represented by symbols VIII in Roman numerals (5)

24 Seaport area of Los Angeles, California, linked to Terminal Island by the Vincent Thomas Bridge (3,5)

25 **and 9 Down** 1975 film drama starring David Niven and Toshirô Mifune (5,5)

Down

1 See 4 Down

2 Small diving duck of northern Eurasia (4)

3 Philip K ___, author of science fiction novels The Man in the High Castle and The Game-Players of Titan (4)

4 **and 1** US state; capital Providence (5,6)

5 Wales and Cardiff Blues wing; 2019 Rugby World Cup top try scorer (4,5)

6 E F ___, author of 1920 novel Queen Lucia (6)

9 See 25 Across

11 **10 Across and 17 Across** 1962 novel by Ray Bradbury (9,6,4,3,5)

13 Seventh letter in the Greek alphabet (3)

15 Parish in Perth and Kinross, Scotland; former site of the Pictish capital (5)

16 Town in Perugia, central Italy; birthplace of St Francis (6)

18 See 1 Across

19 Capital of Gard, France, whose Roman remains include the Maison Carrée (5)

21 1926 debut novel by Vladimir Nabokov published under pseudonym V Sirin (4)

22 Asian palm tree whose feathery leaves are used for thatching (4)

No. 33

Across

1 **and 13 Down** 2011 novel by Patrick deWitt (3,7,8)

8 Highest mountain in the world (7)

9 John ___, first Director-General of the BBC, from 1927-38 (5)

10 Unit of length equal to three feet (4)

11 Olympic sailing class in which Great Britain's Giles Scott was gold medallist in 2016 (4)

12 Old Testament teacher of Samuel (3)

14 Basic SI unit of electric current (6)

15 **and 17 Down** 2002 novel by Ken Follett (6,6)

18 1981 comedy-drama film starring Julie Andrews and William Holden (1,1,1)

20 Enamelled or lacquered metalware popular in the 18th century (4)

21 Robert ___, industrialist and social reformer who formed a model industrial community at New Lanark, Scotland (4)

23 Light semi-transparent silk, rayon or cotton fabric used for dresses and scarves (5)

24 Bushy shrub in the aster family of Mexico and the southwestern US; a source of latex (7)

25 1999 comedy-drama film starring Allan Corduner as Sir Arthur Sullivan (5-5)

Down

1 2011 novel by Michael Connelly (3,4)

2 Anthony ___, prime minister from 1955-57 (4)

3 Peninsula in the north Adriatic Sea; chief city Pula (6)

4 Unfinished opera by Giacomo Puccini first performed in 1926 (8)

5 European river upon which Basel, Strasbourg and Cologne stand (5)

6 2011 romcom featuring Halle Berry and Jessica Biel (3,5,3)

7 Helena ___, Danish supermodel and photographer born in 1968 (11)

13 **See 1 Across**

16 Berkshire horse racecourse established in 1905 (7)

17 **See 15 Across**

19 Arrigo ___, Italian composer of 1868 opera Mefistofele (5)

22 Johnny ___, The Smiths guitarist and co-founder (4)

No. 33

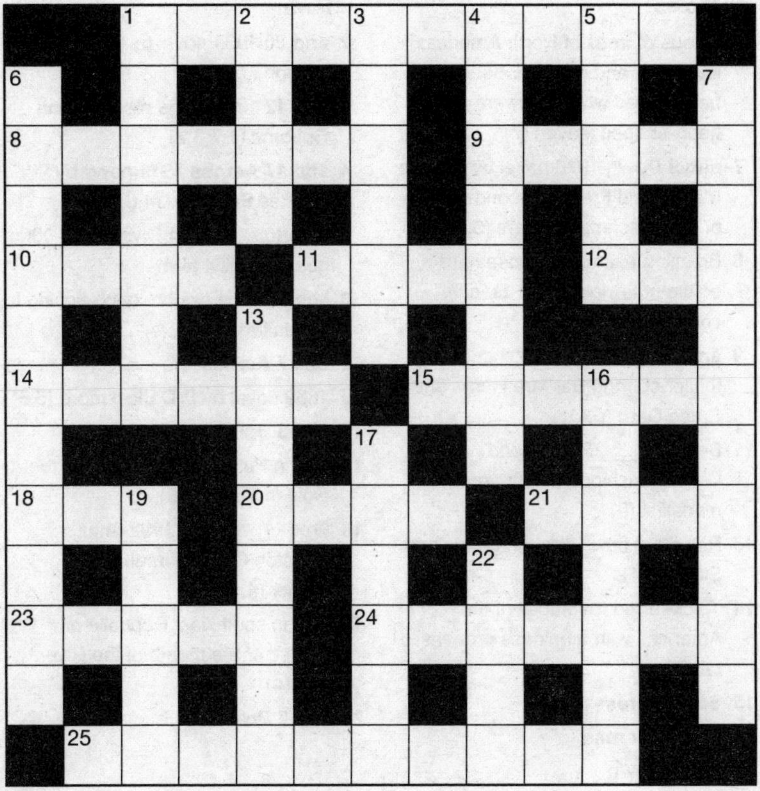

No. 34

Across

1 Genus of trees of North America, East Asia and the Caribbean with bell-shaped whitish flowers and heart-shaped leaves (7)

7 **and 9 Down** 1970 novel by George MacDonald Fraser, second volume of The Flashman Papers (5,5)

8 Brazilian palm tree whose hard edible nuts yield an oil used in cosmetics (7)

9 **and 15** 1976 Alfred Hitchcock film thriller starring Barbara Harris and Bruce Dern (6,4)

11 Berhane ___, 2003 World Championships 10,000m gold medallist (5)

13 River that flows through Leeds and Skipton (4)

14 Thick-furred marsupial of the Americas with a hairless prehensile tail (7)

15 **See 9 Across**

16 **See 22 Across**

17 **See 4 Down**

21 William Inge stage drama; 1956 Tony Award for Best Play nominee (3,4)

22 **and 16** Original title of a 2016 animated film starring the voice talent of Jason Sudeikis and Josh Gad (5,5)

23 Greville ___, jockey who rode 1978 Derby winner Shirley Heights (7)

Down

2 **and 20** 1934 novel by Evelyn Waugh (1,7,2,4)

3 **and 12** 1965 stage play by John Osborne (1,7,3,2)

4 **and 17 Across** 1971 novel by Charles Bukowski (4,6)

5 Alberto ___, 1984 Olympic 10,000m gold medallist (4)

6 Long skirt, dress or coat reaching to the ankles (4)

9 **See 7 Across**

10 1869 novel by R D Blackmore (5,5)

12 **See 3 Down**

13 City in Punjab, India, home to the Golden Temple (8)

18 Fred ___, golfer; 1992 Shell Houston Open tournament winner (4)

19 Port in southwest Republic of Ireland at the mouth of the River Lee (4)

20 **See 2 Down**

No. 35

Across

1 Metal tip or mounting on a sheath or scabbard (5)

4 River in Scotland upon which Stirling stands (5)

10 See 26 Across

11 Secretary of State for Defence from 2010-11 and Secretary of State for International Trade from 2016-19 (4,3)

12 1983 Grand National winner ridden by Ben de Haan (8)

13 Franco ___, Italian actor who played Lancelot Du Lac in 1967 film musical Camelot (4)

15 See 17 Across

17 **and 15** Nick Park 1989 animated film starring Wallace and Gromit (1,5,3,3)

19 Darlene ___, 1960 and 1961 US National Championships singles tennis tournament winner (4)

20 Bushy-tailed rodent such as the red ___ or fox ___ (8)

23 Ancient region on the Adriatic Sea including parts of present-day Albania, Croatia and Montenegro (7)

24 Native American tribe formerly living in an area between the Missouri and Arkansas rivers (5)

25 Joe ___, former Widnes rugby league centre; 1984 Man of Steel award and Lance Todd Trophy winner (5)

26 **and 10** 2006 film comedy starring Jack Black and Ana de la Reguera (5,5)

Down

2 Anke ___, 1996 Australian Open singles tennis championship runner-up (5)

3 2009 film drama starring Gabourey Sidibe in the title role (8)

5 Small port and resort in Argyll and Bute, west Scotland (4)

6 Crisp plain-weave silk or rayon used for women's clothing (7)

7 The ___, 1987 novel by James Ellroy (5,6)

8 County of the Republic of Ireland; county town Ennis (5)

9 1984 comedy-drama film starring Rob Lowe and Ally Sheedy (6,5)

14 Gnaeus Julius ___, Roman general and governor of Britain who died in 93 AD (8)

16 B ___, Australia Test cricketer who took 7-98 against West Indies in Sydney in 1982 (7)

18 Young unfledged pigeon (5)

21 Small European freshwater fish of the carp and minnow family (5)

22 Piece of music composed for three people (4)

No. 36

Across

6 2011 novel by Martina Cole (3,9)

8 **and 17 Down** 1992 novel by Peter Ackroyd (7,5)

9 Australian acacia tree with yellow ball-shaped flowers (5)

10 Russian river that flows to the Caspian Sea at Guryev (4)

12 Deputy to Vincentio in William Shakespeare play Measure for Measure (6)

14 **See 12 Down**

15 Market town in North Yorkshire on the River Ribble (6)

16 1995 novel by Iain Banks (4)

19 African republic; capital Cairo (5)

21 City in Rajasthan, India; historic capital of the kingdom of Mewar (7)

22 The ___, 1968 action film starring Dean Martin and Elke Sommer (8,4)

Down

1 **and 20** 1941 film drama starring Gary Cooper in the title role (8,4)

2 1985 film comedy starring Glenn Close in the title role (5)

3 Georg Ernst ___, German scientist born in 1659 who developed the phlogiston theory of combustion (5)

4 Samuel Langhorne ___, author who used pen name Mark Twain (7)

5 Mountain in Greek mythology sandwiched between Olympus and Pelion by Otus and Ephialtes (4)

6 1935 novel by C S Forester first published in 2011 (3,7)

7 US author of novels Andrew's Brain and Homer and Langley (1,1,8)

11 City in Gelderland, Netherlands, northwest of Arnhem (3)

12 **and 14 Across** Best Actress in a Leading Role Oscar nominee for American Hustle (3,5)

13 2006 novel by Michael Connelly (4,4)

14 Glacier in Switzerland; largest in Europe (7)

17 **See 8 Across**

18 1996 comedy and crime drama film starring Frances McDormand and William H Macy (5)

20 **See 1 Down**

No. 37

Across

3 2003 comedy-drama film starring Paul Kaye and James Cromwell (9)

8 City and railway junction in west Romania once part of Turkey, Austria and Hungary (4)

9 Industrial city in Connecticut, US, housing Yale University (3,5)

10 Capital of Turkey (6)

13 Irene ___, comedy actress who played the title character in 1970s ITV sitcom For the Love of Ada (5)

14 Frankie ___, 1994, 1995 and 2004 flat racing champion jockey (7)

15 Peter ___, star and co-writer of Channel 4 television comedy series Phoenix Nights (3)

16 and 17 Drama starring Catherine McCormack, Rachel Weisz and Anna Friel (3,4,5)

17 See 16 Across

21 ___ IV, pope from 1154-59 born Nicholas Breakspear (6)

22 and 15 Down 2003 action-comedy film starring Jackie Chan and Owen Wilson (8,7)

23 Bury My Heart at Wounded ___, non-fiction book by Dee Brown about the history of Native Americans (4)

24 The ___, 1969 novel by Mary Wesley (5,4)

Down

1 Haruhiro ___, artistic gymnast; 1964 Olympic men's vault and team all-around gold medallist (9)

2 Marcia ___, former personal, political and private secretary to prime minister Harold Wilson (9)

4 Desmond ___, television presenter whose credits include Match of the Day and Countdown (5)

5 M C ___, England Test cricketer who made 148 against West Indies in Port-of-Spain in 1968 (7)

6 Bertolt Brecht stage play first performed in 1923 (4)

7 Sébastien ___, French driver; 2004-12 World Rally Championship winner (4)

11 2010 comedy-drama film starring Riz Ahmed (4,5)

12 Kurt Georg ___, chancellor of West Germany from 1966-69 (9)

14 1981 novel by William Wharton (3)

15 See 22 Across

18 Standard monetary unit of Nigeria (5)

19 Language also called Siamese (4)

20 Protuberance on a tree trunk, also known as a burl (4)

Across

1 See 22 Down

7 Four-wheeled horse-drawn closed carriage with a raised open driver's seat in front (8)

8 General Tom ___, 19th-century circus performer born Charles Sherwood Stratton (5)

10 Large shrub whose fruit is the sloe (10)

12 Benjamin ___, 18th-century American statesman and scientist whose inventions include a lightning rod (8)

14 1939-49 BBC Radio comedy programme starring Tommy Handley (4)

16 Ada ___, owner of Cold Comfort Farm in the 1932 novel of that name by Stella Gibbons (4)

17 City in Osaka, Japan, northeast of Moriguchi housing a campus of Setsunan University (8)

20 See 5 Down

23 Emma ___, Best Actress in a Leading Role Oscar winner for La La Land (5)

24 See 1 Down

25 Town in Mendip, Somerset; birthplace of 2009 F1 World Championship winner Jenson Button (5)

Down

1 and 24 Across 2018 action film starring Bruce Willis and Cole Hauser (4,2,8)

2 Larry ___, actor who played Archie Mitchell in BBC TV soap EastEnders (4)

3 and 19 Comedian and writer who authored 2005 memoir If I Don't Write It, Nobody Else Will (4,5)

4 Capital of Ecuador (5)

5 and 20 Across 1976 film Western directed by and starring Clint Eastwood in the title role (3,6,5,5)

6 and 9 US actress who played Peach Lips in 1953 musical-drama film Lili (6,5)

9 See 6 Down

11 1922 novel by D H Lawrence (6,3)

13 1983 novel by Ed McBain (3)

15 Henry ___, author of novels The Aspern Papers and Roderick Hudson (5)

16 2006 action film starring Denzel Washington and Paula Patton (4,2)

18 Department of southern France; capital Foix (6)

19 See 3 Down

21 Jorge ___, 2011-12 WBO Bantamweight champion (4)

22 and 1 Across Tropical American tree with smooth-skinned edible greenish-purple fruit (4,5)

No. 38

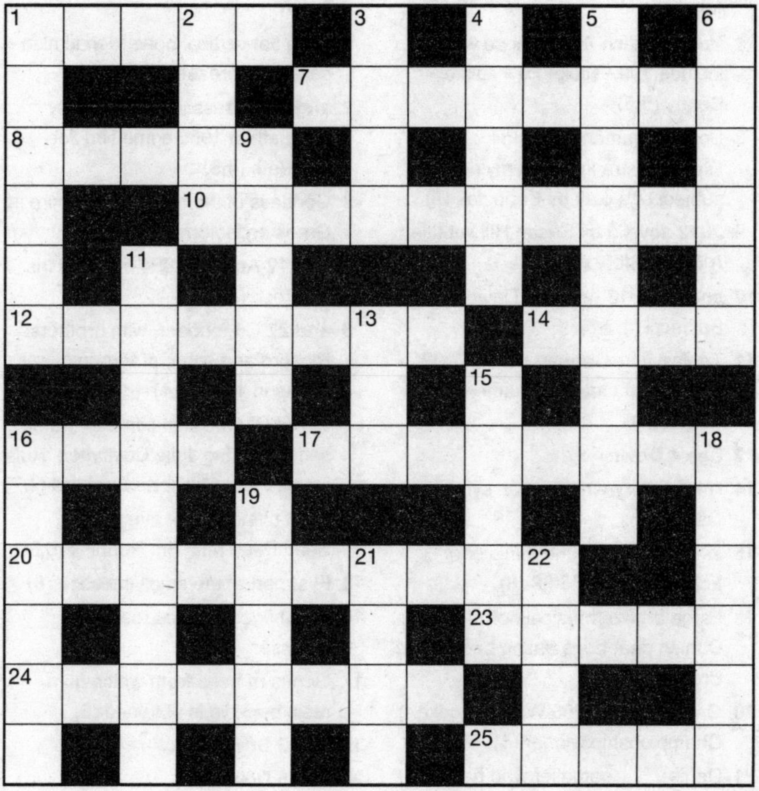

No. 39

Across

1 Young British Artist whose works include 1997 sculpture Pauline Bunny (5,5)

8 Son of Agamemnon and Clytemnestra in Greek mythology; subject of a play by Euripides (7)

9 2012 novella by Susan Hill subtitled A Ghost Story (5)

10 and 25 2013 novel by David Baldacci (4,3,7)

11 Tobias ___, German golfer; 2002 TNT Dutch Open tournament winner (4)

12 See 4 Down

14 Hard silvery-white metal; symbol Os (6)

15 Jacques ___, prime minister of France from 1986-88 (6)

18 Large bronze musical horn found in Danish peat bogs dating back to the Bronze Age (3)

20 Graeme ___, 2006 World Snooker Championship winner (4)

21 Denis ___, footballer who has represented Belgium and played for clubs including OH Leuven, Anderlecht and Fulham FC (4)

23 New town in Drenthe, northeast Netherlands, developed since World War II (5)

24 City in Virginia, US, housing the man-made Mill Mountain Star (7)

25 See 10 Across

Down

1 Long flat vertical bone in man also called the breastbone (7)

2 and 19 Actress who played Lily MacBeth in 1955 crime film Joe MacBeth (4,5)

3 Goddess of the hearth and its fire in Greek mythology (6)

4 and 12 Across 1954 novel by Iris Murdoch (5,3,3)

5 and 22 Co-founder, with brothers Richard and John, of Penguin Books in 1935 (5,4)

6 1970s ITV musical comedy-drama series starring Julie Covington, Rula Lenska and Charlotte Cornwell (4,7)

7 2003 crime drama film starring Sean Penn and Tim Robbins (6,5)

13 First part of the small intestine (8)

16 Small finch such as the Arctic ___ or lesser ___ (7)

17 Genus of trees from which gum resin benzoin is obtained (6)

19 See 2 Down

22 See 5 Down

No. 40

Across

1 and 17 19th-century author of poems The Forsaken Merman and Dover Beach (7,6)

7 and 20 Down Presenter of BBC TV shows It's a Knockout and A Question of Sport who died in 2009 (5,4)

8 King of Pherae, Thessaly, in Greek mythology married to Alcestis (7)

9 British rapper born Joseph Junior Adenuga; 2016 Mercury Prize winner (6)

11 Shane ___, Australia-born former Bristol, Northampton and Worcester rugby union fly-half (5)

13 and 21 2004 novel by Meg Rosoff (3,1,4,3)

14 Frank ___, Best Actor in a Supporting Role Oscar winner for From Here to Eternity (7)

15 Alfred ___, US stage actor who married Lynn Fontanne in 1922 (4)

16 ___ Castle, former home of Andrew Carnegie in Sutherland, Scotland, overlooking Dornoch Firth (5)

17 See 1 Across

21 See 13 Across

22 1989 novel by Hilary Mantel (5)

23 In Japan, a carved toggle of wood or ivory worn dangling from the waist (7)

Down

2 See 3 Down

3 and 2 1947 comedy-drama film starring Rex Harrison and Gene Tierney (3,5,3,3,4)

4 Twelfth month of the Jewish civil year (4)

5 See 9 Down

6 Issa ___, defender who moved from West Ham United to Fulham FC in 2022 (4)

9 and 5 Animated US television series featuring character Eric Cartman (5,4)

10 2012 film thriller starring Sheridan Smith and Ralph Brown (5,5)

12 Sam ___, 1942, 1949 and 1951 PGA Championship winner (5)

13 Steve ___, 1989-99 Liverpool FC defender who later played for Benfica (8)

18 Longest river in Africa (4)

19 Ned ___, supposed Leicestershire weaver alleged to have destroyed industrial machinery in the late 18th century (4)

20 See 7 Across

No. 40

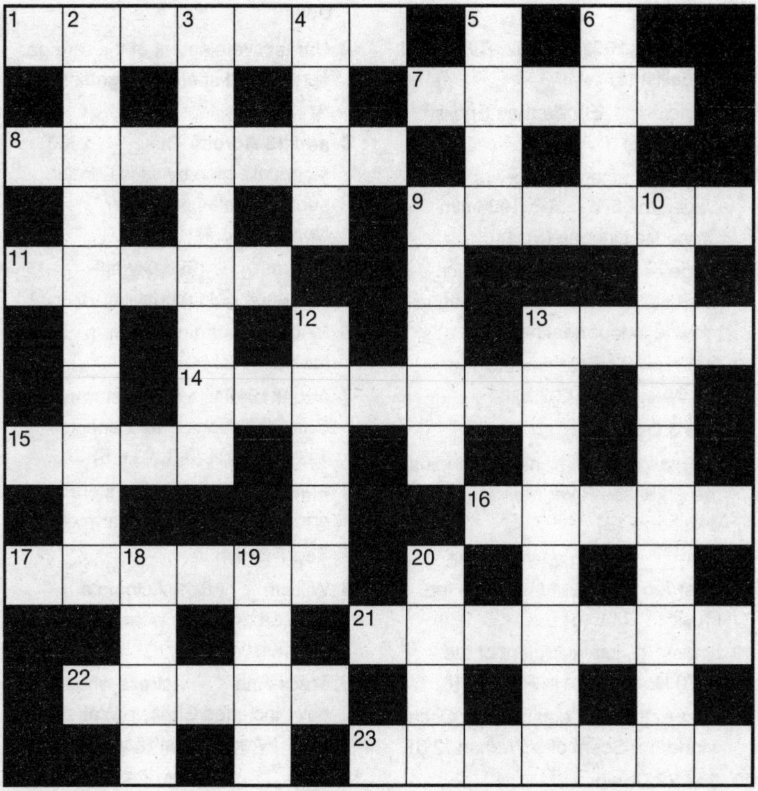

No. 41

Across

1 Mike ___, 1992 Olympic 200m gold medallist (5)

4 Francis ___, Elizabethan English admiral (5)

10 Paul ___, actor who co-wrote and played the title role in 1986 film Crocodile Dundee (5)

11 Large earthenware pot in which charcoal is burnt used in Japan to provide indoor heating (7)

12 2003 novel by Alexander Kent set in the West Indies (3,2,3)

13 See 3 Down

15 US river rising in Kansas that joins the Arkansas River near Muskogee, Oklahoma (6)

17 Bryn ___, Welsh opera singer awarded The Queen's Medal for Music in 2006 (6)

19 Louis ___, joint recipient of the 1970 Nobel Prize in Physics (4)

20 Best Actor in a Leading Role Oscar winner for Scent of a Woman (2,6)

23 See 22 Down

24 Popular name for the machine that randomly selects winning Premium Bonds numbers in Britain (5)

25 Viswanathan ___, winner of the 2008 World Chess Championship (5)

26 Graham ___, actor whose roles included Hercule LaJoy in A Shot in the Dark (5)

Down

2 Unreactive element of the rare gas series used in electric lights; symbol Ar (5)

3 **and 13 Across** The ___, 1900 story collection by Jack London subtitled Tales of the Far North (3,2,3,4)

5 Fatuma ___, 1996 Olympic marathon gold medallist (4)

6 Method of starting play in a game of football (4-3)

7 **and 9** 1949 film thriller starring Charles Laughton as Inspector Jules Maigret (3,3,2,3,6,5)

8 Member of a body of lancers first employed in the Polish army (5)

9 See 7 Down

14 William ___, Best Actor in a Supporting Role Oscar nominee for The Jolson Story (8)

16 Tracy-Ann ___, actress whose roles have included Chrissie Watts in BBC TV soap EastEnders (7)

18 Felix ___, founder of a school of fine art in London in 1871 (5)

21 John ___, 2010 Heineken Open singles tennis champion (5)

22 **and 23 Across** New Zealand-born soprano, violinist and golfer who died in 1996 (4,7)

No. 41

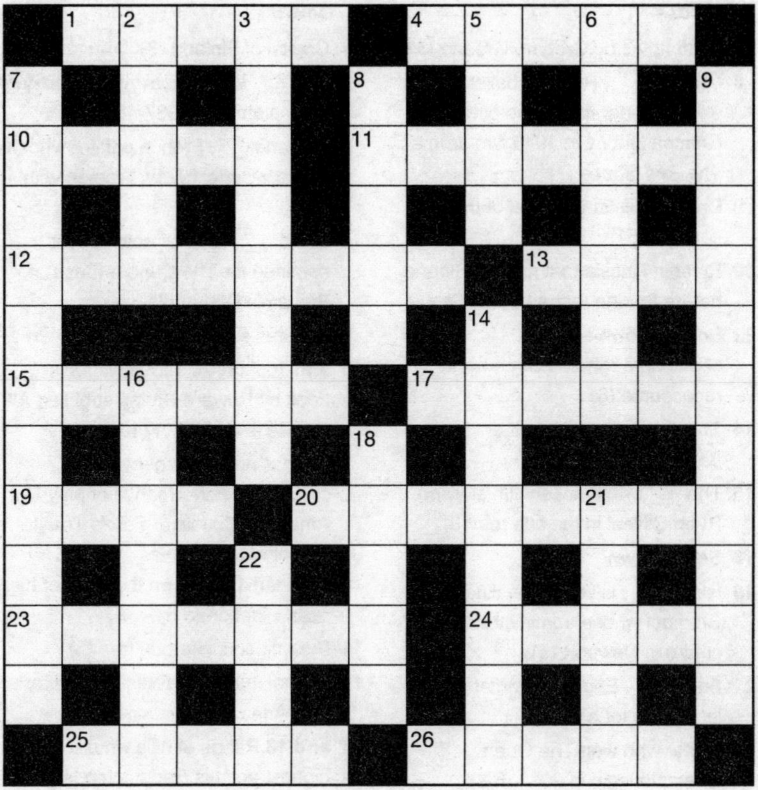

Across

6 1966 novel by Graham Greene (3,9)

8 Léonide ___, Russian ballet dancer and choreographer who played Grischa Ljubov in 1948 film drama The Red Shoes (7)

9 Dried oil-yielding kernel of the coconut (5)

10 River in Russia that rises in Siberia before flowing to the Laptev Sea (4)

12 Seaside town east of Middlesbrough housing a horse racecourse (6)

14 Standard monetary unit of Bahrain (5)

15 The ___, 1978 action film starring Ryan O'Neal in the title role (6)

16 **See 6 Down**

19 Isle of ___, island in the English Channel whose administrative centre is Newport (5)

21 Frank ___, English inventor of the jet engine for aircraft (7)

22 Golfer who won The Open Championship in 2011 (6,6)

Down

1 Capital of Finland (8)

2 Joe ___, World Heavyweight boxing champion from 1937-49 (5)

3 Fernand ___, French painter whose works include 1921's Woman with a Cat (5)

4 David ___, Best Director Oscar nominee for The Curious Case of Benjamin Button (7)

5 Children's card game (4)

6 **and 16 Across** 1939 children's book by Howard Spring subtitled All People and No Plot (10,4)

7 Actress and manager whose company's performance of play Our American Cousin at Ford's Theatre, Washington, DC was attended by Abraham Lincoln on the night of his assassination (5,5)

11 Pyramidal coniferous tree (3)

12 Animal that represents the zodiac sign Aries (3)

13 **and 18** Range of hills whose highest point is Haddington Hill near Wendover, Buckinghamshire (8,5)

14 Frankie ___, 2004 flat racing champion jockey (7)

17 Hilary ___, Best Actress in a Leading Role Oscar winner for Million Dollar Baby (5)

18 **See 13 Down**

20 Pacific island whose capital is Hagåtña (4)

Across

3 One of the tendons at the back of the thigh (9)

8 ___ Napa, Cypriot resort (4)

9 The ___, Rose Tremain novel that won the 2008 Orange Broadband Prize for Fiction (4,4)

10 Mark ___, Russia-born abstract painter whose works include Yellow Band and Number 13 (6)

13 Alfred ___, author of the 1896 stage play play Ubu Roi (5)

14 Monk-detective in novels by Ellis Peters (7)

15 Collective noun for a small group of seals or whales (3)

16 2005 novel by Chuck Palahniuk (7)

17 and 21 Chilean poet who won the 1971 Nobel Prize in Literature (5,6)

21 See 17 Across

22 Chief harpooner on the Pequod in the Herman Melville novel Moby-Dick (8)

23 1996 novel by Frederick Forsyth (4)

24 One of a large breed of gun dogs such as the Golden ___ (9)

Down

1 Rugby Union fly-half whose final Wales Test appearance was against France in 1972 (5,4)

2 and 15 1984 novel by Tom Robbins (9,7)

4 Hank ___, US baseball player who retired in 1976 with a total of 755 home runs (5)

5 A ___, cricketer whose 2010 England Test debut was against Bangladesh at Old Trafford (7)

6 Ernst ___, Nazi co-founder of the Sturmabteilung killed in 1934 (4)

7 Former gold rush town in west Alaska; finishing point of the Iditarod trail sled dog race (4)

11 Italian white, red or rosé wine of the Emilia-Romagna region (9)

12 Jazz singer whose husband John Dankworth died in 2010 (4,5)

14 Cape ___, peninsula in Massachusetts, US housing the resort of Provincetown (3)

15 See 2 Down

18 Member of a people from north Germany who invaded and settled large parts of England in the 5th and 6th centuries (5)

19 Department of France whose capital is Carcassonne (4)

20 Michael ___, war correspondent who authored 1990 novel Walter Winchell (4)

Across

1 The ___, 2013 film thriller starring Ethan Hawke and Lena Headey (5)

7 **and 5 Down** Actress whose roles have included Pam Ewing in US television soap Dallas (8,9)

8 Shrub with fragrant violet, pink or white flowers (5)

10 1934 book by Rex Stout; the first Nero Wolfe detective novel (3-2-5)

12 Imelda ___, Best Actress in a Leading Role Oscar nominee for Vera Drake (8)

14 Movement disorder affecting golfers (4)

16 Alfie ___, comedy actor who co-starred with Bill Fraser in ITV sitcom Bootsie and Snudge (4)

17 US actor who voiced the cartoon characters Daffy Duck and Porky Pig (3,5)

20 City on the River Trent associated with the hosiery industry (10)

23 Former name for both the county of Shropshire and the town of Shrewsbury (5)

24 1999 action film starring Brendan Fraser as Rick O'Connell (3,5)

25 Roman goddess of love (5)

Down

1 Large funnel-shaped structure formed by the hipbones, sacrum and coccyx in man (6)

2 Steffi ___, 1993 US Open singles tennis champion (4)

3 John ___, actor and satirist known for his work with John Fortune (4)

4 **and 21** BBC television sitcom that starred Ford Kiernan and Greg Hemphill (5,4)

5 **See 7 Across**

6 **and 18** 1973 stage play by Alan Bennett (6,6)

9 **and 15** Dorset village above which a famous chalk giant is carved out of the hillside (5,5)

11 1940 film comedy starring Laurel and Hardy (4,2,3)

13 The ___, 2001 action film starring Jet Li and Carla Gugino (3)

15 **See 9 Down**

16 Food fish such as the Pacific ___ or Atlantic ___ (6)

18 **See 6 Down**

19 Close-textured fabric of cotton, silk or spun rayon woven with lengthwise ribs (5)

21 **See 4 Down**

22 Spice made from the dried aril round a nutmeg seed (4)

Across

1 See 21 Across

8 Franz ___, 1976 Olympic downhill skiing gold medallist (7)

9 Coniferous forests that extend across much of subarctic North America and Eurasia (5)

10 In billiards, spin imparted to a ball by striking it off-centre with the cue (4)

11 and 12 Prime Minister of Japan from 2008-09 (4,3)

12 See 11 Across

14 The ___ Venus, painting by Diego Velázquez damaged by the suffragette Mary Richardson in 1914 (6)

15 Secret intelligence service of Israel (6)

18 In cricket, a ball bowled in a slow high arc (3)

20 Flightless bird of New Zealand (4)

21 and 1 F1 driver who won the 2003 European GP (4,10)

23 Board with letters and numbers on it used to seek spiritualistic messages (5)

24 US university town in central Texas associated with the oil refining industry (7)

25 and 4 Down 1910 book by L Frank Baum (3,7,4,2,2)

Down

1 1974 novel by Richard Adams (7)

2 David ___, 18th-century Scottish philosopher whose works include A Treatise of Human Nature (4)

3 Organ ___, character in the Dylan Thomas BBC Radio drama Under Milk Wood (6)

4 See 25 Across

5 Genus of shrubs that includes the heaths and some heathers (5)

6 and 17 1968 novel by Barry Hines (1,7,3,1,5)

7 US golfer; winner of the 2013 PGA Championship (5,6)

13 Town in Blaenau Gwent, Wales formerly associated with the steel and coal industries (4,4)

16 Marine algae such as bladderwrack or kelp (7)

17 See 6 Down

19 Alan ___, Liberal Democrat MP for Berwick upon Tweed from 1973 to 2015 (5)

22 University city in Tuscany, Italy housing a famous leaning tower (4)

No. 46

Across

1 Rachel ___, actress whose roles include Irene Adler in 2009 action film Sherlock Holmes (7)

7 A R ___, England Test cricketer who hit 125 against India at Kanpur in 1973 (5)

8 **and 9** 2013 novel by Wilbur Smith (7,6)

9 **See 8 Across**

11 Christian ___, actor who portrayed Orson Welles in 2008 film drama Me and Orson Welles (5)

13 **and 17** 1961 comedy-musical film starring Elvis Presley as Chad Gates (4,6)

14 1819 novel by Walter Scott (7)

15 Inner and longer of the two bones of the human forearm (4)

16 In heraldry, the colour red (5)

17 **See 13 Across**

21 Neck, liver, heart and gizzard of a fowl (7)

22 **and 23** Dish of soaked and boiled split peas served with ham or pork (5,7)

23 **See 22 Across**

Down

2 Small rodent noted for its fur native to the Andes in South America (10)

3 1741 opera by George Frideric Handel (8)

4 Volcanic island; second largest of the Hawaiian Islands (4)

5 Carlo ___, Italian author of 1945 memoir Christ Stopped at Eboli (4)

6 Bluish-white metallic element with the symbol Zn (4)

9 Fermin ___, 1992 Olympic men's 1,500m gold medallist (5)

10 City in Tasmania; main port for trade with the Australian mainland (10)

12 Island off west Italy in the Bay of Naples (5)

13 The ___, 1971 film drama starring Clint Eastwood and Geraldine Page (8)

18 Tiny brown bird with a finebill and a short narrow tail (4)

19 City in northeast Romania; a former capital of the country (4)

20 Language of Japan with dialects including Hokkaido and Sakhalin (4)

No. 46

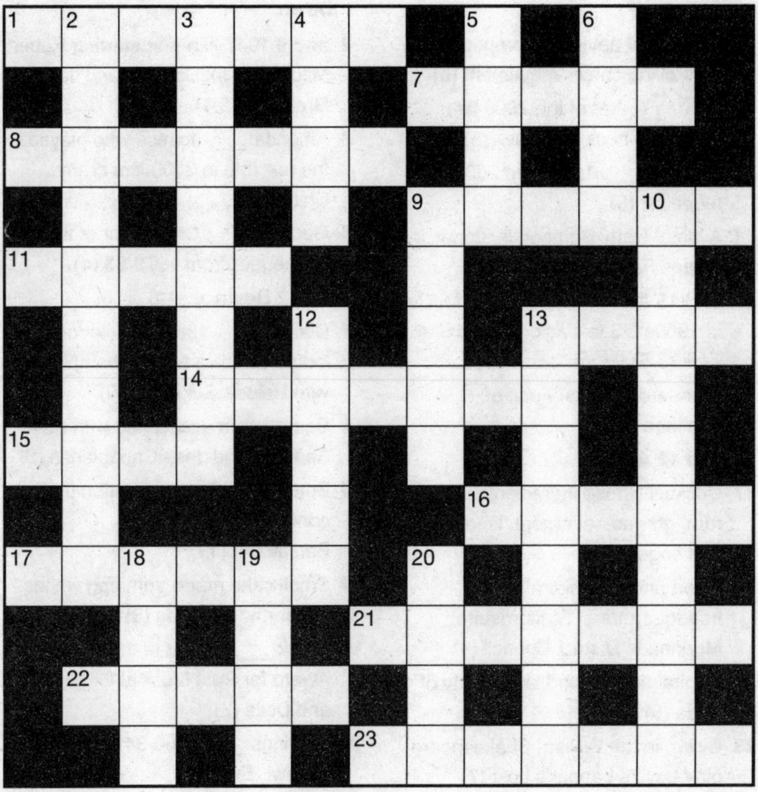

Across

1 Hand-held device in computing for controlling cursor movement (5)

4 Mike ___, star of the 2000 film comedy Chuck and Buck (5)

10 Merlene ___, 100m and 200m gold medallist (5)

11 Alias of Natty Bumppo in stories by James Fenimore Cooper (7)

12 **and 15** Actor who played Dr McCoy in 1960s US television series Star Trek (8,6)

13 Standard monetary unit of Thailand (4)

15 **See 12 Across**

17 Cocktail whose ingredients include rum, grenadine, orgeat, lime juice and sugar (3,3)

19 Town and administrative headquarters of Staffordshire Moorlands District Council (4)

20 Capital and second largest city of Syria (8)

23 Clown in the William Shakespeare play Love's Labour's Lost (7)

24 Evergreen tree of the Mediterranean with edible shiny black fruits (5)

25 **and 26** Harmless European reptile usually found near water (5,5)

26 **See 25 Across**

Down

2 **and 6** 1947 film-noir starring Robert Mitchum, Kirk Douglas and Jane Greer (3,2,3,4)

3 Amanda ___, actress who played the title role in 2009 film drama Chloe (8)

5 Geoffrey ___, Chancellor of the Exchequer from 1979-83 (4)

6 **See 2 Down**

7 Claudia ___, 1987 Wimbledon ladies' doubles tennis champion with Helena Suková (5-6)

8 Board game associated with Boris Spassky and Jose Capablanca (5)

9 Borough of Greater London that contains the Houses of Parliament (11)

14 Small cake made from egg whites, sugar and almonds (8)

16 Frank ___, winner of the 1951 Tony Award for Best Musical for Guys and Dolls (7)

18 Hastings ___, 1966-94 President of Malawi (5)

21 2006 comedy-drama film starring Adam Sandler and Kate Beckinsale (5)

22 Republic in southeast Asia whose capital is Vientiane (4)

No. 47

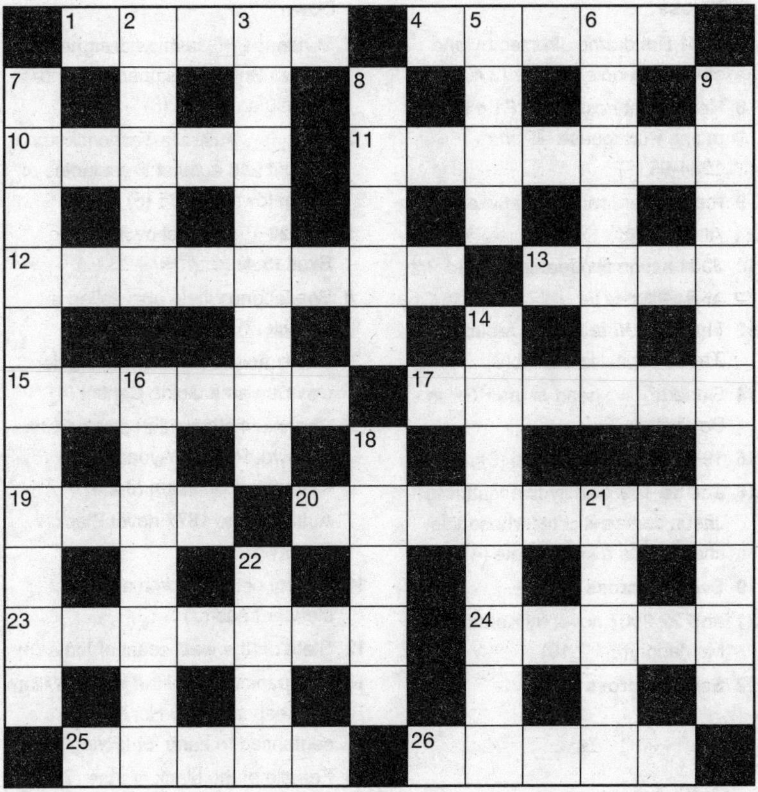

Across

6 1971 film drama directed by and starring Dennis Hopper (3,4,5)

8 Resort that hosted the F1 motor racing Portuguese GP from 1984-96 (7)

9 Playing card ranking between a king and jack (5)

10 2004 action film featuring Brad Pitt as Achilles (4)

12 The ___, West African republic whose capital is Banjul (6)

14 General ___, head of the KGB in six Bond films (5)

15 1985 Jilly Cooper novel (6)

16 and 19 1993 family film featuring Jason James Richter whose title character is a killer whale (4,5)

19 See 16 Across

21 and 22 2007 novel by Katharine McMahon (3,4,2,10)

22 See 21 Across

Down

1 Vivienne ___, fashion designer named British Designer of the Year in 1990 and 1991 (8)

2 W M ___, Australia Test cricketer who hit 210 against West Indies at Bridgetown in 1965 (5)

3 and 20 1985 novel by A S Byatt (5,4)

4 Whalebone whale also called a finback (7)

5 2009 musical film starring Daniel Day-Lewis as Guido Contini (4)

6 Channel 4 sitcom that starred Chris O'Dowd, Richard Ayoade and Katherine Parkinson (3,2,5)

7 Author of the 1877 novel Black Beauty (4,6)

11 Variety of lettuce with a long slender head (3)

12 State on the west coast of India (3)

13 Companion of Falstaff in the William Shakespeare play Henry V sentenced to hang for looting (8)

14 Female of the black grouse (7)

17 Jack ___, Home Secretary from 1997-2001 (5)

18 1983 film drama directed by and starring Barbra Streisand (5)

20 See 3 Down

No. 48

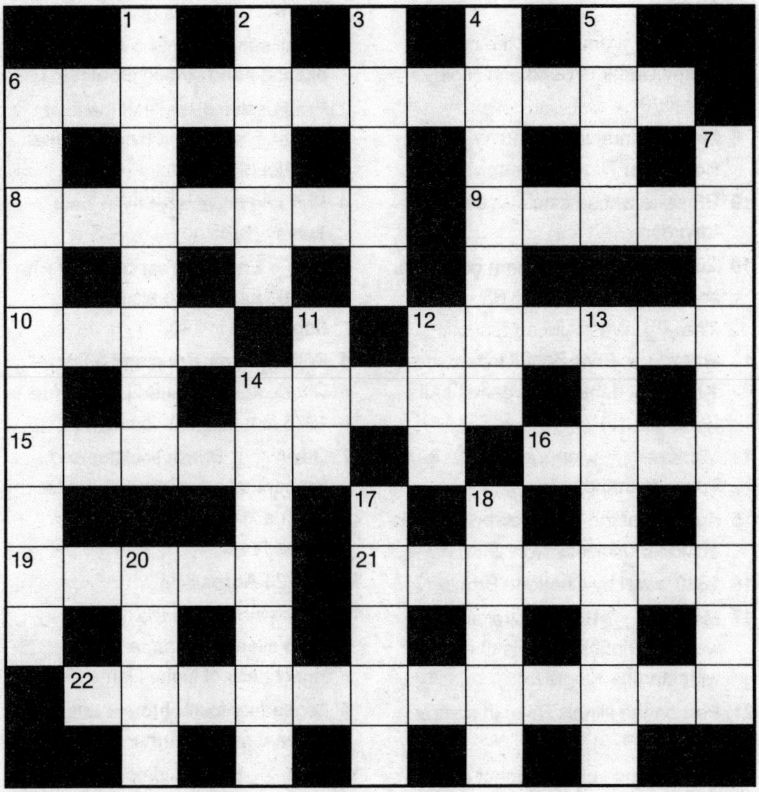

No. 49

Across

3 Patricia ___, author of the novels Ripley Under Ground and Ripley's Game (9)

8 Marvel character played by Anthony Hopkins in Thor: Ragnarok (4)

9 US state whose capital is Jefferson City (8)

10 Antal ___, Budapest-born conductor awarded an honorary KBE in 1983 (6)

13 G R J ___, England cricketer whose 1973 Test debut was against India at Kanpur (5)

14 Michael ___, winner of the 2012 Tokyo marathon (7)

15 Any one of the ten black-belt grades of judo proficiency (3)

16 1849 novel by Charlotte Brontë (7)

17 Mirjana ___, 1998 Australian Open women's doubles tennis champion with Martina Hingis (5)

21 Port on the Illinois River in central Illinois, US (6)

22 Lower house of Parliament of India (3,5)

23 **and 11 Down** French mathematician born in 1596 regarded as the founder of modern philosophy (4,9)

24 The ___, 1978 novel by Emma Tennant (3,6)

Down

1 Small songbird with a dull green plumage and striped crown (9)

2 Progressive disease of the liver sometimes caused by excessive alcohol (9)

4 Port and university city in west Turkey (5)

5 N ___, England Test cricketer who hit 207 against Australia at Edgbaston in 1997 (7)

6 Keith ___, musician and actor whose roles included Uncle Ernie in 1975 film musical Tommy (4)

7 Gavin ___, British sculptor and conceptual artist whose installations include 2004's The Golden Thread (4)

11 **See 23 Across**

12 Actor who played the title role in 1923 silent film drama The Hunchback of Notre Dame (3,6)

14 Legendary foster brother and steward of King Arthur (3)

15 Leo ___, French composer of the ballet Coppélia (7)

18 Card of the highest ranking suit in the game of bridge (5)

19 Port in the Democratic Republic of the Congo; capital of the Belgian Congo until 1926 (4)

20 Ancient Egyptian female fertility goddess usually depicted with a cow's horns (4)

No. 49

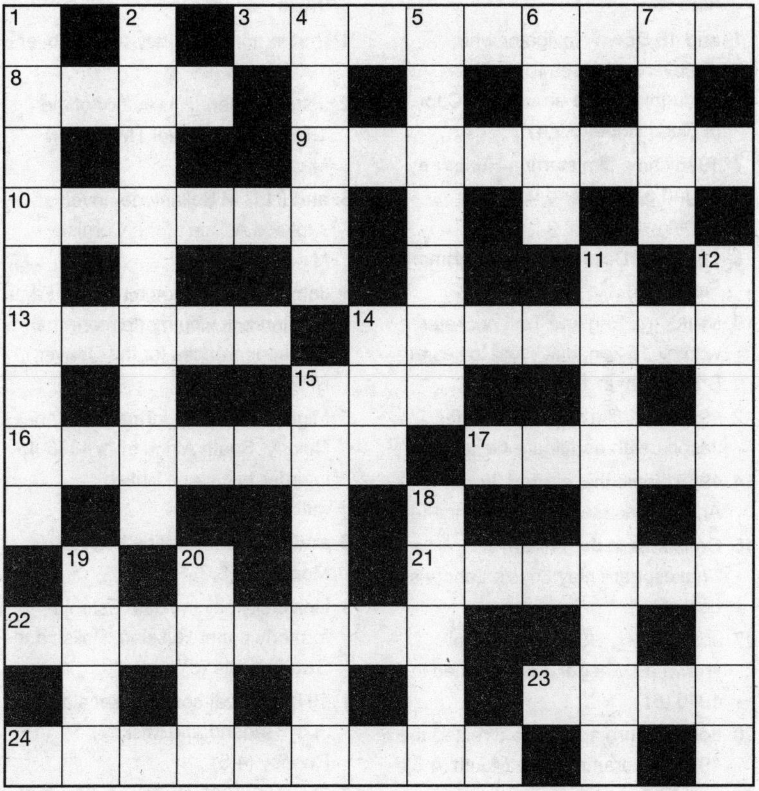

Across

1 and 16 Down Navigator who discovered the sea route from Portugal to India around the Cape of Good Hope (5,2,4)

7 1948 crime film starring Humphrey Bogart and Edward G Robinson (3,5)

8 Capital of Deux-Sèvres department, France (5)

10 Mark ___, England Test cricketer who hit 154 against West Indies at Bridgetown in 1998 (10)

12 1999 sci-fi film starring Jennifer Jason Leigh as Allegra Geller (8)

14 1968 biopic that starred Julie Andrews as Gertrude Lawrence (4)

16 Constable in the William Shakespeare play Love's Labour's Lost (4)

17 Joseph ___, US Army general known as Vinegar Joe who died in 1946 (8)

20 London-born actor who directed the 1997 film drama Nil By Mouth (4,6)

23 and 25 English magician associated with puppet Basil Brush (5,5)

24 Abel ___, Prime Minister of the unrecognized state of Zimbabwe Rhodesia in 1979 (8)

25 See 23 Across

Down

1 Port in northeast Italy built on over 100 islands (6)

2 John Dickson ___, author of the 1935 mystery novel The Hollow Man (4)

3 and 21 R M Ballantyne novel subtitled A Tale of the Cornish Mines (4,4)

4 John ___, Pro Football Hall of Fame quarterback who made more than 200 appearances for the Denver Broncos (5)

5 Migration of Boer farmers in Cape Colony, South Africa from 1836-45 in order to escape British authority (5,4)

6 and 18 1988 novel by Michael Moorcock (6,6)

9 University city in south Estonia formerly under Russian, Polish and Swedish rule (5)

11 1943 musical-comedy film starring Judy Garland and Mickey Rooney (4,5)

13 The ___, 1995 film thriller starring Sandra Bullock as Angela Bennett (3)

15 The ___, Greek epic poem describing the siege of Troy (5)

16 See 1 Across

18 See 6 Down

19 Adrienne ___, actress whose roles include Mrs Alexander in 1971 film drama A Clockwork Orange (5)

21 See 3 Down

22 Mohammad ___, former Afghanistan cricket captain (4)

No. 51

Across

1 1982 film comedy starring Henry Winkler and Michael Keaton (5,5)

8 Kim ___, actress whose roles have included Helga Geerhart in BBC TV sitcom 'Allo 'Allo! (7)

9 Carla ___, singer and actress and wife of former French President Nicolas Sarkozy (5)

10 Stubby ___, actor-comedian whose roles included Nicely-Nicely Johnson in the 1955 film musical Guys and Dolls (4)

11 River that flows into the North Sea at Middlesbrough (4)

12 Small tree or shrub whose leaves are used to make a beverage (3)

14 Longest river in Great Britain (6)

15 Asher Brown ___, US painter whose works include 1868's The Trysting Tree (6)

18 **and 13 Down** 2010 film drama starring Julia Roberts as Liz Gilbert (3,4,4)

20 Y E ___, 2009 US PGA champion (4)

21 **and 2 Down** Type of football played at Eton College for boys (4,4)

23 Word for the letter R in the NATO phonetic alphabet (5)

24 Japanese art of paper folding (7)

25 2006 snooker world champion (6,4)

Down

1 Rudolf ___, Russian-born ballet dancer who died in 1993 (7)

2 **See 21 Across**

3 Roscoe ___, January 1977 Australian singles tennis champion (6)

4 Genus of flowering plants of the mallow family (8)

5 Opera by Charles Gounod that premiered in 1859 (5)

6 **and 17** 1998 comedy-drama film starring Gwyneth Paltrow and Joseph Fiennes (11,2,4)

7 City in west Cuba associated with the tobacco industry (5,3,3)

13 **See 18 Across**

16 Singer and actor born Stuart Goddard in London in 1954 (4,3)

17 **See 6 Down**

19 River that forms most of the border between Cornwall and Devon (5)

22 1953-80 Yugoslavia President born Josip Broz (4)

Across

1 One of two or more atoms with the same atomic number that contain different numbers of neutrons (7)

7 **and 22** David Mitchell novel shortlisted for the 2004 Man Booker Prize (5,5)

8 J E ___, England Test cricketer who took 7-78 against Australia in Sydney in 1987 (7)

9 Draped garment traditionally worn in southeast Asia (6)

11 **and 13 Down** Plant of the lily family with orange bell-shaped flowers (5,8)

13 US state whose capital is Des Moines (4)

14 Ductile white metallic element; symbol Nb (7)

15 **and 17** 1986 film thriller starring Isabella Rossellini and Kyle MacLachlan (4,6)

16 Pseudonym of Belgian strip cartoonist Georges Remi (5)

17 **See 15 Across**

21 Large aquatic bird that stores fish in a pouch below the lower mandible (7)

22 **See 7 Across**

23 Slice of meat rolled around a stuffing and cooked (7)

Down

2 Geraldine ___, actress whose roles have included DS Jane Penhaligon in ITV drama series Cracker (10)

3 Josiah ___, 1996 Olympic marathon gold medallist (8)

4 2002 novel by Michael Crichton (4)

5 Mountainous island off the west coast of Italy (4)

6 National style of wrestling of Japan (4)

9 Fabric of silk and rayon closely woven to give a smooth glossy appearance (5)

10 Region of the northeast United States including Rhode Island and Vermont (3,7)

12 Peggy ___, comedy actress whose roles included Mrs Bumble in 1968 film musical Oliver! (5)

13 **See 11 Across**

18 Henry Francis ___, author of the words of the hymn Abide With Me (4)

19 Jennifer ___, author of the novels The Keep and Look at Me (4)

20 Paula ___, Lisbon-born artist whose works include 1988's The Dance (4)

No. 52

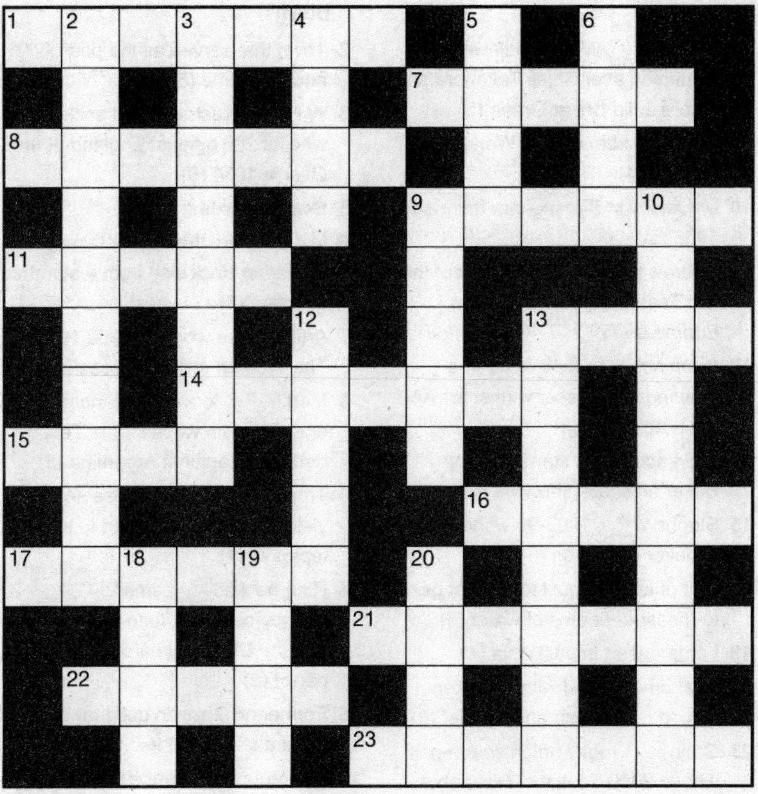

Across

1 William ___, WBA middleweight champion after Shinji Takehara and before Julio César Green (5)

4 German submarine in World Wars I and II (1-4)

10 University in Birmingham founded in 1966 (5)

11 Hebrew prophet whose book of the Old Testament condemns the Edomites (7)

12 Broderick ___, Best Actor in a Leading Role Oscar winner for All the King's Men (8)

13 1964 action film starring Stanley Baker and Jack Hawkins (4)

15 Stephen ___, 1992-96 world snooker champion (6)

17 Unit of length equal to six feet used to measure depths of water (6)

19 Large desert in east Asia (4)

20 Seal ornamented with a sunken design rather than one in relief (8)

23 Greig ___, rugby union scrum-half whose 2010 Scotland Test debut was against New Zealand (7)

24 Young eel (5)

25 **and 5 Down** Neolithic village in the Orkney Islands, northeast Scotland (5,4)

26 Emma ___, actress who played Skeeter Phelan in 2011 film The Help (5)

Down

2 Town that served as the port of ancient Rome (5)

3 W H ___, Australia Test cricketer who hit 266 against England at the Oval in 1934 (8)

5 **See 25 Across**

6 In surveying, the horizontal angle of a bearing clockwise from a standard direction (7)

7 Artist whose works include 1929's The Woman and the Roses (4,7)

8 Martin ___, former England rugby union captain whose 1997 Test debut was against Argentina (5)

9 Tropical Asian tree whose seeds yield an oil formerly used to treat leprosy (11)

14 Ring-necked ___, small, brightly-coloured, long-tailed bird and the UK's only naturalised parrot (8)

16 Former no 9 iron in golf that gave a great deal of lift (7)

18 ___ Mountains, range of peaks within the Australian Alps whose highest point is Mount Kosciuszko (5)

21 Loch ___, body of water in Perth and Kinross, Scotland, housing a castle that was a place of imprisonment of Mary, Queen of Scots (5)

22 In music, a legato performance of a melodic interval of two or more notes in a part (4)

No. 53

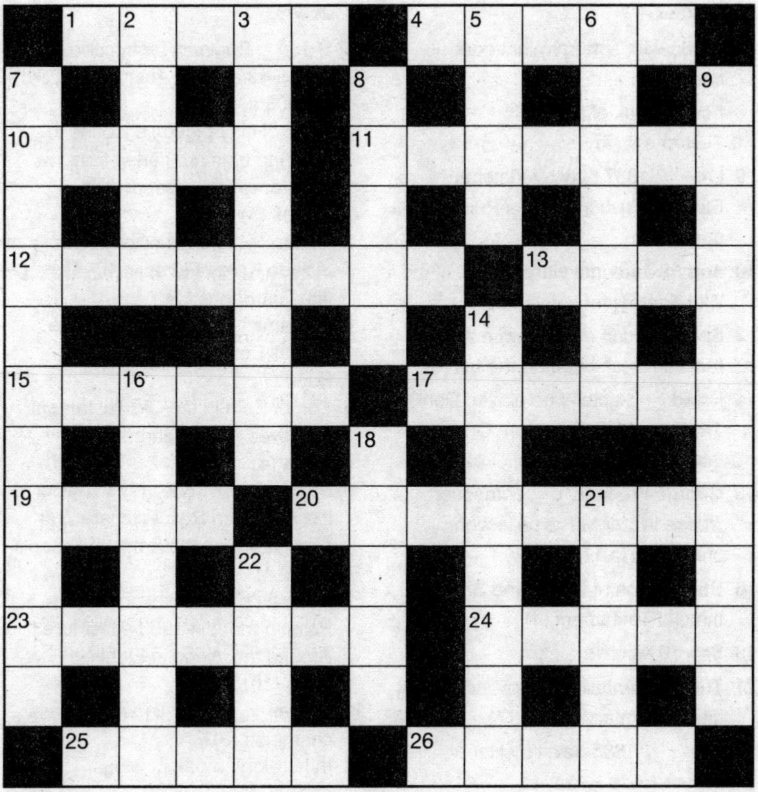

No. 54

Across

6 Shrub with small piquant dark berries (12)

8 Fourth book of the Old Testament (7)

9 La ___, 1887 play by Victorien Sardou which inspired a Puccini opera (5)

10 **and 19** 1861 novel by Ellen Wood (4,5)

12 South African monkey with a reddish patch beneath the tail (6)

14 David ___, actor who played Derek Trotter in BBC TV sitcom Only Fools and Horses (5)

15 George Frederic ___, composer whose Water Music collection premiered in 1717 (6)

16 Second son of Judah and Shua in the Old Testament (4)

19 **See 10 Across**

21 The ___, Anton Chekhov stage play first performed in 1896 (7)

22 The ___, 1888 novel by Henry James (6,6)

Down

1 S J ___, England Test cricketer who took 5-43 against Australia at Lord's in 2005 (8)

2 Form of clay-pigeon shooting in which targets are hurled from two traps at varying speeds and angles (5)

3 Rene ___, actress whose roles include Karen Flores in 1995 crime film Get Shorty (5)

4 Benjamin ___, composer of the operas Peter Grimes and Billy Budd (7)

5 Son of Seth in the Old Testament who lived nine hundred and five years (4)

6 Battle of ___, June, 1775 conflict of the American Revolutionary War also known as the Battle of Breed's Hill (6,4)

7 Mexican comedian who played Passepartout in 1956 adventure film Around the World in Eighty Days (10)

11 Mikhail ___, 1960-61 world chess champion (3)

12 In heraldry, a pair of wings conjoined (3)

13 Denise ___, television presenter whose credits include The Big Breakfast and Who Dares, Sings! (3,5)

14 1938 film drama for which Bette Davis won a Best Actress in a Leading Role Oscar (7)

17 Rafael ___, 1963 US National Singles tennis champion (5)

18 State in Western Asia whose capital is Doha (5)

20 Walter ___, Prime Minister of New Zealand from 1957-60 (4)

Across

3 1992 comedy-drama film starring Eddie Murphy, Robin Givens and Halle Berry (9)

8 Sea of ___, arm of the Black Sea fed chiefly by the River Don (4)

9 The ___, 1994 animated film for which Hans Zimmer won a Best Music, Original Score Oscar (4,4)

10 Iwan ___, rugby union wing whose 1985 Scotland Test debut was against Ireland (6)

13 Tree with red, sugar and Florida varieties (5)

14 Genus of trees including the California redwood (7)

15 Gok ___, television presenter whose credits include Miss Naked Beauty and How to Look Good Naked (3)

16 W Somerset ___, author of The Sacred Flame and The Bread-Winner (7)

17 Piece of music composed for eight singers (5)

21 African republic whose capital is Lilongwe (6)

22 Nadia ___, 1976 and 1980 Olympic balance beam gold medal-winning gymnast (8)

23 Miles ___, actor and comedian who played Archie in Balamory (4)

24 Stew originating from France made with haricot beans and meat (9)

Down

1 Theatrical entertainment performed at Christmas time such as Aladdin or Cinderella (9)

2 Annual period of fasting for Jewish people also called the Day of Atonement (3,6)

4 Deck of HMS Victory where a lamp marks the spot where Horatio Nelson is believed to have died (5)

5 Female of the red grouse (7)

6 Aniseed-flavoured spirit distilled in Turkey and former Yugoslavia (4)

7 Luigi ___, Italian composer of 1960 work Intolleranza (4)

11 Mild semi-soft cow's milk cheese of northwest France (4,5)

12 Wife of Socrates, whose name has come to mean any quarrelsome woman (9)

14 ___ Worthington, actor who plays Jake Sully in the James Cameron film Avatar (3)

15 Jean-Antoine ___, French painter whose works include 1717's The Embarkation for Cythera (7)

18 Perpetually ill character in the Charles Dickens novel Nicholas Nickleby (5)

19 Asian bean plant whose nutritious seeds are used as food and forage (4)

20 1975 film thriller starring Roy Scheider and Robert Shaw (4)

No. 55

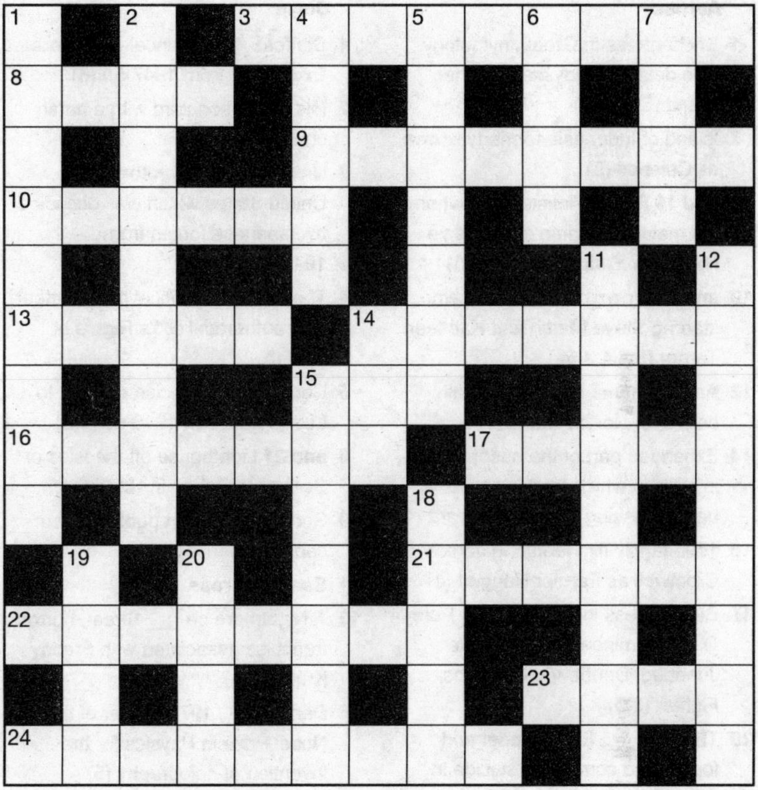

Across

1 Enchantress in Greek mythology who detained Odysseus on her island (5)

7 Island of Indonesia formerly known as Celebes (8)

8 and 19 Down Violinist after whom the main auditorium at Carnegie Hall, New York is named (5,5)

10 and 11 Down 1983 film comedy starring Steve Martin and Kathleen Turner (3,3,4,3,6)

12 Another name for the mountain beaver of North America (8)

14 Expanded part of the oesophagus in birds in which food is stored before passing on to the gizzard (4)

16 1995 family film featuring James Cromwell as Farmer Hoggett (4)

17 Best Actress in a Supporting Role Oscar nominee for The Master, Junebug, Doubt, Vice and The Fighter (3,5)

20 Thomas ___, English poet and forger who committed suicide in 1770 (10)

23 Odilon ___, French painter whose works include 1898's Vierge nimbee (5)

24 White, long-bodied, lop-eared breed of pork pig developed in Denmark (8)

25 Short composition for one instrument intended as an exercise for the improvement of a performer's technique (5)

Down

1 Stafford ___, Chancellor of the Exchequer from 1947-50 (6)

2 Old World songbird with a harsh chattering cry (4)

3 Unincorporated territory of the United States which was occupied by Japanese forces from 1941-44 (4)

4 Thomas ___, political pamphleteer who authored 1791's Rights of Man (5)

5 Cuban-born musician married to Lucille Ball from 1940-60 (4,5)

6 and 21 Lighthouse off the Isles of Scilly established in 1858 (6,4)

9 South American republic whose capital is Santiago (5)

11 See 10 Across

13 A Nightmare on ___ Street, horror franchise associated with Freddy Krueger (3)

15 Dennis ___, 1971 winner of the Nobel Prize in Physics for the invention of holography (5)

16 Lauren ___, Best Actress in a Supporting Role Oscar nominee for The Mirror Has Two Faces (6)

18 Basil ___, British architect who designed Coventry Cathedral (6)

19 See 8 Across

21 See 6 Down

22 Small amphibian whose species include the Palmate, Great Crested and Smooth (4)

Across

1 Wine bottle holding the equivalent of 12 normal bottles (10)

8 and 24 1915 novel by W Somerset Maugham (2,5,7)

9 Frederick ___ composer of the music for the 1947 stage musical Brigadoon (5)

10 River in Devon that flows into the English Channel at Dartmouth (4)

11 Barbara ___ actress whose roles have included Cinnamon Carter in US television series Mission: Impossible (4)

12 Unit of thermal resistance used to measure the power of insulation of a quilt (3)

14 Robert ___ author of novel The Ragged Trousered Philanthropists under the name Robert Tressell (6)

15 Preserver and protector of the universe in the Hindu Trimurti (6)

18 Instance of a batter touching all four bases safely in baseball (3)

20 Kingsley ___, Lucky Jim author (4)

21 Standard unit of currency of Myanmar (4)

23 Seaweeds with varieties such as 'serrated' or 'bladder' (5)

24 See 8 Across

25 Jonah ___ British Open squash champion from 1970-73 (10)

Down

1 President of Indonesia from 1967-98 (7)

2 Capital of Togo (4)

3 Trojan prince and son of Aphrodite in classical mythology who escaped the sack of Troy (6)

4 Legendary continent said to have sunk beneath the ocean west of the Straits of Gibraltar (8)

5 Another name for a catkin (5)

6 British prime minister from 2007-10 (6,5)

7 1824 novel by Sir Walter Scott featuring the story Wandering Willie's Tale (11)

13 S M ___, India Test cricketer who hit 236 n.o. against West Indies at Madras in 1983 (8)

16 The ___, 1821 oil painting by John Constable featuring Flatford Mill (3,4)

17 Small agile ape of forests in south Asia (6)

19 Lake ___, body of water in central Africa at the southern end of the Great Rift Valley (5)

22 Unit of speed of one nautical mile per hour (4)

Across

1 Dom ___ Prime Minister of Malta from 1971-84 (7)

7 and 22 1998 crime film starring George Clooney and Jennifer Lopez (3,2,5)

8 Large feline mammal; the swiftest known to man (7)

9 Ed ___ Best Actor in a Supporting Role Oscar winner for Sweet Bird of Youth (6)

11 Pair of short cloth gaiters covering the instep and ankle (5)

13 See 3 Down

14 Giuseppe Verdi opera composed in 1841 whose title character is king of Babylon (7)

15 Gaming stake put up before the deal in poker (4)

16 and 23 Actor who starred as Timothy Lea in the 1970s Confessions series of British comedy films (5,7)

17 Johan ___ Swedish golfer who won the 2006 Scottish Open (6)

21 Golfer who captained the 1957 British PGA Ryder Cup-winning team (3,4)

22 See 7 Across

23 See 16 Across

Down

2 and 13 Down 1944 film comedy starring Dick Powell and Linda Darnell (2,8,8)

3 and 13 Across 1972 BBC TV drama by Nigel Kneale starring Michael Bryant and Jane Asher (3,5,4)

4 Ship designed for Fridtjof Nansen's 1893 Arctic explorations (4)

5 The ___ Player, title of paintings by Caravaggio and Orazio Gentileschi (4)

6 Book of the Old Testament attributed to the son of Pethuel (4)

9 Tree of temperate regions that bears small edible, triangular nuts (5)

10 The ___ 2010 film drama starring Adrien Brody and Forest Whitaker (10)

12 The ___, 1989 action film starring Ed Harris and Mary Elizabeth Mastrantonio (5)

13 See 2 Down

18 Light slender flexible sword tipped by a button (4)

19 Chief coal mining and industrial region of Germany (4)

20 Roman god of war (4)

No. 59

Across

1 ___ Protocol, 1997 international treaty on climate change, named after the city in which it was adopted (5)

4 Eighth letter of the Greek alphabet (5)

10 In heraldry, the colour blue (5)

11 King of Scotland from 1040-57 (7)

12 Port in southwest Japan (8)

13 Chemical element; symbol Pb (4)

15 William Henry ___ US Secretary of State from 1861-69 (6)

17 Plant with flat clusters of white flower heads whose dried stalks are used for divination (6)

19 2009 family film featuring Kelsey Grammer as Mr Cranston (4)

20 Hindu trinity of the gods Brahma, Vishnu and Shiva (8)

23 Sheila ___ 1966 Tony Award Best Actress in a Play nominee for Entertaining Mr Sloane (7)

24 **25 and 26** 1998 steel sculpture by Antony Gormley erected in Gateshead (5,2,3,5)

25 **See 24 Across**

26 **See 24 Across**

Down

2 Kirsty ___ former presenter of BBC Radio show Desert Island Discs (5)

3 Government department responsible for economic strategy in Britain (8)

5 Joint in the hind leg of a horse between the gaskin and the cannon bone (4)

6 **See 16 Down**

7 **and 9** 2013 novel by Ian Rankin (6,2,3,6,5)

8 Miyoshi ___, Best Actress in a Supporting Role Oscar winner for Sayonara (5)

9 **See 7 Down**

14 Russian sculptor whose works include 1930's Construction in a Niche (4,4)

16 **and 6** 1942 romcom starring Spencer Tracy and Katharine Hepburn (5,2,3,4)

18 Common tree in intertropical Africa which yields a durable wood (5)

21 Peter Mark ___, English physician and lexicographer whose Thesaurus of English Words and Phrases was published in 1852 (5)

22 Page to Don Adriano de Armado in William Shakespeare play Love's Labour's Lost (4)

No. 59

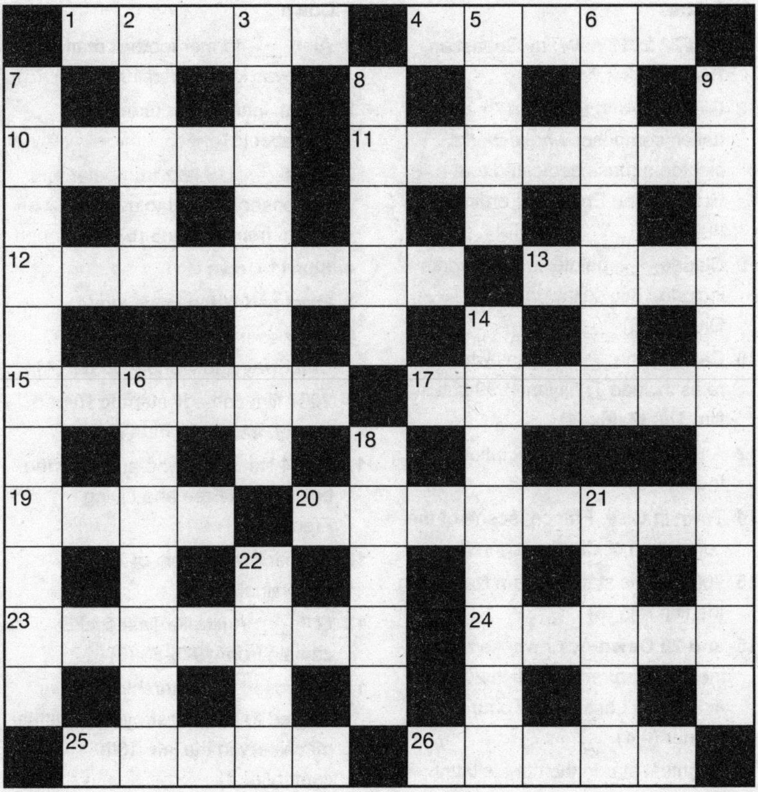

Across

6 and 22 2013 novel by Sebastian Faulks (6,3,3,7,5)

8 Giovanni Antonio ___, 17th-century Italian composer whose works include a mass dedicated to the Holy Roman Emperor Ferdinand III (7)

9 Claude ___, painter whose works include 1886's Haystack at Giverny (5)

10 Carrie-Anne ___, actress whose roles include Trinity in 1999 action film The Matrix (4)

12 Another name for association football (6)

14 Town in Oise, France; scene of the coronation of Charlemagne (5)

15 2004 biopic starring Liam Neeson in the title role (6)

16 and 20 Down Actor whose roles include Manfred Powell in 2001 action film Lara Croft: Tomb Raider (4,4)

19 Brightest star in the constellation Orion (5)

21 Marcus Vipsanius ___, Roman general and son-in-law of Augustus (7)

22 See 6 Across

Down

1 Alex ___, former football manager who was knighted in 1999 (8)

2 Fourth letter in the Greek alphabet (5)

3 Miles ___, US jazz trumpeter and composer married to actress Cicely Tyson from 1981-88 (5)

4 See 11 Down

5 Front part of the lower leg (4)

6 Composer of the music for 1927 Broadway show Show Boat (6,4)

7 2007 film comedy starring Rupert Everett and Colin Firth (2,8)

11 and 4 Naturalist who authored the books Born Free and Living Free (3,7)

12 Former French coin of low denomination (3)

13 G S ___, Australia Test cricket captain from 1975-83 (8)

14 Supposed Leicestershire weaver alleged to have destroyed industrial machinery in the late 18th century (3,4)

17 William ___, US animator who formed a successful partnership with Joseph Barbera (5)

18 Freshwater diving bird with lobed membranes along each toe (5)

20 See 16 Across

No. 61

Across

3 Yellow mineral such as pyrite or chalcopyrite (5,4)

8 Argyll and Bute resort where a whisky distillery has existed since 1794, predating the establishment of the town (4)

9 Genus of perennial plants with slender spikes of small yellow flowers (8)

10 Stringed musical instrument related to the lute (6)

13 Jimmy ___, President of the International Brotherhood of Teamsters from 1957-71 who disappeared in 1975 (5)

14 **and 16** 2013 novel by David Baldacci (4,3,7)

15 Insect such as the mason ___ or carpenter ___ (3)

16 See 14 Across

17 **and 22** Author of the novels Amelia and An Apology for the Life of Mrs Shamela Andrews (5,8)

21 Fanny ___ actress who portrayed Mary of Guise in 1998 film drama Elizabeth (6)

22 See 17 Across

23 **and 6 Down** The ___, 1920 stage play by John Galsworthy (4,4)

24 Richard ___, US actor who played the title role in 1971 film thriller Shaft (9)

Down

1 French horse racecourse that hosts the Prix de l'Arc de Triomphe (9)

2 Best Actor in a Leading Role Oscar winner for biopic Ray (5,4)

4 International airport in Chicago formerly called Orchard Field (5)

5 US city that houses the University of Wyoming (7)

6 See 23 Across

7 **and 20** Actress whose roles include Diane Hirsch in 2010 film drama Remember Me (4,4)

11 Author of the novels The Business and The Wasp Factory (4,5)

12 ___ Rocks, a group in the English Channel southwest of Plymouth (9)

14 **and 18** Golfer who won The Open Championship in 1960 (3,5)

15 Louis ___, French aviator who made the first flight across the English Channel (7)

18 See 14 Down

19 Richard ___, 2001 World Championships 5,000m gold medallist (4)

20 See 7 Down

Across

1 and 3 Down 2008 Olympic decathlon gold medallist (5,4)

7 and 5 Down Scottish actor who played Archie MacDonald in BBC TV comedy series Monarch of the Glen (8,9)

8 Jesse ___, 1936 Olympic 100m and 200m gold medallist (5)

10 Actor who portrayed Ian Brady in 2006 Channel 4 television drama Longford (4,6)

12 Hector ___, US actor whose roles include Barney Thompson in 1990 romcom Pretty Woman (8)

14 and 13 Down 2001 novel by Alan Titchmarsh (4,3)

16 Tropical yellow-flowered plant cultivated for its strong fibre (4)

17 Capital of South Australia (8)

20 Port at the mouth of the River Wear (10)

23 Paavo ___, 1924 Olympic 5,000m gold medallist (5)

24 Caryl ___, author of novels The Final Passage and In the Falling Snow (8)

25 Sharon ___, Best Actress in a Leading Role Oscar nominee for Casino (5)

Down

1 David ___, show jumper who won the 1960 BBC Sports Personality of the Year Award (6)

2 Former Indian copper coin worth one sixteenth of a rupee (4)

3 See 1 Across

4 Arthur ___, bespectacled Liverpudlian comedian who died in 1982 (5)

5 See 7 Across

6 Bing ___, Best Actor in a Leading Role Oscar nominee for The Country Girl (6)

9 Ornamental net loosely holding a woman's hair at the back (5)

11 German Shepherd dog, a Hollywood star of the 1920s who died in 1932 (3,3,3)

13 See 14 Across

15 Jerome ___, actor whose roles have included Sergeant Bennet Drake in BBC TV drama series Ripper Street (5)

16 Biblical character; husband of Mary, the mother of Jesus (6)

18 1987 novel by Gore Vidal (6)

19 Philippe ___, rugby union centre whose 1982 France Test debut was against Romania (5)

21 Member of a nomadic people living chiefly in north Scandinavia and the Kola Peninsula (4)

22 2013 novel by Patricia Cornwell (4)

Across

1 Charles Camille ___, French composer of 1874 symphonic poem Danse Macabre (5-5)

8 Ardal ___, Irish stand-up comedian and actor who authored novel The Talk of the Town (7)

9 David ___, playwright whose stage works include Maydays and Pentecost (5)

10 Wyomia ___, 1964 and 1968 Olympic women's 100m gold medallist (4)

11 Flesh of a calf used as food (4)

12 Unit of length equal to five and a half yards (3)

14 Seventh planet from the sun (6)

15 Standard monetary unit of Russia (6)

18 Resort town in Belgium with medicinal mineral springs (3)

20 **and 21** Holiday resort on the southeast coast of Cyprus (4,4)

21 **See 20 Across**

23 Louis ___, French designer of the modern two-piece swimsuit (5)

24 Word representing the letter C in the NATO phonetic alphabet (7)

25 State capital of Alabama (10)

Down

1 Either of the two large flat triangular bones also called a shoulder blade (7)

2 Eric ___, Monty Python member who wrote the book of Broadway musical Spamalot (4)

3 Gene ___, World Heavyweight boxing champion from 1926-28 (6)

4 **and 19** 1944 war novel by John Hersey (1,4,3,5)

5 West African republic whose capital is Niamey (5)

6 Shipping forecast area north of Fisher off the southwest coast of Norway (5,6)

7 Brad ___, 1996 Olympic 200m backstroke swimming gold medallist (11)

13 Princess ___, Puccini opera role first performed by soprano Rosa Raisa (8)

16 Omar ___, US Army general who was Chairman of the Joint Chiefs of Staff from 1949-53 (7)

17 Ben ___, 1974 Commonwealth 5,000m gold medallist (6)

19 **See 4 Down**

22 Cultivated variety of cabbage with crinkled leaves (4)

Across

1 and 14 2013 novel by Michael Connelly (3,4,2,5)

7 and 22 Pakistan Test cricketer who took 9-56 against England at Lahore in 1987 (5,5)

8 Dennis ___ WBC Light Heavyweight champion from 1990-91 (7)

9 and 13 Down Actor who played the title role in 1970 comedy-adventure film The Private Life of Sherlock Holmes (6,8)

11 Thicker of the two bones of the leg between the knee and ankle (5)

13 River rising in Slovenia that flows to the Danube at Belgrade (4)

14 See 1 Across

15 Berkshire town housing a public school for boys (4)

16 Narcotic drug extracted from the unripe seeds of a poppy (5)

17 Garret ___, 24th vice president of the United States of America (6)

21 and 12 Down 1818 opera by Rossini (5,2,5)

22 See 7 Across

23 Port in northeast Sicily that houses a university (7)

Down

2 Golfer who won the 2011 South African Open (6,4)

3 Zina ___, 1990 Wimbledon singles tennis championship runner-up (8)

4 Nest of a squirrel (4)

5 Longest river entirely within Spain (4)

6 Department of northern France whose capital is Évreux (4)

9 and 19 WBC Super Middleweight champion from 1996-97 (5,4)

10 1985 film drama starring Al Pacino and Donald Sutherland (10)

12 See 21 Across

13 See 9 Across

18 Andy ___, US golfer who won the Doral-Eastern Open Invitational in 1977, 1982 and 1986 (4)

19 See 9 Down

20 Light pink wine such as Mateus (4)

No. 65

Across

1 Berkshire racecourse that hosts the King George VI and Queen Elizabeth Stakes (5)

4 Round yellow edible root called rutabaga in North America (5)

10 Department of southeast France whose capital is Grenoble (5)

11 2012 Olympic men's 5,000 and 10,000m gold medallist (2,5)

12 State capital of Hawaii, US (8)

13 2000 action film featuring Patrick Stewart as Professor X (1-3)

15 Donald ___, Archbishop of Canterbury from 1974-80 (6)

17 **and 26** 2011 novel by David Lodge (1,3,2,5)

19 **See 9 Down**

20 Stavros ___, Greek shipping tycoon who died in 1996 (8)

23 J K ___, author of the Harry Potter heptalogy of novels (7)

24 State capital of Oregon, US (5)

25 Strong polymer first produced by the DuPont firm in the 1930s (5)

26 **See 17 Across**

Down

2 Rick ___, chef and TV presenter with restaurants in Padstow, Cornwall (5)

3 Information ___, psychological state alluded to in Stanley Milgram's experiments in bystander behaviour (8)

5 In weaving, the yarn woven across the width of a fabric (4)

6 1990 horror film starring Liam Neeson in the title role (7)

7 The ___, 1971 film thriller starring Marlon Brando and Stephanie Beacham (11)

8 G C ___, England Test cricketer who took 5-48 against Australia at Melbourne in 1986 (5)

9 **and 19 Across** 1937 adventure film starring Peter Lorre and Virginia Field (5,4,2,4)

14 Food of the gods in Greek mythology (8)

16 2013 action film starring Ethan Hawke and Selena Gomez (7)

18 1927 film drama starring Clara Bow; the first Best Picture Oscar winner (5)

21 Gustav ___, English composer of The Planets suite (5)

22 John ___, photographer who won a Pulitzer Prize in 1971 for his coverage of the Kent State University tragedy (4)

Across

6 Field of geometry concerned with the properties of and relations among the parts of a triangle (12)

8 2005 war film starring Jake Gyllenhaal as Anthony Swofford (7)

9 Ruth ___, actress known from her performances as Gladys Ormphby on US comedy show Rowan and Martin's Laugh-In (5)

10 Main tower within the walls of a medieval castle (4)

12 **and 15** 1941 stage play by Noël Coward (6,6)

14 Best Actor in a Leading Role Oscar nominee for Fiddler on the Roof (5)

15 **See 12 Across**

16 Hideki ___, Japanese PM who was tried by the International Military Tribunal for the Far East in 1948 (4)

19 City in which the Kwame Nkrumah Mausoleum is located (5)

21 John ___, comedian and actor who co-starred as 'Joliet' Jake Blues in 1980 film The Blues Brothers (7)

22 1961 horror film starring Deborah Kerr and Peter Wyngarde (3,9)

Down

1 Benjamin ___, Prime Minister from 1874-80 (8)

2 **See 17 Down**

3 Large round Dutch cheese similar to Edam (5)

4 Team game similar to basketball played mainly by women (7)

5 Nilo ___, author of 2003 Pulitzer Prize for drama-winning stage play Anna in the Tropics (4)

6 Republic bordering on China whose capital is Dushanbe (10)

7 1930 novel by Evelyn Waugh (4,6)

11 Biblical nephew of Abraham whose wife was turned into a pillar of salt (3)

12 Foremost point on a ship (3)

13 Number represented by the letter M in Roman numerals (8)

14 Queen of the fairies in the William Shakespeare play A Midsummer Night's Dream (7)

17 **and 2** The ___, 1974 story collection by John Fowles (5,5)

18 Ball worth seven points in snooker (5)

20 Nik ___, rock music journalist whose books include Need and King Death (4)

Across

3 London borough; site of the original Royal Observatory (9)

8 Old Testament Hebrew prophet of the 8th century BC (4)

9 Town and port in Cornwall linked by ferry to St Mawes (8)

10 and 23 1952 novel by John Steinbeck (4,2,4)

13 and 20 Down 2013 action film whose only cast member is Robert Redford (3,2,4)

14 and 11 Down 1928 Broadway stage play by Eugene O'Neill (7,9)

15 Series of games in a tennis match (3)

16 Ancient region of central Italy between the Rivers Tiber and Arno (7)

17 24th letter of the Greek alphabet (5)

21 Greek mathematician of Alexandria who authored the work Elements (6)

22 1945 Rodgers and Hammerstein Broadway musical based on Ferenc Molnár play Liliom (8)

23 See 10 Across

24 Heath ___, Australian rugby league hooker at Bradford Bulls from 2010-13 (9)

Down

1 2013 film drama starring Josh Duhamel and Julianne Hough (4,5)

2 City in West Flanders, Belgium that has a black Cross of Lorraine on its coat of arms (9)

4 European freshwater fish also called a pope (5)

5 Denholm ___, Best Actor in a Supporting Role Oscar nominee for A Room with a View (7)

6 Natalie ___, Best Actress in a Leading Role Oscar nominee for Love with the Proper Stranger (4)

7 Mike ___, rugby union utility back whose 1994 England Test debut was against Wales (4)

11 See 14 Across

12 and 19 Best Actress in a Leading Role Oscar winner for The Trip to Bountiful (9,4)

14 The ___, 1973 stage play by Edward Bond (3)

15 Region of Europe mainly in Poland centred on the upper Oder valley (7)

18 Movie of 1983 which immediately precedes Broadway Danny Rose in Woody Allen's filmography (5)

19 See 12 Down

20 See 13 Across

139

Across

1 Julianne ___, Best Actress in a Leading Role Oscar nominee for Far from Heaven (5)

7 The ___, Hampshire ground that staged its first Test cricket match in June 2011 (4,4)

8 Roberto ___, 1972-79 WBA Lightweight champion (5)

10 African republic whose capital is Nouakchott (10)

12 The ___, 1971 novel by William Peter Blatty (8)

14 The ___, 1997 film drama starring Anthony Hopkins and Alec Baldwin (4)

16 and 17 Horse that won the 2003, 2006 and 2007 Hennessy Gold Cup at Leopardstown (4,2,6)

17 See 16 Across

20 City in Yvelines, France where the Treaty of Paris was signed in 1919 (10)

23 See 24 Across

24 and 23 US actor whose roles included Gil Westrum in 1962 film western Ride the High Country (8,5)

25 Celia ___, actress who portrayed Doris Speed in 2010 BBC TV drama The Road to Coronation Street (5)

Down

1 and 16 Down 1857 novel by Gustave Flaubert (6,6)

2 Word for number of sheets of paper equal to 20 quires (4)

3 Niels ___, Danish winner of the 1922 Nobel Prize in Physics (4)

4 Edward ___, Prime Minister from 1970-74 (5)

5 Composer of the operas A Flowering Tree and Nixon in China (4,5)

6 and 13 ITV sitcom that starred John Alderton as Bernard Hedges (6,3)

9 City in Meurthe-et-Moselle, France; capital of the dukes of Lorraine in the 12th century (5)

11 2013 action film starring Jason Statham (9)

13 See 6 Down

15 Geoff ___, 1974 and 1978 Commonwealth shot put gold medallist (5)

16 See 1 Down

18 Plant whose jagged leaves are covered with stinging hairs (6)

19 Castrated cock fowl fattened for eating (5)

21 Radu ___, winner of the 1969 Leeds International Pianoforte Competition (4)

22 Alan Clarke television play made into a 1979 film starring Ray Winstone as Carlin (4)

Across

1 See 23 Across

8 Town in North Lanarkshire east of Glasgow (7)

9 See 10 Across

10 **and 9** The ___, 1929 novel by Dashiell Hammett (4,5)

11 Nephew of Lancelot and knight of the Round Table in Arthurian legend (4)

12 Anaïs ___, author of 1954 short novel A Spy in the House of Love (3)

14 James ___, actor who portrayed Lon Chaney in 1957 biopic Man of a Thousand Faces (6)

15 Messenger and herald of the gods in Greek mythology (6)

18 2003 novel by Freya North (3)

20 Colourless gaseous element; symbol Ne (4)

21 A J ___, English philosopher whose works include Language, Truth and Logic (4)

23 **and 1** 1980 action film starring Jason Robards based on a novel by Clive Cussler (5,3,7)

24 1979 adventure film starring Michael Caine and Peter Ustinov (7)

25 Group of standing stones on Salisbury Plain in Wiltshire (10)

Down

1 **and 19** The ___, 1977 film drama starring Shirley MacLaine and Anne Bancroft (7,5)

2 George ___, singer who had a UK no 1 single in 2018 with Shotgun (4)

3 Henry ___, English Parliamentarian general and son-in-law of Oliver Cromwell (6)

4 Roman town in Warwickshire west of Stratford- upon-Avon (8)

5 **and 22** Captain of the 1992 Cricket World Cup-winning Pakistan team (5,4)

6 Horse racecourse in Merseyside that stages the Lancashire Oaks (7,4)

7 French horn player with the Philharmonia Orchestra who died in a car crash in 1957 (6,5)

13 Robert A ___, author of the novels Starship Troopers and The Door into Summer (8)

16 Department of northwest France whose capital is Laval (7)

17 Another name for potassium carbonate (6)

19 See 1 Down

22 See 5 Down

Across

1 and 19 Down Star and co-writer of 2011 comedy film Bridesmaids (7,4)

7 and 22 1978 film comedy starring George C Scott and Trish Van Devere (5,5)

8 Aleksandr ___, author of the short story The Queen of Spades (7)

9 John ___, English artist whose works include 1954 oil Still Life With Chip Frier (6)

11 Come Back, Little ___, film for which Shirley Booth won the Best Actress Oscar at the 25th Academy Awards (5)

13 Erki ___, 1998 European Championships decathlon gold medallist (4)

14 and 15 Author of novels The Judge and The Return of the Soldier (7,4)

15 See 14 Across

16 Stephen of ___, author of the Life of Saint Wilfrid, an eighth-century hagiography (5)

17 Capital of Canada (6)

21 Country in southern Africa whose capital is Windhoek (7)

22 See 7 Across

23 Genus of shrubs and trees that includes the Gebang palm and Talipot palm (7)

Down

2 1996 Grand National-winning horse (5,5)

3 Franz ___, composer of song cycles Winterreise and Die Schöne Müllerin (8)

4 and 10 2000 biopic starring Julia Roberts in the title role (4,10)

5 Period of sixty minutes (4)

6 Perennial herb whose aromatic leaves are used to flavour toothpaste (4)

9 and 13 2013 musical-drama film starring Forest Whitaker and Angela Bassett (5,8)

10 See 4 Down

12 African musical instrument also known as a thumb piano (5)

13 See 9 Down

18 ___ Kirk, landmark of the Royal Mile, Edinburgh (4)

19 See 1 Across

20 Port and resort in southern Portugal (4)

145

No. 71

Across

1 and 17 Author of 1955 novel An Episode of Sparrows (5,6)

4 River in northern Italy that flows to the Adriatic via Verona (5)

10 Wingless parasitic insect that lives on the skin of mammals (5)

11 Plant related to the onion cultivated for its edible bulb (7)

12 Breed of short-legged terriers developed in Wales (8)

13 Resort town in north Wales at the entrance to the Vale of Clwyd (4)

15 Clare ___, singer and actress whose roles include Susan in 1981 comedy-drama film Gregory's Girl (6)

17 See 1 Across

19 1948 Alfred Hitchcock film thriller based on a stage play by Patrick Hamilton (4)

20 In Japanese cookery, a dish of meat basted with soy sauce and rice wine and broiled over an open fire (8)

23 Tony ___, rugby union wing whose 1955 Ireland Test debut was against France (7)

24 Maria ___, US mezzo-soprano; mother of actress Rebecca Hall (5)

25 ___ River, tributary of the Missouri River in the US that flows into the Lake of the Ozarks reservoir (5)

26 John Philip ___, US composer of the march The Stars and Stripes Forever (5)

Down

2 Small fleshy flap of tissue at the back of the throat; an extension of the soft palate (5)

3 Popular English morality play of the early 16th century (8)

5 Sixteenth of an ounce in the avoirdupois system of weights (4)

6 and 9 1965 novel by P G Wodehouse featuring the character Tipton Plimsoll (7,2,9)

7 1980 action film starring Sam J Jones in the title role (5,6)

8 Lion in the The Chronicles of Narnia heptalogy by C S Lewis (5)

9 See 6 Down

14 Cristian ___, actor whose roles have included Jason Turner in ITV drama series Footballers' Wives (8)

16 Poet in Greek mythology who married Eurydice (7)

18 Joseph ___, German conceptual artist whose works include Felt Suit, Sled and Capri Battery (5)

21 Constellation between Pisces and Taurus (5)

22 Type of wooden shoe (4)

147

Across

6 English poet and dramatist whose works include the plays Match Me in London and The Shoemaker's Holiday (6,6)

8 A daughter of Agamemnon and Clytemnestra in Greek mythology (7)

9 Valley in north Argolis, ancient Greece; site of a biennial athletic competition (5)

10 Capital and largest city of Samoa (4)

12 12th sign of the zodiac (6)

14 Sidney ___, Australian painter whose works include 1957's Rainforest (5)

15 Joanna ___, actress who played Purdey in ITV action series The New Avengers (6)

16 ___ Wolfhard, actor who plays Mike Wheeler in sci-fi drama series Stranger Things (4)

19 Wilbert ___, creator of characters including Henry the Green Engine and Sir Topham Hatt (5)

21 Billie ___, US jazz singer whose nickname was Lady Day (7)

22 Author of the novels Nineteen Eighty-Four and Coming Up for Air (6,6)

Down

1 Element produced artificially from Curium; symbol No (8)

2 Grete ___, winner of the women's race in the 1986 London Marathon (5)

3 Large desert-living, African antelope with long twisted horns (5)

4 and 14 1957 comedy-drama film starring, written and directed by Charlie Chaplin (1,4,2,3,4)

5 Golfer whose victory at the 2002 PGA Championship helped his entry into the top 20 of the Official World Golf Ranking (4)

6 and 13 1906 novel by E Nesbit (3,7,8)

7 Rudolf ___, character in the Anthony Hope novel The Prisoner of Zenda (10)

11 Island of the Orkneys group (3)

12 God of fields, woods, shepherds and flocks in Greek mythology (3)

13 See 6 Down

14 See 4 Down

17 The Taming of the ___, Shakespeare comedy (5)

18 Petula ___, singer and actress whose roles include Sharon McLonergan in 1968 film musical Finian's Rainbow (5)

20 Eric ___, Tottenham Hotspur and England footballer (4)

No. 72

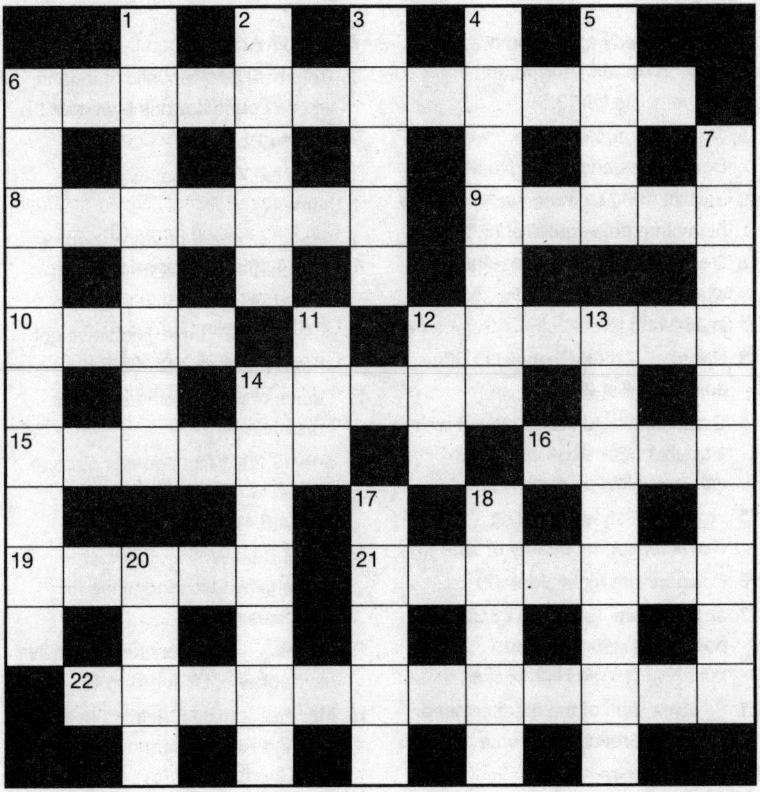

No. 73

Across

3 2013 comedy and crime film starring Robert De Niro and Michelle Pfeiffer (3,6)

8 Greg ___, author of the novels Dead Sleep and Sleep No More (4)

9 **and 22** 1990 Commonwealth men's high jump gold medallist (8,8)

10 S M ___, Australia Test cricketer who hit 125 against India at Sydney in 2004 (6)

13 Noah ___, 2000 Olympic 1,500m gold medallist (5)

14 Game similar to Whist played with a double pack of 64 cards with nothing below a seven (7)

15 ___ canto, style of singing characterised by beauty of tone (3)

16 Polygon with eight sides (7)

17 **and 1 Down** 19th-century US poet whose works include Wild Nights-Wild Nights! (5,9)

21 ___ Sea, arm of the Mediterranean between Greece and Turkey (6)

22 **See 9 Across**

23 Paul ___, Best Actor in a Leading Role Oscar winner for The Story of Louis Pasteur (4)

24 Word in a computer document that can be clicked on in order to move to a related document (9)

Down

1 **See 17 Across**

2 County of the Republic of Ireland whose county town is Mullingar (9)

4 **See 14 Down**

5 2011 2,000 Guineas-winning horse (7)

6 Joe ___, record producer portrayed by Con O'Neill in 2008 biopic Telstar (4)

7 Jeff ___, IBF Super Middleweight champion from 2004-06 (4)

11 Genus of plants comprising the horsetails (9)

12 **and 19** 2001 film comedy starring Rachel Griffiths in the title role (4,5,4)

14 **and 4** Best Writing, Original Screenplay Oscar nominee for Notorious (3,5)

15 James ___, 18th-century Scottish biographer of Dr Johnson (7)

18 Marsha ___, Best Actress in a Leading Role Oscar nominee for The Goodbye Girl (5)

19 **See 12 Down**

20 Joint of the human leg connecting the tibia and fibula with the femur (4)

Across

1 Gabriela ___, 2000 Olympic women's 5,000m gold medallist (5)

7 Black form of carbon used as a fuel (8)

8 Role played by Eric Schweig in 1992 drama The Last of the Mohicans (5)

10 Golfer who won The Open Championship in 1968 (4,6)

12 1987 action-comedy film starring Richard Dreyfuss and Emilio Estevez (8)

14 ___ Gulf, inlet of the Solomon Sea in eastern Papua New Guinea (4)

16 Douglas ___, Germany-born director of the films All That Heaven Allows and Imitation of Life (4)

17 Name given by the Apostles to the Levite Joseph in the New Testament (8)

20 Leather shorts with H-shaped braces worn by men in Austria and Bavaria (10)

23 ___ Spruce, evergreen tree named after a former capital of the Department of Alaska and District of Alaska (5)

24 Political party in Ireland (4,4)

25 Small tree with pink flowers and rounded edible fruit (5)

Down

1 See 13 Down

2 Card game which is an old form of poker (4)

3 Watery liquid that separates from the curd when milk is clotted in cheesemaking (4)

4 Shrimp-like marine crustacean which is the principal food of whalebone whales (5)

5 WBA Heavyweight champion from 1985-86 (4,5)

6 Former British coin equivalent to two shillings (6)

9 1965 stage play by Edward Bond (5)

11 Keith ___, actor who won a Best Music, Original Song Oscar for I'm Easy from 1975's Nashville (9)

13 **and 1 Down** Actress who played Rita in BBC TV sitcom Till Death Us Do Part (3,6)

15 Major mountain system of South America (5)

16 1984 romcom starring Tom Hanks and Daryl Hannah (6)

18 Marrow-like plant whose fruits have an edible flesh (6)

19 Annabel ___, 1984 Girls' Singles winner at the Wimbledon International Junior Championships (5)

21 Elisha Graves ___, American inventor of an elevator who died in 1861 (4)

22 Winged goddess of victory in Greek mythology (4)

Across

1 Mark placed over a vowel such as the o in French (10)

8 Goat antelope from whose hide a soft suede leather was formerly made (7)

9 2008 action film starring Sylvester Stallone in the title role (5)

10 The ___, 1976 novel by Peter Benchley (4)

11 South American republic whose capital is Lima (4)

12 Alastair ___, actor who played the title role in 1951 film drama Scrooge (3)

14 John ___, author of the epic poem Paradise Lost (6)

15 Alice ___, author of 1982 novel The Color Purple (6)

18 1988 film drama starring James Woods as Lloyd Hopkins (3)

20 Patricia ___, Best Actress in a Leading Role Oscar winner for Hud (4)

21 US state whose capital is Salt Lake City (4)

23 Lorenzo ___, Italian artist whose works include Portrait of Giovanni della Volta with his Wife and Children (5)

24 1989 film drama featuring Ian McKellen as John Profumo (7)

25 2009 film comedy starring Jesse Eisenberg and Woody Harrelson (10)

Down

1 James ___, author of the novels Shogun and Tai-Pan (7)

2 Marcelo ___, 1999 Hamburg Masters singles tennis champion (4)

3 and 6 2009 novel by Terry Pratchett (6,11)

4 George ___, author of 1707 stage play The Beaux' Stratagem (8)

5 Charles ___, furniture designer best known for his 1956 'Lounge Chair' (5)

6 See 3 Down

7 1886 stage play by Henrik Ibsen (11)

13 Motor racing driver who died on Loch Ness in 1952 attempting to break the water speed record (4,4)

16 Green long-horned grasshopper of North America (7)

17 R A L ___, Australia Test cricketer who took 8-84 and 8-53 against England at Lord's in 1972 (6)

19 Arboreal nocturnal short-tailed African primate (5)

22 Lake known as Llyn Tegid in Welsh (4)

Across

1 and 23 1895 novel by H G Wells (3,4,7)

7 Daniel ___, author of 1719 novel Robinson Crusoe (5)

8 Louise ___, actress whose roles have included Rosa Di Marco in BBC TV soap EastEnders (7)

9 and 14 2007 film comedy starring Will Ferrell and Jon Heder (6,2,5)

11 Hardy ___, dressmaker by appointment to Queen Elizabeth II who founded his own fashion house in 1946 (5)

13 'American Tribal Love Rock Musical' that opened on Broadway in 1968 (4)

14 See 9 Across

15 ___ gun, light 9 mm submachine gun formerly used in the British Army (4)

16 Group or set of twenty (5)

17 In heraldry, the colour silver (6)

21 Sally ___, 1986 Commonwealth 100m hurdles gold medallist (7)

22 Sylvia ___, US poet whose volumes include The Colossus and Ariel (5)

23 See 1 Across

Down

2 See 3 Down

3 and 2 1982 children's book by Gillian Cross (3,5,10)

4 Robert ___, US engineer who died in 2005 after whom a type of musical synthesizer is named (4)

5 Term for a villainous character in professional wrestling who fulfils the role of antagonist (4)

6 ___ Hill, location in Ulverston of a monument to John Barrow (4)

9 Metalloid element used in hardening steel; symbol B (5)

10 Author of the novels Three Weeks and The Price of Things (6,4)

12 Wading bird similar to the heron (5)

13 ___ Bucket, Patricia Routledge's role in television comedy Keeping Up Appearances (8)

18 Eric ___, British sculptor and typographer whose works include 1914 print Slaughter of the Innocents (4)

19 1987 film drama starring Barbra Streisand and Richard Dreyfuss (4)

20 Island in the Inner Hebrides separated from the Scottish mainland by the Sound of ___ (4)

Across

1 City and state capital of Western Australia (5)

4 **See 25 Across**

10 **See 6 Down**

11 Standard monetary unit of Afghanistan (7)

12 1977 action film starring Roy Scheider based on the novel Le Salaire De La Peur by Georges Arnaud (8)

13 Lembit ___, Liberal Democrat MP for Montgomeryshire from 1997-2010 (4)

15 Dark grey rain-bearing cloud (6)

17 Former name of Iran (6)

19 David ___, author of the stage plays Gethsemane and The Vertical Hour (4)

20 James A ___, author of novel Chesapeake and The Bridges at Toko-Ri (8)

23 Island country in the Caribbean Sea whose capital is St George's (7)

24 The ___, 1997 horror film starring Penelope Ann Miller and Tom Sizemore (5)

25 **and 4** Best Actress in a Supporting Role Oscar nominee for The World According to Garp (5,5)

26 **and 9 Down** US Ambassador to the United Nations from 1981-85 (5,11)

Down

2 Edward ___, composer of 1900 oratorio The Dream of Gerontius (5)

3 1949 film drama starring Robert Ryan and Audrey Totter (3,3-2)

5 Racing toboggan on which riders lie supine (4)

6 **and 10 Across** 1981 novel by Bernard Cornwell (7,5)

7 Thomas ___, 1982 European Championships 5,000m gold medallist (11)

8 George ___, Archbishop of Canterbury from 1991-2002 (5)

9 **See 26 Across**

14 Marine fish with a bony-plated body (8)

16 Andrew ___, 17th-century poet and satirist whose works include The Mower's Song and Last Instructions to a Painter (7)

18 Legendary Greek king able to turn what he touched into gold (5)

21 Christopher ___, author of 1999 novel The Banyan Tree (5)

22 Leslie ___, actress whose roles have included Robin Harris in 1996 film comedy The Cable Guy (4)

No. 78

Across

6 Actress whose roles include Esmeralda in 1939 film drama The Hunchback of Notre Dame (7,5)

8 and 6 Down 1899 novel by H G Wells (4,3,2,8)

9 Rich Japanese sauce made from soy beans naturally fermented with wheat or barley (5)

10 James ___, darts player who won the 2007 World Matchplay tournament (4)

12 The ___, peninsula in Cornwall containing the southernmost point in mainland Great Britain (6)

14 Capital of Seine-et-Marne department, France (5)

15 Karen ___, 1962 Wimbledon singles tennis champion (6)

16 Type of creature named Everest in 2019 animation Abominable (4)

19 Diane ___, US photographer portrayed by Nicole Kidman in 2006 film drama Fur (5)

21 Manuel ___, 1975 US Open singles tennis champion (7)

22 and 4 Down The ___, 1982 novel by P D James (5,7,3,4)

Down

1 Henryk Sienkiewicz novel first published in book form in 1896 (3,5)

2 Edgar ___, painter and sculptor whose works include 1877's Dancers Practicing at the Barre (5)

3 Positive electrode in an electrolytic cell (5)

4 See 22 Across

5 2012 film thriller directed by and starring Ben Affleck (4)

6 See 8 Across

7 Best Actor in a Supporting Role Oscar nominee for his role as Dr Berger in Ordinary People (4,6)

11 Monetary unit of Malaysia worth one-hundredth of a ringgit (3)

12 Derived SI unit of illumination (3)

13 ___ Islands, chain of over 150 islands in the Bering Sea off mainland Alaska (8)

14 Nigel ___, 1992 Formula 1 motor racing world champion (7)

17 City that houses the University of Malawi (5)

18 US state whose capital is Augusta (5)

20 City in which the Heydar Aliyev Centre is located (4)

No. 78

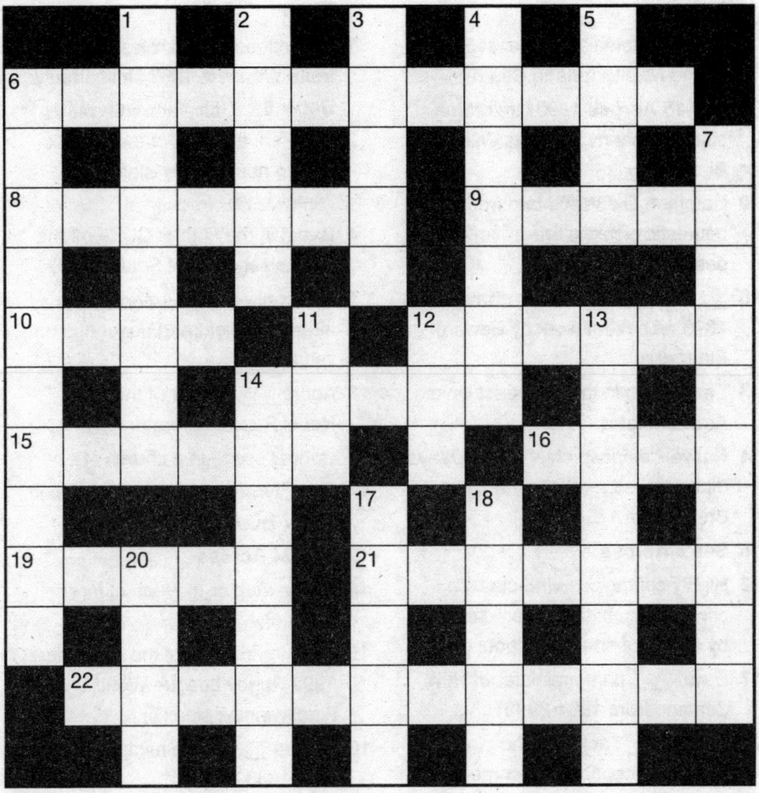

No. 79

Across

3 City in Catalonia, northeast Spain on the Mediterranean Sea (9)

8 and 15 Across 1995 film drama starring Johnny Depp as William Blake (4,3)

9 Common Old World bird from which domestic pigeons are descended (4,4)

10 ___ Variations, popular name for an 1899 orchestral work by Edward Elgar (6)

13 Sheikhdom in the northeast United Arab Emirates (5)

14 Native American chief of the Ottawa tribe who led a rebellion against the British from 1763-66 (7)

15 See 8 Across

16 Highly contagious viral disease common in children characterized by a rash of small red spots (7)

17 David ___, prime minister of New Zealand from 1984-89 (5)

21 Jessica ___, actress who plays a medical receptionist in comedy drama Doc Martin (6)

22 Roman name for Ireland (8)

23 Ben ___, marooned pirate in the R L Stevenson novel Treasure Island (4)

24 and 12 Down 1976 Olympic women's high jump gold medallist (9,9)

Down

1 US actress whose roles included Dr Irene Wilson in 1963 film comedy Under the Yum Yum Tree (4,5)

2 ___ Sea, that part of the Atlantic Ocean housing the island of Jamaica (9)

4 Island in the Firth of Clyde off the southwest coast of Scotland (5)

5 Mammal of North America with alternating light and dark rings on its tail (7)

6 André ___, winner of the 1947 Nobel Prize in Literature (4)

7 Central space in a church (4)

11 ___ I, tyrant of Syracuse who died in 367 BC (9)

12 See 24 Across

14 Dance step or movement in ballet (3)

15 Mal ___, captain of the Australia 1992 Rugby League World Cup Final-winning side (7)

18 Bettino ___, prime minister of Italy from 1983-87 (5)

19 Steve ___, South African civil rights leader who died in Pretoria in 1977 (4)

20 The Venerable ___, saint who died in 735 AD (4)

Across

1 Rainer Maria ___, Prague-born poet whose works include Duino Elegies (5)

7 Italian dessert made with sponge soaked in coffee and Marsala, soft cheese and powdered chocolate (8)

8 ___ piano, another name for the African musical instrument mbira (5)

10 Ignacy Jan ___, pianist and composer who became Prime Minister of Poland in 1919 (10)

12 1992 action film starring Emilio Estevez and Mick Jagger (8)

14 Basic unit of the renminbi in Chinese currency (4)

16 Eurasian plant with bright yellow flowers whose seeds yield a useful oil (4)

17 See 11 Down

20 Author of 1971 novel The Winds of War (6,4)

23 Christina ___, actress who played Maggie Ryan in US television series Pan Am (5)

24 Cave in Cantabria, Spain famous for its Palaeolithic paintings (8)

25 Nick ___, Liberal Democrat leader from 2007-2015 (5)

Down

1 **and 18** The ___, ballet with music by Igor Stravinsky first performed in 1913 (4,2,6)

2 Ross ___, actor who played Grant Mitchell in BBC TV soap EastEnders (4)

3 **and 21** 1988 novel by David Lodge (4,4)

4 Cud-chewing mammal of desert regions that can survive long periods without food or water (5)

5 1888 play by August Strindberg first performed the following year (4,5)

6 Asian tree with edible oval fruit (6)

9 Stringed musical instrument with a long fretted neck and circular body (5)

11 **and 17 Across** 1871 novel by Thomas Hardy featuring the character Edward Springrove (9,8)

13 ___ for Treason, 1940 children's historical novel by Geoffrey Trease (3)

15 Bone of the body also called a thighbone (5)

16 Hasim ___, WBC, IBF and IBO Heavyweight champion from April to November 2001 (6)

18 See 1 Down

19 City in Emilia-Romagna, Italy associated with cheese and ham manufacture (5)

21 See 3 Down

22 Port and capital of Schleswig-Holstein, Germany (4)

No. 80

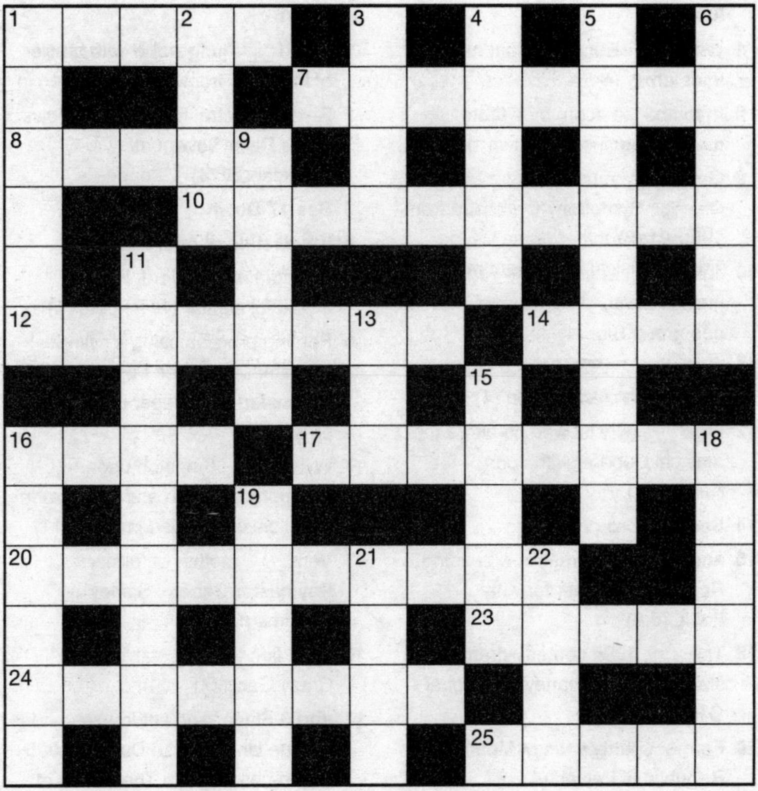

No. 81

Across

1 White ___, Eurasian plant of the mint family (4-6)

8 In football, a score by a team member against their own side (3,4)

9 Georg ___, music director of the Chicago Symphony Orchestra from 1969-91 (5)

10 Julian ___, artist whose works include prints of the members of the pop group Blur (4)

11 Carlos ___, 1998 French Open singles tennis champion (4)

12 Fred ___, lyricist who co-wrote the musical Cabaret with John Kander (3)

14 See 15 Across

15 **and 14** Best Actress in a Leading Role Oscar winner for Kitty Foyle (6,6)

18 The ___, 1996 comedy-drama film starring Colm Meaney and Donal O'Kelly (3)

20 Former county town of Meath, Republic of Ireland (4)

21 Capital of Norway (4)

23 Spanish wine with a vanilla bouquet produced around the Ebro river (5)

24 Matt ___, actor who played the title role in US television sitcom Joey (7)

25 Formal name for the game played by Venus and Serena Williams (4,6)

Down

1 Alfred ___, judge who was Master of the Rolls from 1962-82 (7)

2 River of central England that flows to the River Severn at Tewkesbury (4)

3 **See 17 Down**

4 Island state of Australia (8)

5 Industrial city in Nord, France; medieval capital of Flanders (5)

6 Printing process using a cylinder with small recesses from which ink is transferred to paper in a rotary press (11)

7 William ___, Kingston upon Hull-born politician and slave trade abolitionist who died in 1833 (11)

13 Vera ___, mother of former Paymaster General Shirley Williams (8)

16 1941 film comedy starring The Crazy Gang (7)

17 **and 3** Singer and actor whose roles include Uncle Jesse Duke in 2005 action-comedy film The Dukes of Hazzard (6,6)

19 City in north Zambia; centre of a rich copper-mining area (5)

22 Port in west Scotland on the Firth of Lorne (4)

Across

1 Bruce ___, F1 motor racing driver who won the 1968 Belgian GP (7)

7 Samuel ___, British diarist and naval administrator who died in 1703 (5)

8 Flesh of a deer used as food (7)

9 **and 13 Down** 2010 US Open golf champion (6,8)

11 David ___, singer and actor who starred as Jim MacLaine in 1973 film drama That'll Be the Day (5)

13 Island of the Inner Hebrides whose largest settlement is Port Mòr (4)

14 1997 film drama starring Leonardo DiCaprio and Kate Winslet (7)

15 Woodwind instrument whose mouthpiece has a double reed (4)

16 James ___, author of the novels Finnegans Wake and Ulysses (5)

17 Republic in southwest Africa whose capital is Luanda (6)

21 Most populous department in Lorraine, France (7)

22 Philip ___, composer of the operas Satyagraha and Akhnaten (5)

23 Judy ___, Best Actress in a Supporting Role Oscar nominee for Judgment at Nuremberg (7)

Down

2 Spiral-shaped currant cake decorated with sugar (7,3)

3 Liqueur flavoured with aniseed (8)

4 God of love in Greek myth (4)

5 Widely cultivated tree with a gritty-textured juicy fruit (4)

6 **and 10** Actor who played Special Agent Dale Cooper in 1990s US TV show Twin Peaks (4,10)

9 Hugh ___, actor whose roles include Daniel Cleaver in 2001 romcom Bridget Jones's Diary (5)

10 **See 6 Down**

12 German Junkers-87 dive-bomber first used in combat in the Spanish Civil War (5)

13 **See 9 Across**

18 Metallic element; symbol Au (4)

19 **See 20 Down**

20 **and 19** 1986 crime drama film starring Bob Hoskins and Cathy Tyson (4,4)

No. 82

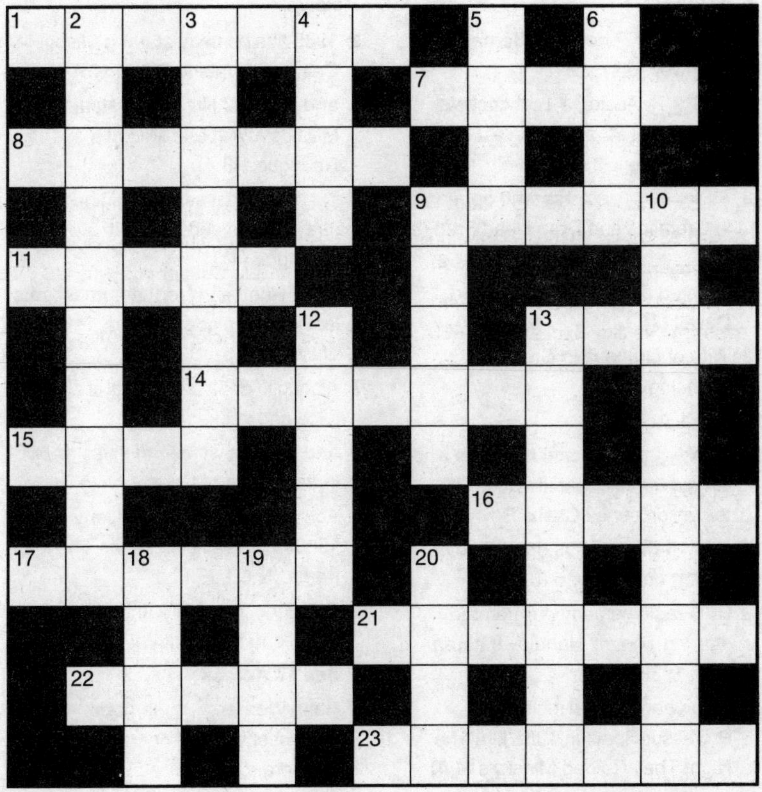

No. 83

Across

1 **and 13** 2007 novel by Bernard Cornwell (5,4)

4 M G ___, Australia Test cricketer who took 6-82 against West Indies at Adelaide in 1997 (5)

10 Phoebe ___, actress who appeared in Gremlins and Drop Dead Fred (5)

11 The ___, 1997 film drama written, directed by and starring Robert Duvall (7)

12 Wife of Orpheus in Greek mythology (8)

13 **See 1 Across**

15 Micky ___, actor and musician who played the title role in 1950s US television series Circus Boy (6)

17 **and 16 Down** 1893 operetta by Gilbert and Sullivan (6,7)

19 BBC radio comedy programme starring Tommy Handley that ran from 1939-49 (4)

20 Actor whose roles included Professor Spats in 1968 film The Night They Raided Minsky's (4,4)

23 Emilio ___, actor whose roles include William H Bonney in 1988 action film Young Guns (7)

24 Former province of South Africa whose capital was Pietermaritzburg (5)

25 Nicholas ___, 16th-century English playwright who authored the comedy Ralph Roister Doister (5)

26 John Logie ___, Scottish engineer and television pioneer who died in 1946 (5)

Down

2 1985 film comedy starring Michael Caine and Valerie Perrine (5)

3 **and 22** 2002 film thriller starring Milla Jovovich and Michelle Rodriguez (8,4)

5 ___ Mess, dessert containing strawberries and crushed meringue (4)

6 Stately home in Northamptonshire; last resting place of Diana, Princess of Wales (7)

7 Alcoholic drink consisting of orange juice and vodka (11)

8 **and 21** First woman to sit as an MP in the House of Commons (5,5)

9 Actor who played Mr Waverly in 1960s US television series The Man from U.N.C.L.E. (3,1,7)

14 Fractional monetary unit of Bulgaria worth one hundredth of a lev (8)

16 **See 17 Across**

18 Hans Werner ___, German composer of 2007 opera Phaedra (5)

21 **See 8 Down**

22 **See 3 Down**

No. 84

Across

6 and 22 The ___, 1907 stage play by J M Synge (7,2,3,7,5)

8 River of the Democratic Republic of the Congo; a headstream of the Congo River (7)

9 Fast powerful overhead stroke in tennis (5)

10 Republic on the Persian Gulf whose capital is Baghdad (4)

12 and 2 Down Pakistan Test cricketer who hit 274 against England at Edgbaston in 1971 (6,5)

14 Neil ___, golfer who won the 1966 Dunlop Masters (5)

15 Final honours examination for a BA degree at Cambridge University (6)

16 Amorphous form of hydrated silica used as a gemstone (4)

19 Long-barrelled firearm with a spirally grooved interior (5)

21 Continents of Europe and Asia considered as a whole (7)

22 See 6 Across

Down

1 ___ Desert, arid plateau of South Africa, Namibia and Botswana (8)

2 See 12 Across

3 Jane ___, Best Actress in a Leading Role Oscar winner for Johnny Belinda (5)

4 Horse racecourse in Wales that opened in 2009 (4,3)

5 ___ Perlman, Carla in the sitcom Cheers (4)

6 Chazz ___, Best Actor in a Supporting Role Oscar nominee for Bullets Over Broadway (10)

7 Actress who played Kris Munroe in US television series Charlie's Angels (6,4)

11 Internationally recognised distress signal used by ships and aircraft (3)

12 Branch of Mahayana Buddhism stressing the role of meditation in pursuing enlightenment (3)

13 2008 Mal Peet novel (8)

14 French author of 1933 novel The Cat (7)

17 Justin ___, Best Actor in a Supporting Role Oscar nominee for Kramer vs Kramer (5)

18 Town and major railway junction in Cheshire (5)

20 Small wingless blood-sucking insect noted for its power of leaping (4)

No. 84

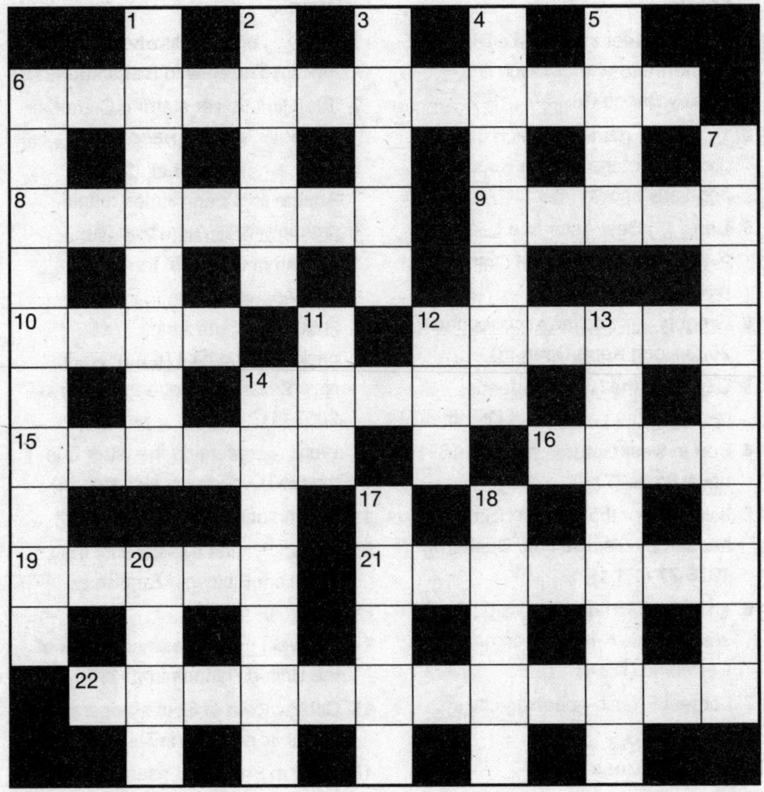

Across

3 Body of water in the Lake District at the northern end of which lies Pooley Bridge (9)

8 ___ Adde, name by which the first president of the Somali Republic is popularly known (4)

9 Dan ___, Best Actor in a Leading Role Oscar nominee for 1954's Robinson Crusoe (8)

10 Grégory ___, golfer who won the 2009 Hong Kong Open (6)

13 City in northeast Netherlands; capital of the province of Drenthe (5)

14 Port in west Greece; site of a 1571 naval battle (7)

15 Initialism for the federal US bureau headed by George H W Bush from 1976-77 (1,1,1)

16 and 21 1985 comedy-drama film starring Kris Kristofferson and Keith Carradine (7,2,4)

17 Largest French-speaking city in Belgium (5)

21 See 16 Across

22 The ___, 1957 Meredith Wilson Broadway musical set in River City, Iowa (5,3)

23 Aromatic Eurasian plant whose leaves are used for flavouring in pickles (4)

24 Radioactive chemical element; symbol Bk (9)

Down

1 J K ___, economist whose books include The New Industrial State (9)

2 1965 film thriller starring Catherine Deneuve and Ian Hendry (9)

4 John ___, December, 1977 Australian Open singles tennis championship runner-up (5)

5 Abandoned baby in the Popeye cartoon series (7)

6 H M ___, South Africa Test cricketer who hit 176 n.o. against New Zealand at Johannesburg in 2007 (4)

7 Word representing the letter E in the NATO phonetic alphabet (4)

11 Inflammation of the intestine (9)

12 Miles ___, first translator of the complete Bible into English in 1535 (9)

14 Trygve ___, Secretary-General of the United Nations from 1946-52 (3)

15 County town of South Tipperary, Republic of Ireland (7)

18 River in Brazil that rises on the Mato Grosso plateau before flowing north to the Amazon delta (5)

19 John Stuart, Earl of ___, British Prime Minister from 1762-63 (4)

20 Stewart ___, golfer who won The Open Championship in 2009 (4)

175

Across

1 Ancient Athenian statesman whose code of laws prescribed death for almost every offence (5)

7 Follower of Don John in the William Shakespeare play Much Ado About Nothing (8)

8 Sacred book of Islam (5)

10 Hana ___, 1987 Australian Open singles tennis champion (10)

12 British bronze coin that ceased to be legal tender in 1960 (8)

14 2008 animated film starring the voice talent of John Cusack in the title role (4)

16 First king of Israel in the Old Testament (4)

17 Large hard grains of wheat that are used for puddings and soups (8)

20 **and 5 Down** 1992 film drama starring Craig Sheffer and Brad Pitt (1,5,4,7,2)

23 Lake ___, body of water in northwest Russia between Lake Ladoga and the White Sea (5)

24 Socialistic movement in England from 1837-48 whose programme demanded vote by secret ballot (8)

25 London Underground station on the District Line between Barking and Becontree (5)

Down

1 **and 18** Husband of Goneril in the William Shakespeare play King Lear (4,2,6)

2 Steve ___, 1986 Commonwealth 800m gold medallist (4)

3 **and 21** The ___, 1925 film directed, written by and starring Charlie Chaplin (4,4)

4 Head of a gang of thieves in Charles Dickens novel Oliver Twist (5)

5 **See 20 Across**

6 Long soft silky hair that makes up the outer coat of an Angora goat (6)

9 In Mexican cookery, a snack consisting of a piece of tortilla topped with cheese and peppers and grilled (5)

11 Richard ___, author of the novels In Watermelon Sugar and Trout Fishing in America (9)

13 Simon ___, creator of the ITV sitcoms Is It Legal? and Hardware (3)

15 2002 novel by Irvine Welsh (5)

16 2000 crime film starring Benicio Del Toro and Dennis Farina (6)

18 **See 1 Down**

19 Sauce for pasta consisting of crushed basil leaves, nuts, garlic, Parmesan cheese and oil (5)

21 **See 3 Down**

22 Card game (4)

Across

1 The ___, 1965 stage play by Harold Pinter (10)

8 Guy ___, French fashion designer who died in 1989 (7)

9 Tapered log about 19 feet long that is tossed in an event at a modern Highland Games (5)

10 Tracey ___, conceptual artist whose works include 1998's My Bed (4)

11 River that flows to the North Sea at Sunderland (4)

12 and 1 Down Best Actress in a Leading Role Oscar nominee for Holiday (3,7)

14 Desmond ___, author of the novels Windfall, Juggernaut and The Snow Tiger (6)

15 US television sitcom set in a Boston bar (6)

18 Rodgers ___, 2002 New York City and Boston Marathon winner (3)

20 John ___, Scottish author of novels The Ayrshire Legatees and Annals of the Parish (4)

21 Small constellation in the northern hemisphere containing the star Vega (4)

23 Tourist island of the Balearics in the Mediterranean (5)

24 François ___, winner of the 1952 Nobel Prize in Literature (7)

25 Division of the vertebrate brain in man above the medulla oblongata (10)

Down

1 **See 12 Across**

2 David ___, Scottish artist whose work includes 1999 installation Big Heids (4)

3 Dick ___, Vice President of the United States from 2001-09 (6)

4 Joseph ___, Republican US Senator from Wisconsin from 1947-57 (8)

5 Ancient region of northeast Africa (5)

6 Actress whose roles include Calamity Jane in 1995 film drama Wild Bill (5,6)

7 Motor racing circuit at which the 1986 F1 British GP was held (6,5)

13 Capital and largest city of Serbia (8)

16 Dwelling place of the blessed after death in Greek mythology (7)

17 Reiner ___, 1984 Olympic individual dressage gold medallist (6)

19 Graham ___, rugby union prop whose 1975 Wales Test debut was against France (5)

22 Island off the west coast of Scotland whose chief town is Tobermory (4)

Across

1 Official language of Ethiopia (7)

7 **and 22** Prime minister of Egypt assassinated in 1981 (5,5)

8 Secretary of State for Northern Ireland from 1985-89 (3,4)

9 **See 12 Down**

11 Rhys ___, Welsh actor who portrayed Howard Marks in 2010 biopic Mr Nice (5)

13 River that forms part of the border between Germany and Poland (4)

14 Des ___, entertainer who authored 2001 autobiography Bananas Can't Fly! (7)

15 River in southwest Australia that flows to the Indian Ocean below Perth (4)

16 ___ Islands, group off the coast of Northumberland that house a bird sanctuary (5)

17 City in Northern Ireland southeast of Dungannon (6)

21 Stanley ___, Prime Minister from 1935-37 (7)

22 **See 7 Across**

23 1973 film comedy starring, directed and co-written by Woody Allen (7)

Down

2 Night-blooming tropical American climbing plant (10)

3 Rowan ___, comic actor who played the title role in films Bean and Johnny English (8)

4 Island in the Inner Hebrides; site of an abbey founded by St Columba (4)

5 Smallest wild buffalo species found on the Indonesian islands of Sulawesi and Buton (4)

6 Type of melancholy Portuguese folk song (4)

9 Male bee in a colony whose function is to mate with the queen (5)

10 1955 novel by Thomas B Costain (3,7)

12 **and 9 Across** US state whose capital is Bismarck (5,6)

13 Fine slightly stiff cotton fabric used for dresses (8)

18 Ancient kingdom in the Old Testament east of the Dead Sea (4)

19 Animal that represents the constellation Capricorn (4)

20 Fine-grained sedimentary rock containing silt that is used as a fertiliser (4)

Across

1 Josiah ___, 18th-century founder of a pottery manufactory in Stoke (5)

4 Genus of small terrestrial lizards that inhabit warm regions of the Old World (5)

10 Georges ___, French author of 1881 novel Serge Panine (5)

11 One of the two immortal gorgons in Greek mythology (7)

12 **and 5 Down** 2007 novel by Peter Ho Davies (3,5,4)

13 Small sawbill sometimes called 'white nun' (4)

15 **and 25** 2008 crime drama film starring Melissa Leo as Ray Eddy (6,5)

17 **and 26** 1939 novel by Arthur Ransome (6,5)

19 Pseudonym of 19th-century illustrator Hablot Knight Browne (4)

20 Arboreal amphibian such as the gray ___ of the US and Canada (4,4)

23 The ___, 1797 novel by Mrs Ann Radcliffe subtitled The Confessional of the Black Penitents (7)

24 1979 sci-fi film starring Tom Skerritt and Sigourney Weaver (5)

25 **See 15 Across**

26 **See 17 Across**

Down

2 Mike ___, Governor of Indiana from 2013-17 and former vice president of the United States (5)

3 Medium-sized plover whose adult female is brighter in colour than the male (8)

5 **See 12 Across**

6 Asian republic also known as Burma; capital Nay Pyi Taw (7)

7 Capital of Trinidad and Tobago (4,2,5)

8 Market town in the Scottish Borders at the confluence of the Rivers Teviot and Tweed (5)

9 1997 film drama starring Federico Luppi and Damián Delgado (3,4,4)

14 River in Guyana flowing north to the Atlantic at Georgetown (8)

16 Art form practised by the character of Gaff throughout the 1982 neo-noir film Blade Runner (7)

18 Black partially dried plum with a wrinkled appearance (5)

21 Craig ___, poet whose volumes include 1979's A Martian Sends a Postcard Home (5)

22 River in Normandy, France, that flows through Saint-Lô (4)

Across

6 **and 14** 1860 novel by George Eliot (3,4,2,3,5)

8 **12 and 22** 1944 adventure film starring Maria Montez and Jon Hall (3,4,3,3,5,7)

9 Lemuroid primate of Madagascar also called a babakoto (5)

10 City and state capital of Perak, Malaysia (4)

12 **See 8 Across**

14 **See 6 Across**

15 **and 4 Down** Cricket team; 2017, 2019 and 2020 IPL champions (6,7)

16 Compact brownish soil deposit of partially decomposed organic matter used as a fuel (4)

19 Yma ___, Peru-born singer and actress who played Kori-Tica in 1954 adventure film Secret of the Incas (5)

21 1986 Cheltenham Gold Cup winner ridden by Jonjo O'Neill (4,3)

22 **See 8 Across**

Down

1 Coastal resort northeast of Alicante, Spain (8)

2 City in Lombardy; chief financial centre of Italy (5)

3 Metropolitan city in South Korea on the Taehwa River (5)

4 **See 15 Across**

5 African republic; capital N'Djamena (4)

6 The ___, 1890 novel by Henry James (6,4)

7 1991 film comedy starring, directed and co-written by Mel Brooks (4,6)

11 The Book of ___, 2010 post-apocalyptic film starring Denzel Washington (3)

12 Mammal of the horse family also called a donkey (3)

13 1997 film drama starring Johnny Depp and Marlon Brando (3,5)

14 1972 film drama starring Stacy Keach and Jeff Bridges (3,4)

17 Clifford ___, author of stage plays Waiting for Lefty and Clash by Night (5)

18 Joe ___, snooker player; 2009 Welsh Open tournament runner-up (5)

20 Robert ___, US engineer after whom a type of musical synthesiser is named (4)

Across

3 **and 13** 1991 stage play by Edward Albee; 1994 Pulitzer Prize for Drama winner (5,4,5)

8 David ___, Best Director Oscar winner for The Bridge on the River Kwai (4)

9 Friedrich ___, German poet who authored stage plays The Robbers and Maria Stuart (8)

10 **and 14** Best Actress in a Leading Role Oscar nominee for My Man Godfrey (6,7)

13 **See 3 Across**

14 **See 10 Across**

15 **and 20 Down** London-born ventriloquist whose dolls included Lord Charles (3,4)

16 Genus of flowering plants in the grass family grown for grain and fodder (7)

17 Oily secretion of the sebaceous glands (5)

21 K R ___, Australia Test cricketer who took 5-26 against West Indies in Sydney in 1952 (6)

22 Capital of Sardinia (8)

23 Samantha ___, actress who played Miss Moneypenny in 1995 action film GoldenEye (4)

24 US state; capital Nashville (9)

Down

1 1986 film comedy starring John Cleese and Penelope Wilton (9)

2 Drew ___, actress who played the title role in 1992 film drama Poison Ivy (9)

4 Old Testament Hebrew prophet of the 8th-century BC (5)

5 2014 children's novel by Matt Haig (4,3)

6 White, grey, brown or pale green mineral found in metamorphic rocks (4)

7 A Z ___, 2014 Cricket Writers' Club Young Cricketer of the Year (4)

11 1965 comedy Western film starring Jane Fonda in the title role (3,6)

12 US actor who played Benjamin Danz in 2005 action film Mr and Mrs Smith (4,5)

14 Pat ___, Bristol Rugby coach appointed in 2017 (3)

15 Animated television series for children featuring characters Tommy Pickles and Susie Carmichael (7)

18 Character played by Jamie Bell in the 2003 film version of Nicholas Nickleby (5)

19 Christian ___, Best Actor in a Supporting Role Oscar winner for The Fighter (4)

20 **See 15 Across**

Across

1 Sharon ___, actress who replaced Meg Foster as Christine Cagney in US television series Cagney and Lacey (5)

7 Attilio ___, 1990-97 Italy midfielder; Sampdoria 1990 European Cup Winners' Cup Final winner (8)

8 **and 21 Down** The ___, 1922 stage play by Noël Coward (5,4)

10 Battle of ___, conflict of the American Civil War fought in July, 1863 (10)

12 Stand-up comedian who performs as The Pub Landlord (2,6)

14 ___ Stillman, Oscar-nominated writer and director of 1990 romantic drama film Metropolitan (4)

16 Substance which is traditionally layered with string and leather to make a cricket ball (4)

17 Another name for the eardrum (8)

20 The ___, 1955 novel by Leon Uris (5,5)

23 ___ Cup, international tennis tournament between Team Europe and Team World, founded in 2017 (5)

24 West Yorkshire town northwest of Bradford on the River Worth (8)

25 **and 13 Down** Actress who played Chardonnay Lane-Pascoe in ITV drama series Footballers' Wives (5,3)

Down

1 Republic in South America; capital Georgetown (6)

2 2016 animated film starring the voice talent of Matthew McConaughey and Reese Witherspoon (4)

3 Waterbird of Europe, Asia and North America with a white bill and forehead (4)

4 The ___, English title of the Marguerite Yourcenar novel which won the 1968 Prix Femina (5)

5 Area in the London Borough of Haringey that shares its name with a 1980 Stephen King short story (6,3)

6 Chewy sweet containing chopped nuts and cherries (6)

9 Frank ___, Canada-born architect who designed the Guggenheim Museum in Bilbao, Spain (5)

11 Natalie ___, singer and actress who played Lorna Campbell in 2003 film Johnny English (9)

13 **See 25 Across**

15 Rafe ___, actor who portrayed William Holman Hunt in 2009 BBC TV drama series Desperate Romantics (5)

16 Charles ___, Home Secretary from 2004-06 (6)

18 Marilyn ___, singer and actress who played Sugar Kane Kowalczyk in 1959 film comedy Some Like It Hot (6)

19 Town in Kent; one of the original Cinque Ports (5)

21 **See 8 Across**

22 Actor who played the title role in 1937 film drama Elephant Boy (4)

No. 92

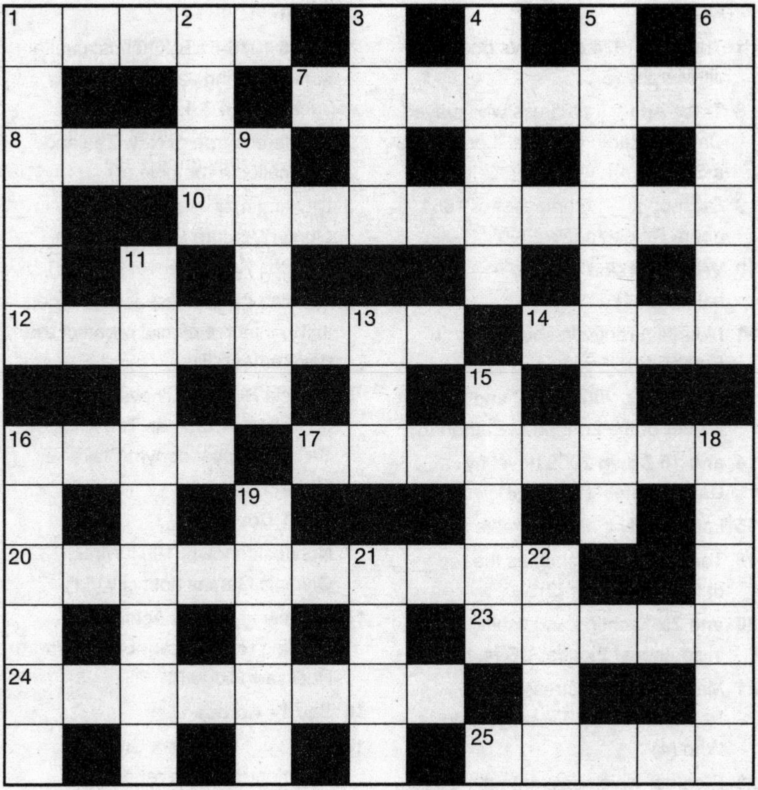

Across

1 The ___, 1974 children's book by Jill Murphy (5,5)

8 Tracy-Ann ___, actress who played Carol Carter in Channel 4 drama It's a Sin (7)

9 Giuseppe ___, composer of 1851 opera Rigoletto (5)

10 Very short skirt worn by a ballerina (4)

11 Mountain range in south central Europe (4)

12 Martin ___, 2005, 2007 and 2008 winner of the London Marathon (3)

14 **and 16 Down** 2009 novel by Danielle Steel (3,3,2,1,4)

15 Largest city in Saudi Arabia (6)

18 Terrestrial newt such as the red ___ of North America (3)

20 **and 25** Yachting and fishing resort in southeast Florida, US (4,10)

21 Mary ___, first actress to play Romana in BBC TV series Doctor Who (4)

23 Steamer which delivered the Statue of Liberty to New York and shares its name with a department of France (5)

24 Dorothy ___, actress who played the title role in 1958 biopic The Bonnie Parker Story (7)

25 **See 20 Across**

Down

1 **and 6** 1976-81 BBC TV drama series starring James Bolam as Jack Ford (4,3,4,5,2)

2 Coniferous tree of New Zealand also called a red pine (4)

3 City and major railway junction in Guntur, Andhra Pradesh, India, near the Krishna River delta (6)

4 Russian daily newspaper founded in 1917 as the official organ of the government (8)

5 Patricia Highsmith novel first published in 1951 as The Price of Salt under pseudonym Claire Morgan (5)

6 **See 1 Down**

7 Norwegian town; 1994 Winter Olympic Games host city (11)

13 Andrew ___, Best Actor in a Leading Role Oscar nominee for Hacksaw Ridge (8)

16 **See 14 Across**

17 Ruth ___, New York City-born monologist whose repertoire included The Italian Lesson and Opening a Bazaar (6)

19 Letter which precedes iota in the Greek alphabet (5)

22 1977 novel by Robin Cook (4)

No. 93

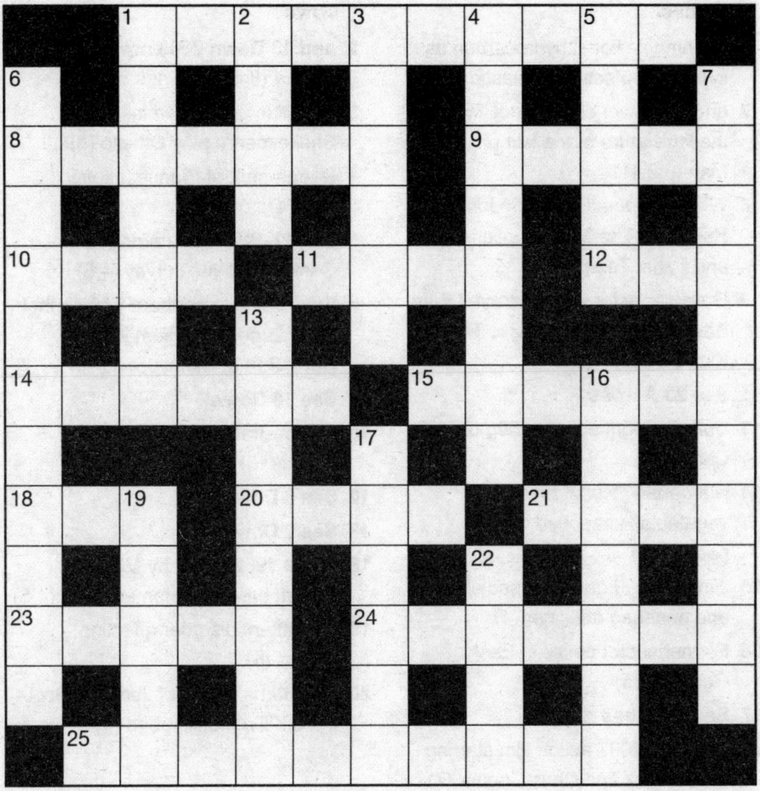

Across

1 Flammable liquid hydrocarbon used in the manufacture of plastic (7)

7 **and 17** Lower chamber of Tynwald, the legislature of the Isle of Man (5,2,4)

8 Wim ___, director of film dramas Hammett, The Million Dollar Hotel and Paris, Texas (7)

9 Guy ___, actor who portrayed King Edward VIII in 2010 biopic The King's Speech (6)

11 **See 23 Across**

13 Unit of weight equal to 50g used in China (4)

14 Hungarian stew of meat and vegetables seasoned with paprika (7)

15 Jimmy ___, London-based shoe and handbag designer (4)

16 Former secret police in East Germany (5)

17 **See 7 Across**

21 The ___, 2007 action film starring Jamie Foxx and Chris Cooper (7)

22 Medium-sized wading bird with a long straight bill (5)

23 **and 11** Horse that won the Hennessy Gold Cup at Leopardstown a record four times between 1999 and 2004 (7,5)

Down

2 **and 13 Down** 2003 novel by Tom Clancy (3,5,2,3,5)

3 Venetian gentleman in William Shakespeare play Othello (8)

4 Department of France; capital Lille (4)

5 **and 12** 1990 film starring Jeff Daniels and Judith Ivey (4,5)

6 River rising in northern France that flows through Belgium into the North Sea at Nieuwpoort (4)

9 **See 18 Down**

10 Administrative headquarters of Essex (10)

12 **See 5 Down**

13 **See 2 Down**

18 **and 9** 1962 opera by Michael Tippett based on Homer's Iliad (4,5)

19 Movement disorder affecting golfers (4)

20 ___ Harris, friend of Jem and Scout in To Kill a Mockingbird (4)

No. 94

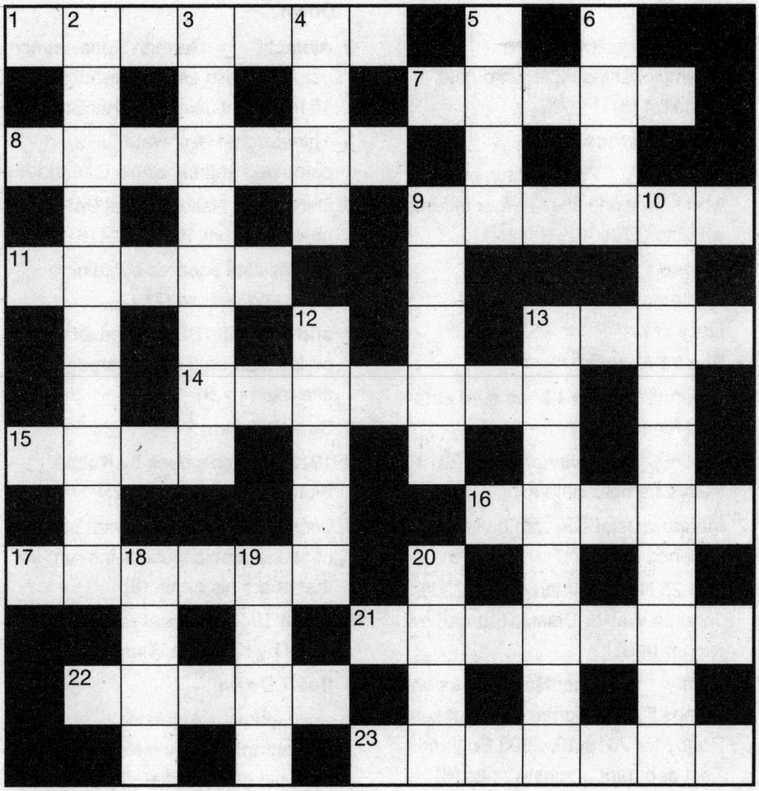

No. 95

Across

1 Phillips ___, 2009 World Championships triple jump gold medallist (5)

4 See 26 Across

10 Roberto ___, Panamanian boxer who held world titles at four different weights (5)

11 Alberto ___, author of novels Contempt and The Indifferent Ones (7)

12 See 23 Across

13 Unfermented soya-bean curd eaten as a foodstuff (4)

15 Jason ___, US winner of the 2013 PGA Championship (6)

17 Marine crustacean with a slender flattened body and large tail (6)

19 and 25 New Zealand golfer; 2008 Johnnie Walker Classic tournament winner (4,5)

20 Danny ___, former Sale Sharks and Wasps fly-half signed by Gloucester Rugby for 2018-19; 2008 England Test debutant against Wales (8)

23 and 12 Founder of the Academy of St Martin in the Fields chamber orchestra in 1958 (7,8)

24 ___ National Park, part of the Willandra Lakes Region in New South Wales, Australia (5)

25 See 19 Across

26 and 4 1987 film thriller starring Mickey Rourke and Robert De Niro (5,5)

Down

2 Albrecht ___, German Renaissance painter whose engravings include 1514's Saint Jerome in His Study (5)

3 Third-largest freshwater lake contained entirely within Canada (8)

5 Derek ___, National Coal Board chairman from 1972-82 (4)

6 Small pasta squares containing meat and cheese (7)

7 and 18 1960s BBC TV adventure series starring Gerald Harper in the title role (4,7,5)

8 See 16 Down

9 1922 children's book by Ruth Plumly Thompson (7,2,2)

14 Leon ___, Russian inventor in 1920 of an electronic musical instrument that bears his name (8)

16 and 8 1944 historical romance novel by Kathleen Winsor (7,5)

18 See 7 Down

21 ___ Leibovitz, American photographer known for her portraits of celebrities (5)

22 2001 biopic starring Johnny Depp as George Jung (4)

Across

6 **and 7 Down** 1913 novel by Sax Rohmer (3,7,2,2,2-6)

8 Slender fish of the snake mackerel family with an almost uniformly dark brown body (7)

9 Surname of acting sisters Eva, Magda and Zsa Zsa (5)

10 Central block or hub of a wheel (4)

12 Jean-Philippe ___, French composer of 1733 opera Hippolyte et Aricie (6)

14 Jo ___, 2014 European Championships 10,000m gold medallist for Great Britain (5)

15 Tiina ___, 1983 World Championships javelin gold medallist (6)

16 Idris ___, actor who played the title role in BBC TV drama series Luther (4)

19 Japanese dish of cold cakes of rice with a topping of raw fish (5)

21 Justin ___, Wales and Ospreys flanker; 2013 and 2017 British and Irish Lions tourist (7)

22 Republic in West Africa known as Portuguese Guinea until 1974 (6-6)

Down

1 Spencer ___, British prime minister assassinated in 1812 (8)

2 Australian acacia with hard scented wood used for fences (5)

3 Johannes ___, Bavaria-born winner of the 1919 Nobel Prize in Physics (5)

4 South American republic; capital Montevideo (7)

5 Ty ___, Detroit Tigers baseball player and manager known as The Georgia Peach (4)

6 **and 14** 1996 film drama starring Ralph Fiennes and Juliette Binoche (3,7,7)

7 **See 6 Across**

11 Evergreen or deciduous tree or shrub whose fruit is the acorn (3)

12 Stephen ___, Best Actor in a Leading Role Oscar nominee for The Crying Game (3)

13 Perennial submerged marine plant of the genus Zostera with long narrow green leaves (8)

14 **See 6 Down**

17 ___ Mountains, range in North Africa whose highest peak is Toubkal (5)

18 Banana ___, dessert topped with syrup, nuts and whipped cream (5)

20 Better Call ___, TV crime drama; a spin-off to the Breaking Bad franchise (4)

Across

3 and 13 1943 Alfred Hitchcock film thriller starring Teresa Wright and Joseph Cotten (6,2,1,5)

8 Marco ___, Germany and Borussia Dortmund forward; 2012 Footballer of the Year in Germany (4)

9 Todd ___, golfer who won The Open Championship in 2004 (8)

10 and 24 Actress who played Nora Tyler Bing in US television sitcom Friends (6,9)

13 See 3 Across

14 In Argentina, one hundredth of a peso (7)

15 Muslim festival, such as ___ ul-Fitr or ___ ul-Adha (3)

16 Singer and actress whose roles include Nine Ball in 2018 action comedy film Ocean's Eight (7)

17 and 20 Down The ___, 2002 novel by Frederic Tuten (5,4)

21 and 15 Down Comedian who played Mr Harman in BBC TV sitcom Are You Being Served? (6,7)

22 Vladimir ___, virtuoso pianist; posthumous winner of a Grammy Lifetime Achievement Award in 1990 (8)

23 ___ Strait, channel between southeast India and Sri Lanka (4)

24 See 10 Across

Down

1 Arabian camel with a single hump (9)

2 William ___, author of novels The Soft Machine and Nova Express (9)

4 Chris ___, Liberal Democrat MP for Eastleigh from 2005-13 (5)

5 2014 novel by Amy Reed (7)

6 1976 novel by Tom Sharpe (4)

7 Unit of length equal to twelve inches (4)

11 Port on the River Tyne opposite Newcastle (9)

12 Common Eurasian rail of fields and meadows with light yellowish-brown plumage (9)

14 Federal US bureau created in 1947 to conduct espionage activities (1,1,1)

15 See 21 Across

18 Temperate tree or large shrub with rounded leaves and edible brown nuts (5)

19 Émile ___, French author of novels Germinal and Thérèse Raquin (4)

20 See 17 Across

No. 98

Across

1 Term for the colour red on a coat of arms, eg (5)

7 Michael ___, stand-up comedian; 2011 judge on ITV talent show Britain's Got Talent (8)

8 Lowest deck of a warship having at least four decks (5)

10 See 14 Across

12 1994 Jack Ketchum novel also published as Joyride (4,4)

14 **and 10** 1982 novel by Antonia Fraser (4,10)

16 ___ in the Water, spiritual song associated with the Underground Railroad (4)

17 Northeasterly that blows down the southwest slope of Cross Fell in Cumbria (4,4)

20 Former BBC TV tennis commentator and British Davis Cup team coach who died in 1992 (3,7)

23 **and 1 Down** Golfer; 2009 US Open Championship winner (5,6)

24 Former Glasgow Warriors prop; 2012 Scotland Test debutant against Wales (2,6)

25 Republic in West Africa; capital Porto-Novo (5)

Down

1 See 23 Across

2 ___ Handicap, flat race run at York (4)

3 Mark on the floor behind which a darts player must stand to throw (4)

4 **and 18** Actress who played Angie Watts in BBC TV soap EastEnders (5,6)

5 1918 novel by Willa Cather (2,7)

6 Michael ___, actor who plays Kevin Webster in ITV soap Coronation Street (2,4)

9 Puppet pig, companion of Pinky, created by Jan and Vlasta Dalibor (5)

11 Wassily ___, painter whose works include 1925's Swinging (9)

13 'I cannot tell a ___', mythical statement attributed to a young George Washington (3)

15 The God of ___ Things, Arundhati Roy's debut novel (5)

16 ___ Sea, area extending along the North Sea coasts of The Netherlands, Germany and Denmark (6)

18 See 4 Down

19 2008 animated film starring the voice talent of Ben Burtt (4-1)

21 Moise ___, Italian footballer who moved to Everton FC in 2019 (4)

22 Olympic sport first contested at the 1964 Winter Games (4)

No. 98

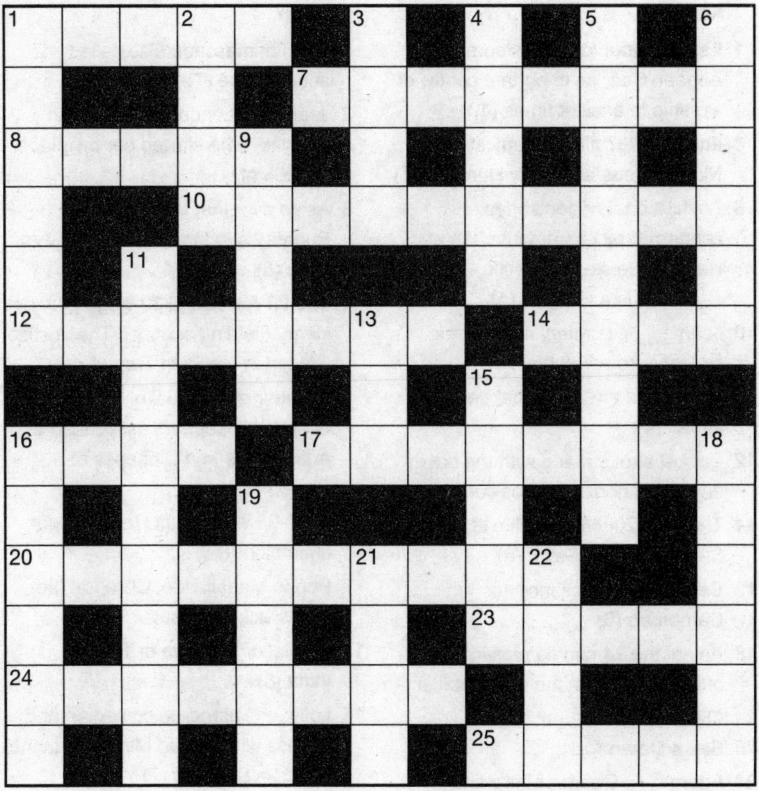

Across

1 Largely mountainous island in the Aegean Sea; an important centre of worship in ancient times (10)

8 and 24 1987 film comedy starring Nicolas Cage and Holly Hunter (7,7)

9 Animated television series conceived by Otmar Gutmann and Harald Muecke whose title character is a penguin (5)

10 John ___, Secretary of State for Defence from 1981-83 (4)

11 Member of the aboriginal people of Japan (4)

12 Cricket stroke made with the bat in an almost horizontal position (3)

14 The ___, 2004 horror film starring Sarah Michelle Gellar (6)

15 Seaport and largest city of Cameroon (6)

18 Any of the 24 curved elastic arches of bone that form the chest wall in man (3)

20 See 4 Down

21 Adam ___, George Eliot's first novel (4)

23 Spanish wine normally made mainly using the Tempranillo grape (5)

24 See 8 Across

25 US golfer; 1991 Phoenix Open tournament winner (5,5)

Down

1 Form of massage also called acupressure (7)

2 Jean ___, London-born fashion designer who started her own label in 1966 (4)

3 Asian river that flows to the Euphrates to form the Shatt al-Arab delta (6)

4 and 20 Across 1730 stage play by Henry Fielding subtitled The Justice Caught in His Own Trap (4,4,4)

5 Member of a school of ancient Greek philosophers associated with Antisthenes and Diogenes of Sinope (5)

6 2001-03 WBA Light Heavyweight champion (5,6)

7 Port in Magallanes, Chile, on the Brunswick Peninsula (5,6)

13 Capital of the state of Tripura, India (8)

16 Lolly ___, stand-up comedian and actress who played Mimi in Channel 4 sitcom Damned (7)

17 Splish ___, Bobby Darin novelty song of 1958 (6)

19 Victor ___, Best Actor in a Supporting Role Oscar nominee for What Ever Happened To Baby Jane? (5)

22 Nathan ___, Australia-born New Zealand half back; 2008 Rugby League World Cup Final winner (4)

Across

1 Julian ___, comedian and actor who played Howard Moon in BBC TV series The Mighty Boosh (7)

7 **and 8** Writer and actor who played Igor in 1974 film comedy Young Frankenstein (5,7)

8 See 7 Across

9 1970s US Western television series starring David Carradine and Keye Luke (4,2)

11 **and 22** US actor and comedian who wrote and directed 1998 film Sour Grapes (5,5)

13 **and 17** 2001 novel by Ben Elton (4,6)

14 City in Washington that hosted the 1962 World's Fair (7)

15 Wavy-edged Indonesian or Malaysian knife (4)

16 City in Sri Lanka home to the ___ International Stadium, a Test cricket venue known as The Esplanade (5)

17 See 13 Across

21 Jacob ___, Flemish painter whose works include 1643's David Bearing the Head of Goliath (3,4)

22 See 11 Across

23 See 9 Down

Down

2 Chief port and second largest city of Egypt (10)

3 International Committee of the ___, humanitarian organisation formally established following the Geneva Convention of 1863 (3,5)

4 Large tree of the East Indies that yields a valuable wood (4)

5 Capital of Azerbaijan (4)

6 Male of a red deer (4)

9 **and 23 Across** Pennsylvania-born US jazz pianist and composer; 2003 Polar Music Prize winner (5,7)

10 19th-century Hungarian composer of symphonic poems Hungaria and Orpheus (5,5)

12 Alfred ___, actor who played Albert Hackett in 1970s ITV sitcom Albert and Victoria (5)

13 Frances ___, 2006 Tony Award Best Featured Actress in a Play winner for The History Boys (2,2,4)

18 Alcoholic drink made by fermenting a solution of honey (4)

19 River in Scotland that flows to the North Sea at Peterhead (4)

20 Rooney ___, Best Actress in a Leading Role Oscar nominee for The Girl with the Dragon Tattoo (4)

No. 100

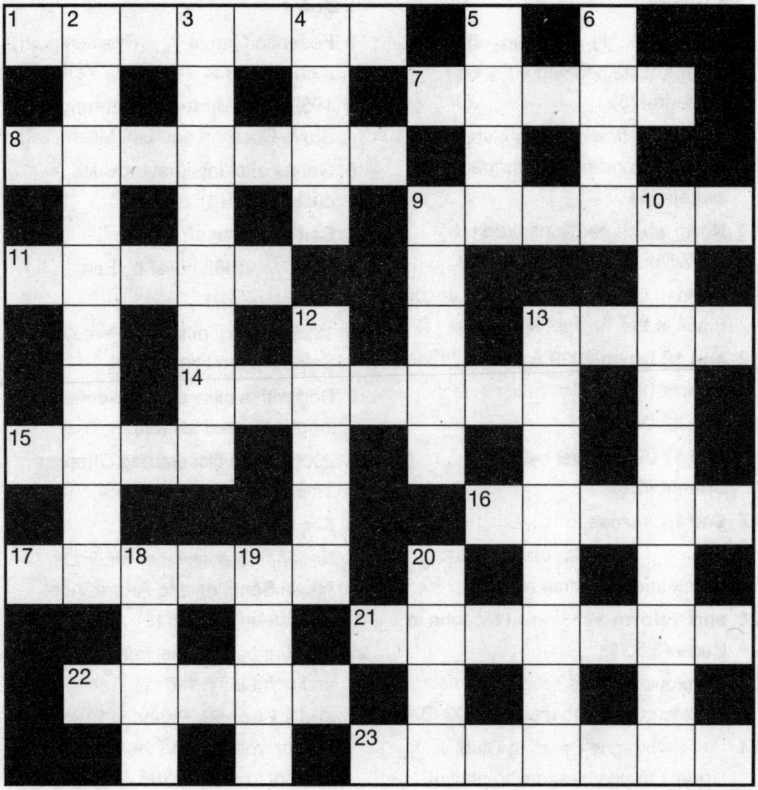

Across

1 Town in Moray, Scotland, on the River Lossie housing a ruined cathedral (5)

4 ___ violet, flower which gives its name to fragrant disc-shaped sweets (5)

10 Novel which partly inspired the 2017 film T2 Trainspotting (5)

11 Taylor ___, actor who played Jacob Black in the Twilight film series (7)

12 **and 16 Down** 2009 novel by Jeffery Deaver (8,7)

13 **See 22 Down**

15 **and 17** 2009 novel by Sarah Dunant (6,6)

17 **See 15 Across**

19 The ___, 1990 film drama starring Derek Jacobi in dual roles (4)

20 **and 6 Down** 1993 novel by John le Carré (3,5,7)

23 US pioneer of the solid-body electric guitar who died in 2009 (3,4)

24 ___ Olympique Sporting Club, Ligue 1 football team who play at the Stade Pierre-Mauroy (5)

25 Port and largest city in Kansai, Japan (5)

26 Yellow-flowered North American plant such as the smooth ___ (5)

Down

2 Federico García ___, Spanish poet; author of 1934 stage play Yerma (5)

3 1959 crime drama film starring Steve Cochran and Lita Milan (1,7)

5 Genus of plants that includes cuckoo pint (4)

6 **See 20 Across**

7 The ___, 1962 novel by Len Deighton (7,4)

8 1998 action film starring Wesley Snipes in the title role (5)

9 Dog with a silky dark red coat and a long feathered tail (5,6)

14 2005 action film starring Charlize Theron in the title role (4,4)

16 **See 12 Across**

18 National football team for whom Alexis Sánchez and Arturo Vidal have been capped (5)

21 Fielding position between the slips and point in cricket (5)

22 **and 13 Across** Period in European history from around the late 5th century to about 1100 AD (4,4)

Across

6 2005 romcom starring Diane Lane and John Cusack (4,4,4)

8 Emma ___, author of novels Alice Fell and Pemberley (7)

9 Celia ___, actress who played Una Alconbury in the Bridget Jones film trilogy (5)

10 and 14 Across 2010 Outstanding Lead Actress in a Comedy Series Emmy winner for Nurse Jackie (4,5)

12 Best Director Oscar winner for Brokeback Mountain and Life of Pi (3,3)

14 See 10 Across

15 Brad ___, US actor who played Todd Bowden in 1998 film drama Apt Pupil (6)

16 The ___, insect character who appears in Lewis Carroll's Through the Looking-Glass, and What Alice Found There (4)

19 Kel ___, golfer who won The Open Championship in 1960 (5)

21 Dark yellow pigment obtained from the gum resin of certain trees of southeast Asia (7)

22 First Sunday in Lent (12)

Down

1 Capital of Paraguay (8)

2 John ___, Denver Broncos quarterback; Super Bowl XXXIII MVP (5)

3 Steve ___, 1980 Olympic 800m gold medallist (5)

4 2000-10 Brazil forward footballer at Internazionale from 2004-09 (7)

5 Carbohydrate obtained from seaweeds used in ice cream as a thickening agent (4)

6 François ___, French president from 1981-95 (10)

7 Elena ___, 2008 Olympic singles tennis gold medallist (10)

11 Official language of Laos (3)

12 Playing card with one spot (3)

13 Best Actress in a Supporting Role Oscar nominee for Enemies, A Love Story (4,4)

14 1994-2004 US television sitcom starring Jennifer Aniston, Courteney Cox and Lisa Kudrow (7)

17 Ancient Celtic writing system used in Britain and Ireland, consisting of straight lines drawn or carved perpendicular to one another (5)

18 Town in the northeast Netherlands near the border with Germany, developed since the Second World War (5)

20 2001 novel by Irvine Welsh (4)

No. 102

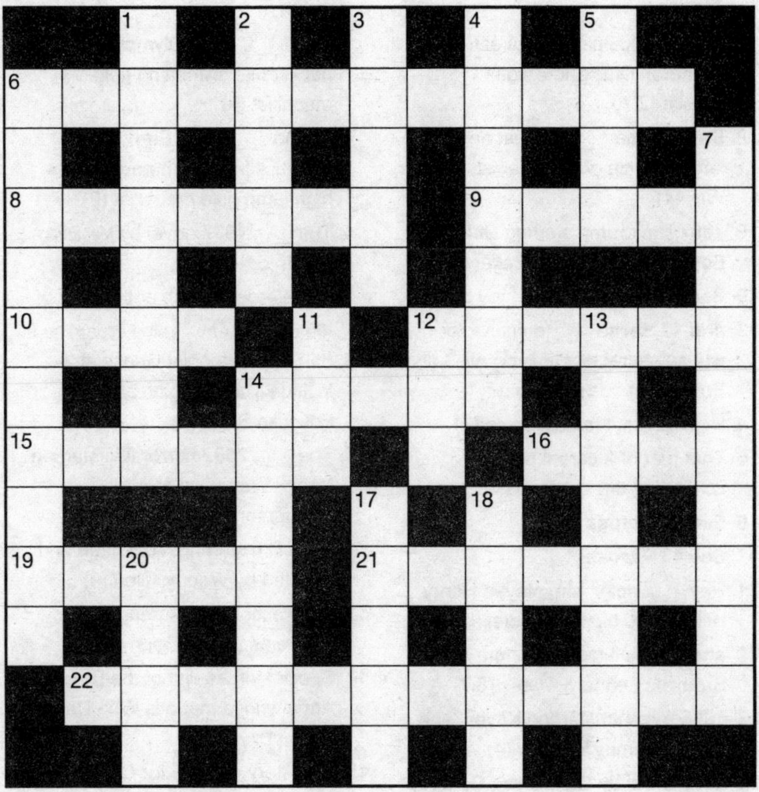

Across

3 and 10 2009 film drama starring Cameron Diaz and Abigail Breslin (2,7,6)

8 Battle of the ___, longest and largest battle of the Spanish Civil War (4)

9 1967 film drama starring Dirk Bogarde and Stanley Baker (8)

10 See 3 Across

13 and 17 Sacha ___, comic actor whose characters include Ali G and Borat (5,5)

14 Highest adult female voice (7)

15 That part of a cereal plant containing the seeds (3)

16 See 22 Across

17 See 13 Across

21 Ray ___, actor who played Henry Hill in 1990 biopic Goodfellas (6)

22 and 16 2008 biopic starring Adrien Brody as Leonard Chess (8,7)

23 1993 romcom starring Kevin Kline and Sigourney Weaver (4)

24 2009 novel by Glen David Gold (9)

Down

1 Mark ___, 1992 Olympic 100m backstroke swimming gold medallist (9)

2 Ariane ___, 2009 European Athletics Indoor Championships high jump gold medallist (9)

4 The ___, 1937 novel by Virginia Woolf (5)

5 Chisel-edged tooth at the front of the mouth (7)

6 Bill ___, cartoonist whose strips include The Cloggies and The Fosdyke Saga (4)

7 The ___, 2002 horror film starring Naomi Watts and Martin Henderson (4)

11 1979 film starring, co-written and directed by Woody Allen (9)

12 1979 action film starring Roger Moore as James Bond (9)

14 Special forces unit of the British Army whose motto is Who Dares Wins (1,1,1)

15 Secretary of State for Children, Schools and Families from 2007-10 (2,5)

18 1961 film drama starring Charlton Heston and Sophia Loren (2,3)

19 Island in central Hawaii; chief town Honolulu (4)

20 Steven ___, Middlesex County Cricket Club's youngest-ever debutant in first-class cricket (4)

Across

1 One of the basic patterns of the human fingerprint (5)

7 Fabric made of silk and wool or cotton and rayon used especially for coats (8)

8 Nikolai ___, author of 1842 novel Dead Souls (5)

10 Large arboreal Australian kingfisher also called a laughing jackass (10)

12 The ___, 1909 novel by L Frank Baum (4,2,2)

14 Sammy ___, Chicago Cubs MLB player who hit 179 home runs in the three seasons between 1998-2000 (4)

16 John ___, 2015 action film starring Keanu Reeves in the title role (4)

17 ___ Ocean, body of water bounded by the Americas, Africa and Europe (8)

20 Composition by Gustav Holst subtitled A Homage to Thomas Hardy (5,5)

23 King of Judaea from 37-4 BC (5)

24 1973 no 1 single by The Simon Park Orchestra (3,5)

25 2006 film drama starring Heath Ledger and Abbie Cornish (5)

Down

1 Richard ___, German composer of operas Parsifal and Lohengrin (6)

2 Large Eurasian bird of the crow family (4)

3 Kirsty ___, television presenter whose credits include Newsnight and The Late Show (4)

4 Rhys ___, actor and comedian who played Murray Hewitt in US television series Flight of the Conchords (5)

5 and 18 Assassin of Jean-Paul Marat executed in 1793 (9,6)

6 River of South America formed at the confluence of the Paranaiba and Grande Rivers in Brazil (6)

9 Lorenzo ___, Italian Renaissance painter after whom a style of lacy patterned carpet from Turkey is named (5)

11 Fictional girl detective who first appeared in 1930 novel The Secret of the Old Clock by Carolyn Keene (5,4)

13 Erect annual grass grown for its edible seed (3)

15 Third planet from the sun (5)

16 E D ___, West Indies Test cricketer who hit 206 against England in Port of Spain, Trinidad in 1954 (6)

18 See 5 Down

19 Deborah Kara ___, actress who played Dahlia Gillespie in 2006 horror film Silent Hill (5)

21 Barbara ___, I Dream of Jeannie star (4)

22 Queen of the Olympian gods in Greek mythology (4)

No. 105

Across

1 Author of 1957 novel Room at the Top (4,6)

8 General ___, The Adventures of Tintin character whose archenemy is General Tapioca (7)

9 **and 17 Down** Motor racing driver; F1 1999 Australian GP winner (5,6)

10 Kenyan lioness cared for by George and Joy Adamson from 1956-61 (4)

11 Sidney ___, British economist and social historian who co-founded magazine The New Statesman with wife Beatrice (4)

12 Judy ___, famous mother of actress Kate Beckinsale (3)

14 Clive ___, actor who played Mike Barratt in Casualty and Holby City (6)

15 **and 3 Down** Former Saracens rugby union flanker; 2003 South Africa Test debutant against Georgia (6,6)

18 Genus of evergreen shrubs including the common ___ whose bitter leaves are used in herbal medicine (3)

20 Vince ___, actor who played Ron Dixon in Channel 4 soap Brookside from 1990-2003 (4)

21 2011 film comedy starring Simon Pegg and Nick Frost (4)

23 Rev W ___, creator of Thomas the Tank Engine (5)

24 The ___, 1961 novel by Mary Stewart (3,4)

25 1996 comedy-drama film starring Pete Postlethwaite, Tara Fitzgerald and Ewan McGregor (7,3)

Down

1 Thomas Jonathan 'Stonewall' ___, Confederate brigadier general associated with the First Battle of Bull Run of 1861 during the American Civil War (7)

2 City in Shandong, China, known for peony cultivation (4)

3 **See 15 Across**

4 Frank ___, Berlin-born artist whose works include 1965's Mornington Crescent (8)

5 Rafael ___, 2008 and 2010 Wimbledon singles tennis championship winner (5)

6 Women's British Open Squash Championship winner from 1950-59 (5,6)

7 US author of 1903 autobiography The Story of My Life; subject of 1962 biopic The Miracle Worker (5,6)

13 **See 16 Down**

16 **and 13** 1873 novel by Thomas Hardy whose heroine is Elfride Swancourt (1,4,2,4,4)

17 **See 9 Across**

19 Shrub or small tree with red, purple or black berry-like fruits (5)

22 Laura ___, US singer-songwriter whose 1967 album debut was More Than a New Discovery (4)

Across

1 Branch of science concerned with the study of the properties of space, time, matter and energy (7)

7 **See 21 Across**

8 Charles ___, 19th-century French acrobat born Jean-François Gravelet (7)

9 Country of Central America between Costa Rica and Colombia (6)

11 Capital of Bulgaria (5)

13 SI unit of power (4)

14 **and 10 Down** The ___, 1968 film drama starring Alain Delon and Marianne Faithfull (4,2,1,10)

15 Highest adult male voice (4)

16 **and 22** 1873 novel by R M Ballantyne (5,5)

17 Young swan (6)

21 **and 7** Actress who played the title role in 2007 BBC TV series Fanny Hill (7,5)

22 **See 16 Across**

23 Ruslan ___, 2007-09 WBA Heavyweight champion (7)

Down

2 1969 film musical starring Barbra Streisand in the title role (5,5)

3 Port in southern California, US, north of Tijuana (3,5)

4 Tiny wafer of semiconductor material used in the manufacture of electronic equipment (4)

5 Standard unit of currency of Turkey (4)

6 Wife of Cronus and mother of Zeus in Greek mythology (4)

9 Genus of flowering plants native to North America including moss ___ and creeping ___ (5)

10 **See 14 Across**

12 David ___, host of 1960s BBC TV satire show That Was the Week That Was (5)

13 Mark ___, Best Actor in a Supporting Role Oscar nominee for The Departed (8)

18 Michael ___, Secretary of State for Education from 2010-14 (4)

19 Richard ___, director of films Iris and Notes on a Scandal (4)

20 Third son of Adam in the Old Testament (4)

No. 106

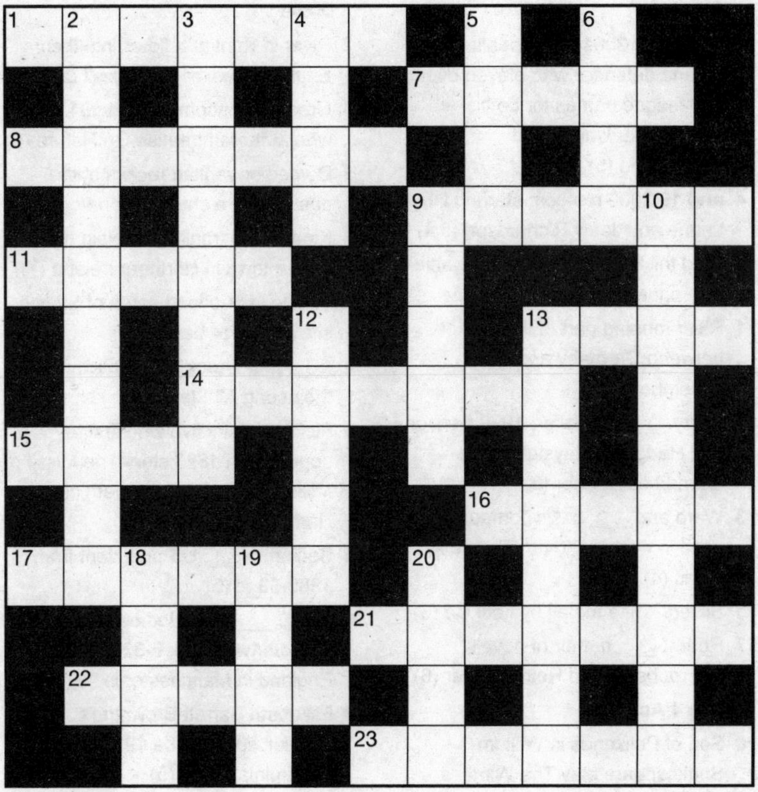

Across

1 John ___, 2001-18 Republic of Ireland defender who played over 200 league games for both Manchester United and Sunderland (5)

4 **and 19** 2000 romcom starring Hugh Laurie and Joely Richardson (5,4)

10 Cold thick sauce made from garlic with eggs and olive oil (5)

11 River forming part of the border between Germany and Luxembourg (7)

12 Gerry ___, US golfer; 1999 Benson and Hedges Malaysian Open tournament winner (8)

13 Warp and ___, basic components used in weaving to turn thread into fabric (4)

15 Silvery-white metal; symbol Ce (6)

17 Robert ___, author of novels Necrophenia and Retromancer (6)

19 **See 4 Across**

20 Son of Polixenes in William Shakespeare play The Winter's Tale (8)

23 Screen or wall decoration at the back of an altar (7)

24 Lizard of tropical Asia and Africa with reduced limbs (5)

25 Junko ___, 1993 World Championships women's marathon gold medallist (5)

26 2012 St Leger winner ridden by Mickael Barzalona (5)

Down

2 River in Kent that flows into the English Channel at Pegwell Bay (5)

3 Greek philosopher born in 341 BC who authored treatise On Nature (8)

5 Domed or vaulted recess at the east end of a church (4)

6 Kind of thin fragile porcelain named after a town in Northern Ireland (7)

7 Village in Scotland south of Stirling; site of a 1314 battle (11)

8 ___ Mouth, rock band known for their song All Star (5)

9 Fictional detective who first appeared in 1893 story The Missing Millionaire by Hal Meredeth aka Harry Blyth (6,5)

14 Benjamin ___, US president from 1889-93 (8)

16 A M E ___, West Indies Test cricketer who took 6-37 against England in Manchester in 1976 (7)

18 Elizabeth Barrett Browning's spaniel; subject of a 1933 biography by Virginia Woolf (5)

21 Edward ___, director of films Glory, Defiance and The Siege (5)

22 River in central Germany upon which Felsberg and Fritzlar stand (4)

No. 107

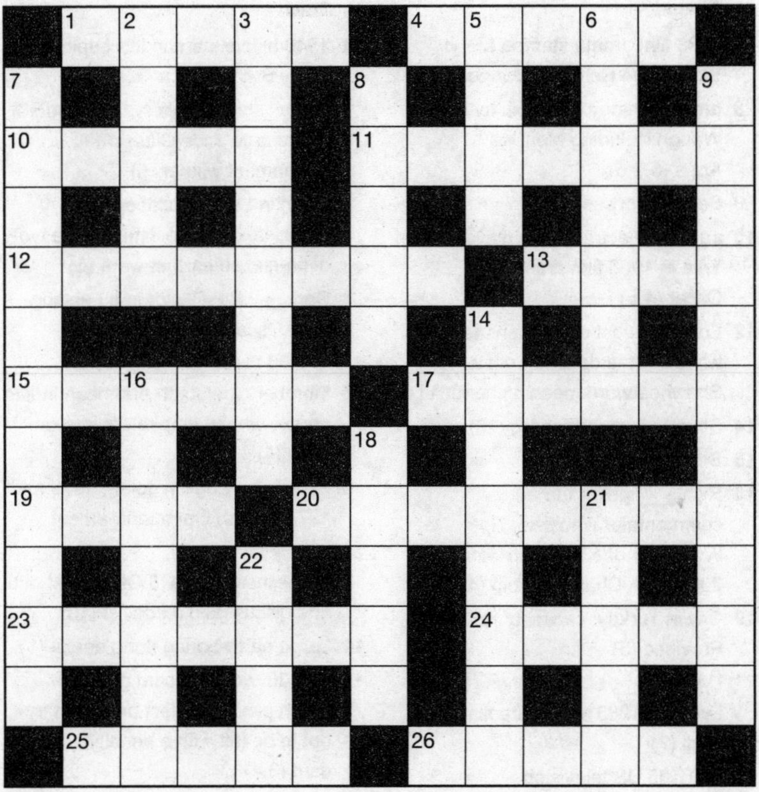

Across

6 1998 film drama starring Meryl Streep and Renée Zellweger (3,4,5)

8 **and 15** Trilogy of novels by Evelyn Waugh including Men at Arms (5,2,6)

9 **See 10 Across**

10 **and 9** US actress who played Trina Yale in 1966 film drama The Oscar (4,5)

12 Fourth largest city in Kansas, US, whose name derives from a Shawnee word meaning beautiful (6)

14 SI unit of work or energy (5)

15 **See 8 Across**

16 Rich ___, golfer turned commentator who beat Tiger Woods by one stroke to win the 2002 PGA Championship (4)

19 City in Turkey; capital of Kocaeli Province (5)

21 Lysette ___, actress whose played Lyssa in 1983 adventure film Krull (7)

22 2001-05 US television comedy-drama series starring Peter Krause and Michael C Hall (3,4,5)

Down

1 1946 biopic starring Ida Lupino as Emily Brontë (8)

2 Dicky ___, US golfer; 1994 Federal Express St Jude Classic tournament winner (5)

3 Town in South Holland, Netherlands, associated with a type of tin-glazed earthenware (5)

4 Don ___, Best Actor in a Leading Role Oscar nominee for Hotel Rwanda (7)

5 Member of a South American Indian people whose empire centred on Peru (4)

6 Peter ___, English golfer; 1973 and 1974 French Open tournament winner (10)

7 Micheline ___, 1948 Olympic shot put and discus gold medallist (10)

11 Large earth-boring dung beetle (3)

12 **and 20** Victorian card game in which players collect pairs and try not to be left with a penalty card (3,4)

13 2007 novel by Harlan Coben (3,5)

14 American racehorse; 2018 Triple Crown winner (7)

17 Spiny Mediterranean plant with edible flower buds (5)

18 Rex ___, author of mystery novels The Broken Vase and The Hand in the Glove (5)

20 **See 12 Down**

No. 108

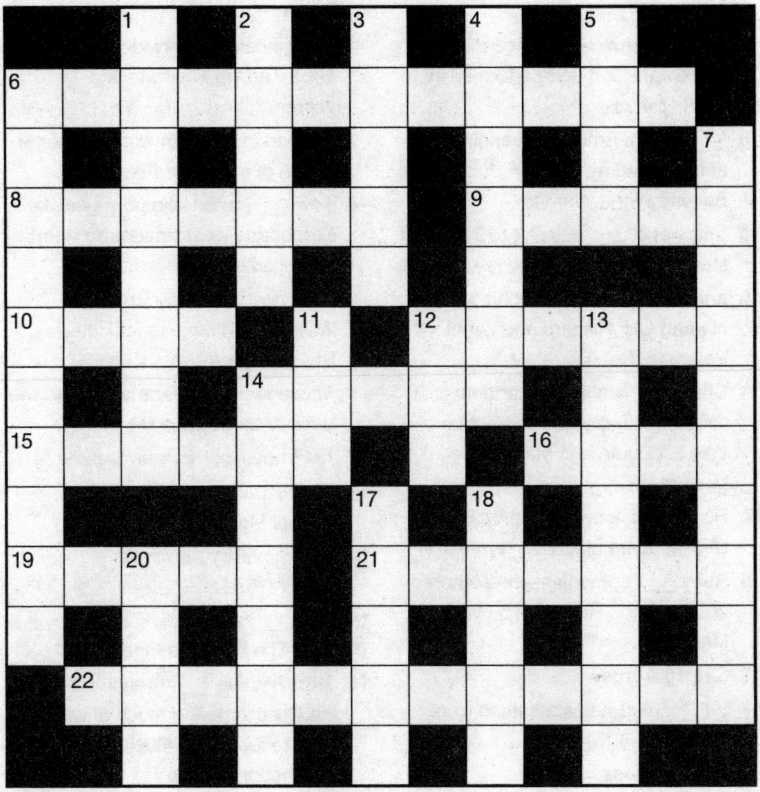

Across

3 and 21 Opera by Arthur Sullivan and Basil Hood first performed in 1899 (3,4,2,6)

8 ___ Anson, British twin-engined aircraft used by the RAF during the Second World War (4)

9 Sherwood ___, author of 1919 short story collection Winesburg, Ohio (8)

10 and 16 1963 musical comedy film starring Cliff Richard and Lauri Peters (6,7)

13 Chuck ___, animated cartoon director who created characters Wile E Coyote and Marvin Martian (5)

14 Honest old counsellor in William Shakespeare play The Tempest (7)

15 Ruby ___, comedian who authored 2002 memoir How Do You Want Me? (3)

16 See 10 Across

17 V I ___, Russian statesman who died in 1924 (5)

21 See 3 Across

22 Hydrocarbon found in carrots and sweet potatoes; main dietary source of vitamin A (8)

23 and 24 1986, 1987, 1991 and 1993 World Rally Drivers' Championship winner (4,9)

24 See 23 Across

Down

1 Scotland centre-forward; Liverpool 1965 FA Cup Final winning scorer (3,2,4)

2 Seaport in Western Australia at the mouth of the Swan River (9)

4 John ___, actor who portrayed Jack Kerouac in 1980 film drama Heart Beat (5)

5 2006 no 1 album by Robbie Williams (7)

6 Island in the English Channel whose two main parts are linked by isthmus La Coupée (4)

7 1847 novel by Herman Melville (4)

11 Silvery-white metallic element; symbol Mg (9)

12 1954 novel by Alexander Trocchi (5,4)

14 John ___, author of 1728 stage work The Beggar's Opera (3)

15 Jean-Antoine ___, French artist of the Rococo period much of whose work reflects the influence of the commedia dell'arte (7)

18 John Hanning ___, Devon-born explorer who discovered Lake Victoria in 1858 (5)

19 Plantation in 1936 Margaret Mitchell novel Gone with the Wind (4)

20 Flesh of a pig used as food (4)

No. 109

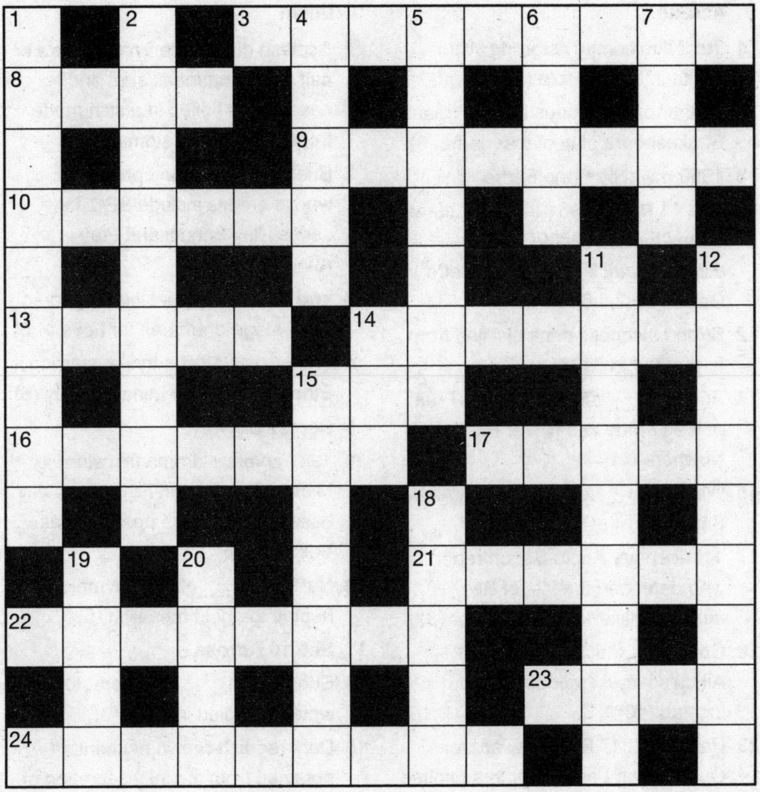

Across

1 2005 film comedy starring Will Smith in the title role (5)

7 Mother of Coriolanus in the William Shakespeare play of that name (8)

8 1950 novel by Edna Ferber (5)

10 and 11 Down 1961 three-act stage drama by Tennessee Williams starring Patrick O'Neal and Bette Davis (3,5,2,3,6)

12 Strong alcoholic drink distilled from fermented fruits (8)

14 Andrea ___, author of novels Fruit of the Lemon and Never Far from Nowhere (4)

16 Whip My ___, 2010 song by Willow Smith (4)

17 11th-century Anglo-Saxon rebel who defended the Isle of Ely against William the Conqueror (8)

20 Country in which Ben Amera, Africa's largest monolith, is located (10)

23 Riz ___, 2017 Emmy Award for Outstanding Lead Actor in a Limited Series or Movie winner for The Night Of (5)

24 2016 Olympics individual field event won by US athletes Jeff Henderson and Tianna Bartoletta (4,4)

25 Henrik ___, author of stage plays Hedda Gabler and The League of Youth (5)

Down

1 Scottish dish made from sheep's or calf's offal, oatmeal, suet and seasonings boiled in a skin made from the animal's stomach (6)

2 Brian ___, actor and presenter whose credits include BBC TV series Play School and Play Away (4)

3 and 18 English poet who authored 1677 stage drama All for Love (4,6)

4 The ___, 2013 film thriller starring Ethan Hawke and Lena Headey (5)

5 See 21 Down

6 1987 comedy-drama film starring Mickey Rourke and Faye Dunaway based on the life of poet Charles Bukowski (6)

9 Nafissatou ___, 2020 Olympic heptathlon gold medallist (5)

11 See 10 Across

13 Edgar Allan ___, US short-story writer who died in 1849 (3)

15 Dark reddish-brown pigment obtained from the inky secretion of the cuttlefish (5)

16 Mark ___, actor who starred as Luke Skywalker in 1977 action film Star Wars (6)

18 See 3 Down

19 One skilled in the Japanese martial art of ninjutsu (5)

21 and 5 1894 stage play by George Bernard Shaw whose heroine is Raina Petkoff (4,3,3,3)

22 Biblical king of Israel and husband of Jezebel (4)

No. 110

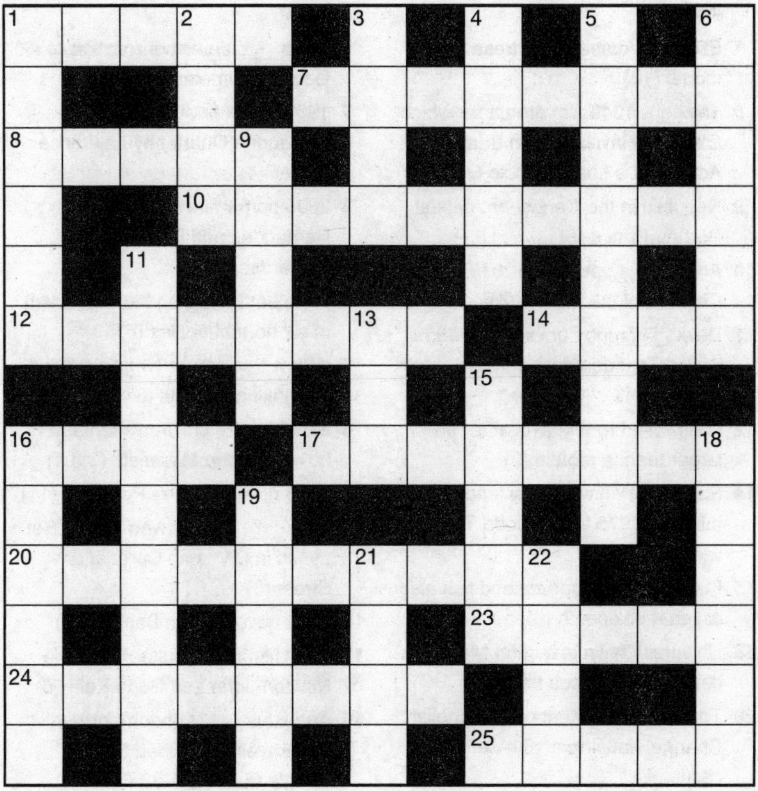

No. 111

Across

1 Elle ___, Australian actress and model (10)

8 The ___, 1949 film drama for which Olivia de Havilland won Best Actress in a Leading Role Oscar (7)

9 Republic in the Caribbean; capital Port-au-Prince (5)

10 Andrew ___, author of 2015 novel Children of the Master (4)

11 Dewi ___, rugby union wing; 1959 Wales Test debutant against England (4)

12 Long-tailed rodent similar to, but larger than, a mouse (3)

14 Ray ___, Widnes rugby league fullback; 1975 Lance Todd Trophy winner (6)

15 Freshwater European food fish also called a pikeperch (6)

18 University town in central Nigeria; a centre of the cocoa trade (3)

20 Tourist town in Kent on the English Channel housing a 16th-century castle (4)

21 L Frank ___, author of 1900 children's novel The Wonderful Wizard of Oz (4)

23 Industrial city and port in North Rhine-Westphalia, Germany, noted for the Cranger Kirmes funfair (5)

24 1960s US animated television character created by Hanna-Barbera (4,3)

25 Light cotton or linen fabric whose name derives from the Persian words for milk and sugar (10)

Down

1 Jules ___, detective creation of Georges Simenon (7)

2 1960 novel; final part of The Alexandria Quartet by Lawrence Durrell (4)

3 2005 horror film starring Jay Hernandez and Derek Richardson (6)

4 Wine bottle holding the equivalent of six normal bottles (8)

5 Willow tree whose twigs are used for making baskets (5)

6 **and 22** 1927 children's fantasy novel by John Masefield (3,8,4)

7 2006 novel by Terry Pratchett (11)

13 Julie ___, actress who played Bet Lynch in ITV soap Coronation Street (8)

16 2002 novel by Iain Banks (4,3)

17 1980 film musical starring Olivia Newton-John and Gene Kelly (6)

19 Augustus ___, London-born artist and traveller attached to HMS Beagle from 1831-32 (5)

22 **See 6 Down**

Across

1 Insect related to the grasshoppers, the male of which makes chirping noises by rubbing its forewings together (7)

7 See 9 Across

8 Cue sport originating in India (7)

9 and 7, 12 Down 1935 comedy film starring Groucho Marx as Otis B Driftwood (1,5,2,3,5)

11 Jean ___, F1 motor racing driver; 1995 Canadian GP winner (5)

13 John ___, English admiral executed in 1757 after failing to relieve Minorca (4)

14 Eighth planet from the sun (7)

15 1976 Elmore Leonard novel (4)

16 D ___, South Africa Test cricketer who hit 199 against Bangladesh in Potchefstroom in 2017 (5)

17 Eye defect also known as near-sightedness (6)

21 Derek ___, 1992 winner of the Nobel Prize in Literature (7)

22 Alex ___, Czechoslovakia-born golfer; 2002 Trophee Lancome tournament winner (5)

23 Roberto ___, Italian author of 2006 non-fiction book Gomorrah (7)

Down

2 Location near Castletown of Isle of Man Airport (10)

3 and 18 2009 film drama starring Harrison Ford and Ray Liotta (8,4)

4 Heaviest modern fencing weapon (4)

5 The ___ Rifles, 1979 song by The Jam (4)

6 Member of the English political party that opposed the succession to the throne of James, Duke of York (4)

9 River of southwest France that enters the Bay of Biscay below Bayonne (5)

10 Seaside resort in Norfolk on the southeast shore of the Wash (10)

12 See 9 Across

13 Thomaz ___, 2009 and 2012 Swiss Open singles tennis tournament winner (8)

18 See 3 Down

19 Jacky ___, Belgian motor racing driver; 1972 F1 German GP winner (4)

20 New Zealand forest tree of the myrtle family with crimson flowers and hard wood such as the northern ___ (4)

No. 113

Across

1 Muriel ___, author of novels The Girls of Slender Means and The Finishing School (5)

4 **and 18 Down** Central character in 1840s W M Thackeray novel Vanity Fair (5,5)

10 **and 17** The ___, 1937 novel by C S Forester (5,6)

11 Louis ___, 19th-century French inventor of a system of raised writing for blind people (7)

12 Northernmost island of a famous Florida archipelago known for its diving and snorkelling opportunities (3,5)

13 Greenish-blue colour complementary to red (4)

15 Richard ___, prime minister of New Zealand from 1893-1906 (6)

17 **See 10 Across**

19 Jennifer ___, actress who portrayed Myrtle Logue in 2010 biopic The King's Speech (4)

20 **See 22 Down**

23 Mount ___, volcano and highest mountain in Washington state, US (7)

24 Margaret ___, Kenyan athlete who set a New York City marathon course record in 2003 (5)

25 Port in Germany at the confluence of the Rivers Rhine and Main (5)

26 Jorn ___, Danish architect; designer of the Sydney Opera House (5)

Down

2 **and 7** 2006 novel by Clare Allan (5,11)

3 Secretary of State for Northern Ireland from 1976-79 (3,5)

5 Mild yellow Dutch cheese (4)

6 Actress who played The Sorceress in 2002 action film The Scorpion King (5,2)

7 **See 2 Down**

8 Victor ___, rugby union prop; 1992 England Test debutant against Canada (5)

9 Oskar ___, Swedish golfer; 2009 Moravia Silesia Open tournament winner (11)

14 Plant of North America such as the large-flowered ___ or perfoliate ___ (8)

16 1971 film drama starring Carol White and John Mills (7)

18 **See 4 Across**

21 US state; capital Boise (5)

22 **and 20 Across** Welsh actress who played Livia in 1976 BBC TV drama series I, Claudius (4,8)

No. 114

Across

6 US bandleader known as The King of Jazz who died in 1967 (4,8)

8 City in Florida, US, housing Lake Eola Park (7)

9 John ___, author of 1935 novel BUtterfield 8 (1,4)

10 ___ pile carpet, popular piece of home decor during the 1970s (4)

12 and 15 1848 Charles Dickens novel featuring characters Walter Gay and Dr Parker Peps (6,3,3)

14 Auguste ___, artist whose Monument to Balzac is located in the museum which bears his name (5)

15 See 12 Across

16 Hindu goddess of destruction (4)

19 Slow-moving Australian marsupial that feeds on eucalyptus leaves (5)

21 Town in West Sussex housing an 11th-century castle (7)

22 2006 novel by Roddy Doyle (5,7)

Down

1 Édouard ___, French painter whose works include 1894's Les deux écoliers (8)

2 Donald ___, composer and lyricist best known for his collaborations with Michael Flanders (5)

3 French city; capital of the former duchy of Burgundy (5)

4 Main field of riders in a cycling road race (7)

5 Code word for the letter P in the NATO phonetic alphabet (4)

6 1915 short film written by and starring W C Fields (4,6)

7 1958 novel by Ed McBain (4,6)

11 Unit of weight equal to 2,240 pounds (3)

12 Otto ___, German artist whose paintings include 1920's Skat Players (3)

13 James J ___, 1935-37 World Heavyweight boxing champion nicknamed The Cinderella Man (8)

14 Georges ___, French painter whose works include 1891 oil The Way to Calvary (7)

17 Tony ___, rugby union centre; 2001 France Test debutant against South Africa (5)

18 SI unit of luminous flux (5)

20 Son of Telamon; Greek hero of the Trojan War (4)

No. 114

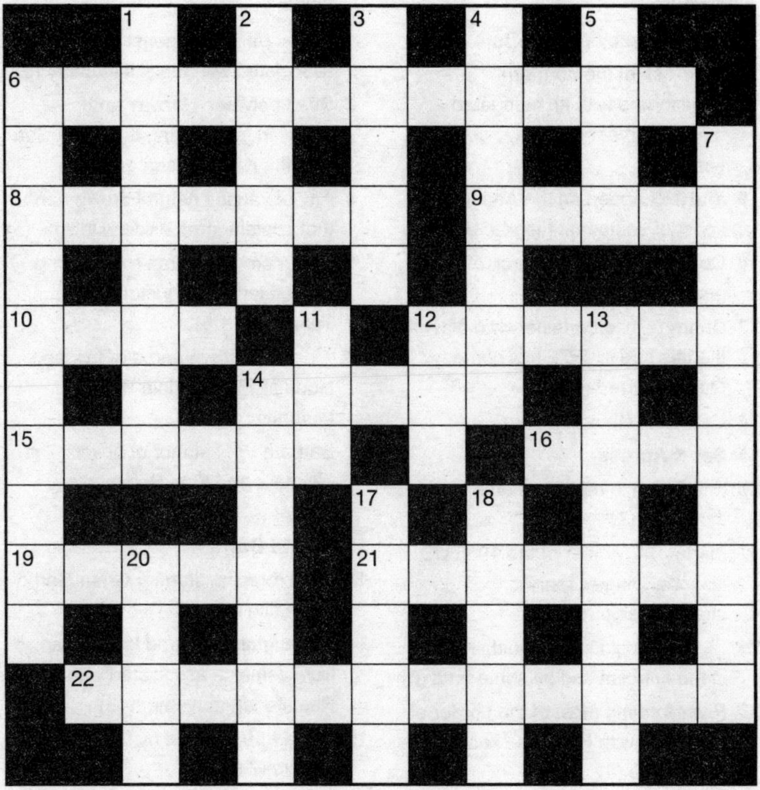

Across

3 1995 novel by Gordon Burn (9)

8 Food fish of the northern hemisphere with an elongated body, large head and two dorsal fins (4)

9 and 15 Lagoon on the Atlantic coast of southeast Florida, US (8,3)

10 Collective noun for a flock of geese (6)

13 Danny ___, entertainer who played the title role in 1972 film comedy Our Miss Fred (2,3)

14 Capital of Libya (7)

15 See 9 Across

16 Silvery-white metallic element; symbol U (7)

17 Maria ___, winner of the 1959 US National Singles tennis championship (5)

21 ___ acid, colourless liquid present in the fluid emitted by some ants (6)

22 River forming most of the border of Colombia with Peru also known as the Rio Içá (8)

23 James K ___, president of the US from 1845-49 (4)

24 Type of patterned carpet named after a town in East Devon (9)

Down

1 City in Bihar, northeast India, associated with the silk industry (9)

2 Strait between Norway and Denmark connecting the North Sea with the Kattegat sea area (9)

4 Any of various natural brown earths that contain ferric oxide with lime (5)

5 1991 comedy-drama film starring Steve Martin and Victoria Tennant (1,1,5)

6 ___ Belly, stage name of folk and blues pioneer Huddie William Ledbetter (4)

7 Barbara ___, author of novels The Minotaur and King Solomon's Carpet (4)

11 See 15 Down

12 1939 romcom starring Greta Garbo in the title role (9)

14 Tall brightly-coloured knitted cap from Jamaica associated with the Rastafarian movement (3)

15 and 11 1937 novel by Dorothy L Sayers (7,9)

18 Benik ___, footballer who has represented DR Congo and played for clubs including Bournemouth, Wolverhampton Wanderers and Stoke City (5)

19 Dick ___, 1976 Olympic 5,000m silver medallist for New Zealand (4)

20 Hungarian dog breed similar in appearance to the Komondor but smaller (4)

235

Across

1 Hoyt ___, singer and actor who played Randall Peltzer in 1984 film comedy Gremlins (5)

7 1998 action film starring Jackie Chan and Chris Tucker (4,4)

8 Costantino ___, Italian golfer; 1997 Canon European Masters tournament winner (5)

10 **and 1 Down** 1981 debut novel by William Boyd (1,4,3,2,6)

12 1928 collection of stories by W Somerset Maugham subtitled The British Agent (8)

14 Eddie ___, footballer who spent most of his playing career at AFC Bournemouth and then went on to manage them (4)

16 National security organisation in South Africa from 1969-80 (4)

17 The ___, 2006 Martin Scorsese film drama; 2007 Best Picture Oscar winner (8)

20 Australian genus of trees that includes the blue gum (10)

23 Fine-grained metamorphic rock split into flat plates for roofing material (5)

24 Greek poet and comic dramatist who authored stage play Dyskolos (8)

25 Asian climbing plant whose leaves are chewed as a narcotic (5)

Down

1 **See 10 Across**

2 Large mammal also known as a killer whale (4)

3 Fighting style contested by rikishi (4)

4 Parsley, Sage, Rosemary and ___, Simon and Garfunkel album (5)

5 1978 comedy Western film directed by and starring Jack Nicholson (4,5)

6 **See 9 Down**

9 **and 6** Highly poisonous herbicide used as a spray for defoliation and crop destruction by the US during the Vietnam War (5,6)

11 **and 19** 2008 collection of essays by Martin Amis (3,6,5)

13 Laverne ___, 2002 Commonwealth javelin gold medallist (3)

15 River that flows to the Atlantic at Lisbon, Portugal (5)

16 Andreas ___, Germany midfielder and defender; 1990 FIFA World Cup Final scorer (6)

18 Anthony ___, director of the Royal Ballet from 1986-2001 (6)

19 **See 11 Down**

21 Claude ___, Leicester City FC manager from 2017-2019 (4)

22 Small blue-black fruit of the blackthorn (4)

Across

1 1992 film drama starring Tom Cruise and Nicole Kidman (3,3,4)

8 The ___, 1981 horror film starring Dee Wallace and Patrick Macnee (7)

9 Jack ___, Taoiseach of Ireland from 1977-79 (5)

10 Biblical character murdered by brother Cain (4)

11 Buffalo endemic to Indonesia comprising the species the mountain ___ and lowland ___ (4)

12 Fifth note of a major scale in tonic sol-fa (3)

14 2000s BBC TV comedy drama series starring Ricky Gervais and Ashley Jensen (6)

15 1997 stage play by Patrick Marber (6)

18 Global governing body of cricket (1,1,1)

20 ___ Castle, the largest Anglo-Norman fortification in Ireland (4)

21 2006 musical film drama starring Glen Hansard and Markéta Irglová (4)

23 ___ Merritt, winner of the gold medal in the men's 110 metres hurdles at the 2012 Summer Olympics (5)

24 Howard ___, author of stage plays Christie in Love and The Churchill Play (7)

25 Industrial town in County Durham northeast of Bishop Auckland (10)

Down

1 Farrah ___, US actress who played Jessie Dewey in 1997 film drama The Apostle (7)

2 Bjarne ___, Danish cyclist; 1996 Tour de France winner (4)

3 Japanese host city of the 1998 Winter Olympics (6)

4 1982-92 BBC TV sitcom set during World War II (4,4)

5 Adrián ___, 2002 European Championships hammer gold medallist (5)

6 **and 16** 1877 novel by Anthony Trollope (3,8,7)

7 **and 17** 1954 novel by C S Lewis (3,5,3,3,3)

13 Troy ___, US golfer; 2005 Virginia Beach Open tournament winner (8)

16 **See 6 Down**

17 **See 7 Down**

19 Quentin ___, author of 1968 autobiography The Naked Civil Servant (5)

22 John F ___, US artist whose works include 1885 oil The Poor Man's Store (4)

No. 117

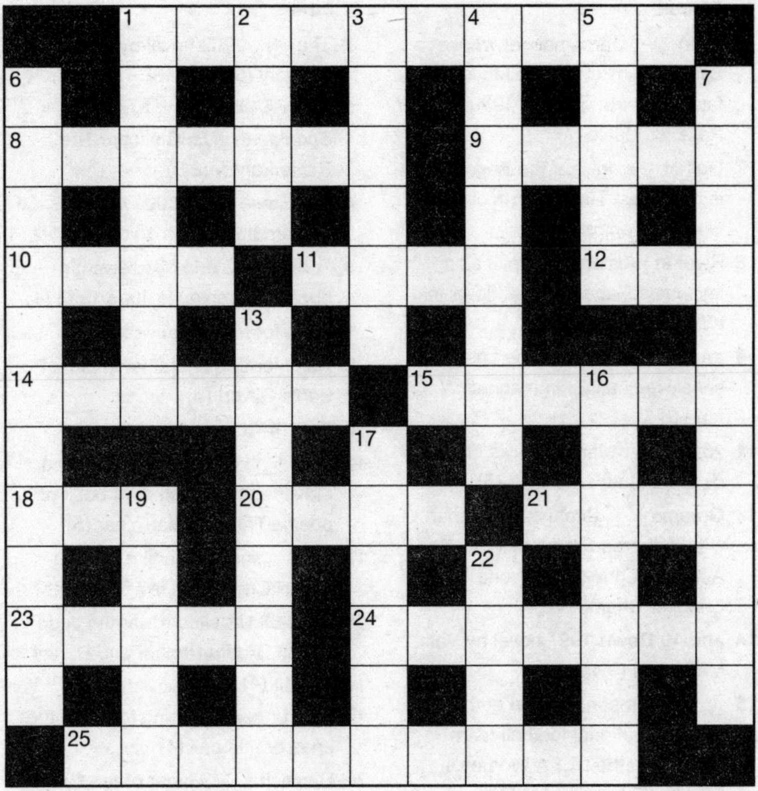

No. 118

Across

1 Ellen ___, US composer whose Symphony no 1 (Three Movements for Orchestra) won the 1983 Pulitzer Prize for Music (7)

7 Gulf of ___, inlet of the Aegean Sea in northwest Turkey north of the Gallipoli Peninsula (5)

8 River in Western Australia also known as Raparapa that flows into King Sound (7)

9 and 22 Red powder used as a sensitive coating on magnetic tape (6,5)

11 2014 biopic starring David Oyelowo as Martin Luther King Jr (5)

13 Graeme ___, Scottish sportsman who authored Frame of Mind: The Autobiography of the World Snooker Champion (4)

14 and 10 Down 1997 novel by Val McDermid (3,4,2,3,5)

15 ___ Williamson, captain of the England national football team which won the UEFA Women's Euro 2022 tournament (4)

16 Bill ___, actor who played Dr David Banner in 1977-82 US TV series The Incredible Hulk (5)

17 2011 action film starring Justin Timberlake and Amanda Seyfried (2,4)

21 Amy ___, British aviator who flew solo from England to Australia in 1930 (7)

22 See 9 Across

23 Salvador ___, president of Chile from 1970-73 (7)

Down

2 The ___, 2009 novel by Philippa Gregory (5,5)

3 Actress who played Norma Speakman in BBC sitcom The Royle Family (3,5)

4 Stephanie ___, 2000 Olympic modern pentathlon gold medallist (4)

5 Tony ___, World Middleweight boxing champion in June 1948 (4)

6 Term for a male guinea pig (4)

9 Ron Moody's character in Lionel Bart's Oliver! (5)

10 See 14 Across

12 John ___, a leader of the Oxford Movement and author of book of poems The Christian Year (5)

13 2008 action-drama film starring Daniel Craig and Liev Schreiber (8)

18 1978-83 US sitcom starring Judd Hirsch, Marilu Henner and Danny DeVito (4)

19 Skirt or coat reaching to below the knee or mid-calf (4)

20 Heinrich ___, winner of the 1972 Nobel Prize in Literature (4)

No. 118

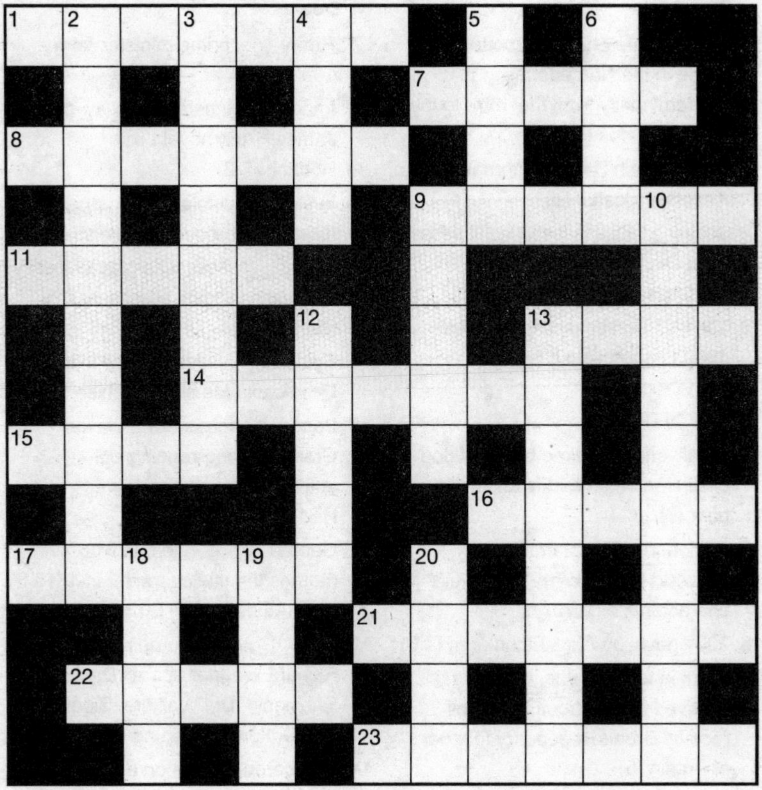

No. 119

Across

3 Type of blue and white pottery made in the Netherlands predominantly from the 16th- to the 18th-centuries (9)

8 City in which Hamad International Airport is located (4)

9 Judy ___, Best Actress in a Leading Role Oscar winner for Born Yesterday (8)

10 1961-67 Scotland defender; Arsenal 1969 League Cup Final runner-up (3,3)

13 **See 20 Down**

14 Small smooth-haired breed of dog of African origin that is unable to bark (7)

15 1972 horror film starring Lee Harcourt Montgomery whose title character is a rat (3)

16 2001 novel by Alan Titchmarsh (4,3)

17 Giant in folklore who, with Gog, survived the destruction of their race by Brutus, legendary founder of Britain (5)

21 F ___, author of novels The Tinted Venus and Vice Versa (6)

22 Alfredo ___, 19th-century composer of operas La Wally and Loreley (8)

23 Area of vulnerability for Achilles in Greek mythology (4)

24 Christian celebration on 2 February also known as the Presentation of Jesus at the Temple (9)

Down

1 Henry ___, prime minister from 1801-04 (9)

2 Imaginary Himalayan valley in 1933 James Hilton novel Lost Horizon (7-2)

4 In Greek mythology, the upper regions of the atmosphere (5)

5 Corey ___, actor who played Teddy Duchamp in 1986 adventure film Stand By Me (7)

6 Kristen ___, voice of Lucy in the Despicable Me film franchise (4)

7 Irene ___, actress who played Granny in long-running US television sitcom The Beverly Hillbillies (4)

11 George ___, gentleman who marries the title character in 1815 Jane Austen novel Emma (9)

12 The ___, collective name given to Richard Wagner operas Das Rheingold, Die Walküre, Siegfried and Götterdämmerung (4,5)

14 Numbered section on a dartboard (3)

15 Charles ___, inventor born in 1791 who built a calculator that anticipated the computer (7)

18 One of two types of coin used in Nigerian currency, the other being the kobo (5)

19 Island of Indonesia; capital Jakarta (4)

20 **and 13 Across** 2009 novel by Martina Cole (4,5)

Across

6 1953 novel by Samuel Beckett (3,9)

8 Aaron ___, US actor who played Harvey Dent in 2008 action film The Dark Knight (7)

9 ___ and Judy, traditional British puppet show (5)

10 See 12 Down

12 D K ___, Australia Test cricketer who took 5-84 against England in Adelaide in 1971 (6)

14 Elizabeth ___, author of novels The Last September and Eva Trout (5)

15 ___ passport, popular name for the travel document issued to stateless persons by the League of Nations after WWI (6)

16 Dominic ___, UK First Secretary of State from July 2019 - September 2021 (4)

19 Michael ___, first chair of the Committee on Standards in Public Life whose surname is used as shorthand for the principles it established (5)

21 Ralph ___, actor who starred as Daniel in 1980s action film series The Karate Kid (7)

22 1998 film drama starring Brad Pitt in the title role (4,3,5)

Down

1 Max ___, German Expressionist painter whose works include 1950 oil Hotel Lobby (8)

2 Sam ___, golfer who won the Masters three times (5)

3 Ballroom dance in triple time (5)

4 Name given to the eldest son of the king of France during the majority of the period 1350-1830 (7)

5 and 14 Down Author of stage plays Allelujah! and The Habit of Art (4,7)

6 1977 novel by Stephen King (3,7)

7 Charlotte ___, zoologist whose BBC TV credits include Cousins and Safari School (10)

11 River that rises in the Cairngorm Mountains before flowing east to the North Sea (3)

12 and 10 Across 1956 Australian Championships men's singles tennis title winner (3,4)

13 Cloris ___, Best Actress in a Supporting Role Oscar winner for The Last Picture Show (8)

14 See 5 Down

17 Ancient nation of the Old Testament whose chief city was Rabbah (5)

18 Underwater breathing apparatus utilising compressed gas supplied at a regulated pressure (5)

20 Peter ___, Australian swimmer who won eight medals at the 2008 Beijing Paralympics (4)

Across

3 Alan ___, playwright; author of Channel 4 series GBH and Jake's Progress (9)

8 Gabriel's ___, Ennio Morricone composition which features in Palme d'Or-winning film The Mission (4)

9 Stargate ___, sci-fi TV series starring Joe Flanigan as John Sheppard (8)

10 **and 20 Down** British pastry with a filling of dried fruit (6,4)

13 Rene ___, actress who played Frigga in 2011 action film Thor (5)

14 Hendrick ___, 2004 New York City Marathon winner (7)

15 Woodland bird of the crow family (3)

16 Silvery metal chemical element; symbol Cs (7)

17 C J ___, Australia cricketer who took 5-33 against Sri Lanka in the 3rd ODI in Brisbane in 2010 (5)

21 Bela ___, actor who played the title role in 1931 horror film Dracula (6)

22 2009 animated film featuring the voice talent of Dakota Fanning in the title role (8)

23 Tobin ___, actor who played Jigsaw in the Saw horror film series (4)

24 Ellen ___, comedian and actress who hosted the 2007 Academy Awards ceremony (9)

Down

1 1971 novel by Dick Francis (9)

2 Town in South Yorkshire on the River Don (9)

4 Capital of Tibet (5)

5 Village in South Ayrshire, Scotland; birthplace of poet Robert Burns (7)

6 Jim ___, US artist whose lithographs include 1973's Big Red Wrench in a Landscape (4)

7 Émilie ___, 2007 Mexican Open singles tennis tournament winner (4)

11 Kimi ___, 2007 F1 World Drivers' Championship winner (9)

12 2001 novel by Jane Green (9)

14 Ovine animal associated with the Egyptian god Ammon (3)

15 1957 Lawrence Durrell novel: first volume of The Alexandria Quartet (7)

18 Area of land used to support a parish priest (5)

19 ___ Basin, that area of Hudson Bay between Baffin Island and Melville Peninsula (4)

20 **See 10 Across**

No. 122

Across

1 Southernmost of the islands of the Inner Hebrides off the Scottish coast (5)

7 Robert ___, villain in 1748 Samuel Richardson novel Clarissa (8)

8 Sidney ___, Best Director Oscar nominee for 12 Angry Men (5)

10 Arthur ___, Poland-born pianist and honorary KBE who died in 1982 (10)

12 Novel by Charles Williams which inspired a 1989 film of the same name directed by Phillip Noyce (4,4)

14 See 21 Down

16 Scottish island of the Inner Hebrides southeast of Rùm (4)

17 Author of novels Shark, The Butt and Dorian (4,4)

20 Antoine-Augustin ___, agronomist who introduced the use of potatoes as food into France (10)

23 Former name for both the county of Shropshire and the town of Shrewsbury (5)

24 1980 comedy and crime film starring Burt Reynolds and Lesley-Anne Down (5,3)

25 **and 6 Down** Best Actress in a Supporting Role Oscar winner for Who's Afraid of Virginia Woolf? (5,6)

Down

1 **and 16 Down** 2006 film drama starring Laura Dern and Jeremy Irons (6,6)

2 A J ___, English philosopher known for promoting logical positivism (4)

3 Aloo ___, Indian potato and cauliflower dish (4)

4 Microscopic fungus used in beer and bread manufacture (5)

5 1985 film Western directed by and starring Clint Eastwood (4,5)

6 **See 25 Across**

9 Stanley ___, actor who appeared in, co-wrote and co-directed 1996 film drama Big Night (5)

11 ___ Liaisons, 1988 romantic drama film directed by Stephen Frears (9)

13 Garland of flowers worn around the neck in Hawaii (3)

15 The ___, 1943 stage play by Jean-Paul Sartre (5)

16 **See 1 Down**

18 Joseph ___, Australian author of novel Such is Life: Being Certain Extracts from the Diary of Tom Collins, published in 1903 (6)

19 River in Hades in Greek mythology that caused forgetfulness in those who drank from it (5)

21 **and 14 Across** 1994 action film starring Arnold Schwarzenegger and Jamie Lee Curtis (4,4)

22 Basic melodic mode in Indian classical music (4)

No. 122

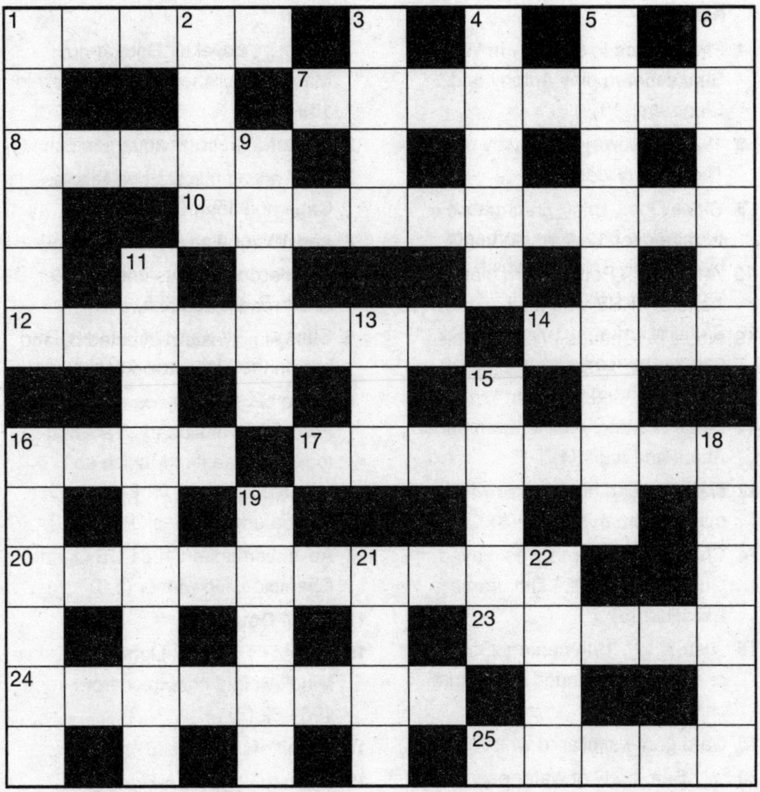

No. 123

Across

1 Pirate friend to Pompey in William Shakespeare play Antony and Cleopatra (10)

8 1938 Broadway stage play by Thornton Wilder (3,4)

9 We're Going to ___, Vengaboys no 1 single based on Barbados by Typically Tropical, which also topped the charts (5)

10 Battle of Lake ___, War of 1812 engagement also known as the Battle of Put-in-Bay (4)

11 Large predatory feline mammal of Africa and India (4)

12 New Zealand honeyeater which mimics human speech (3)

14 Cherie ___, actress who played Guenevere in 1981 film drama Excalibur (6)

15 Justus ___, 19th-century German chemist who founded agricultural chemistry (6)

18 Card game similar to whist (3)

20 ___ Sea, body of water east of the Caspian Sea straddling Uzbekistan and Kazakhstan whose eastern basin is now called the Aralkum Desert (4)

21 ___ Wintour, fashion editor who was made a dame in 2017 (4)

23 Bird with types including cattle, little and snowy (5)

24 European republic; capital Zagreb (7)

25 1978, 1985 and 1989 Women's PGA Championship winner (5,5)

Down

1 The ___, novel by George du Maurier published posthumously in 1897 (7)

2 ___ tetra, popular aquarium fish (4)

3 1997 action film starring Nicolas Cage and John Cusack (3,3)

4 and 13 2009 adventure-comedy film starring Carter Jenkins and Austin Butler (6,2,3,5)

5 George ___, author of novels The Mill on the Floss and Adam Bede (5)

6 Battle of ___, 1800 conflict of the French Revolutionary Wars that took place east of Munich and resulted in victory for France over Austria and its allies (11)

7 Australian golfer; 1981 US Open Championship winner (5,6)

13 See 4 Down

16 Wilfred ___, WBC Light Middleweight champion from 1981-82 (7)

17 SI unit of pressure (6)

19 Lorenzo ___, WBA Flyweight champion from 2003-07 (5)

22 US television sitcom that featured the Tate and Campbell families (4)

No. 123

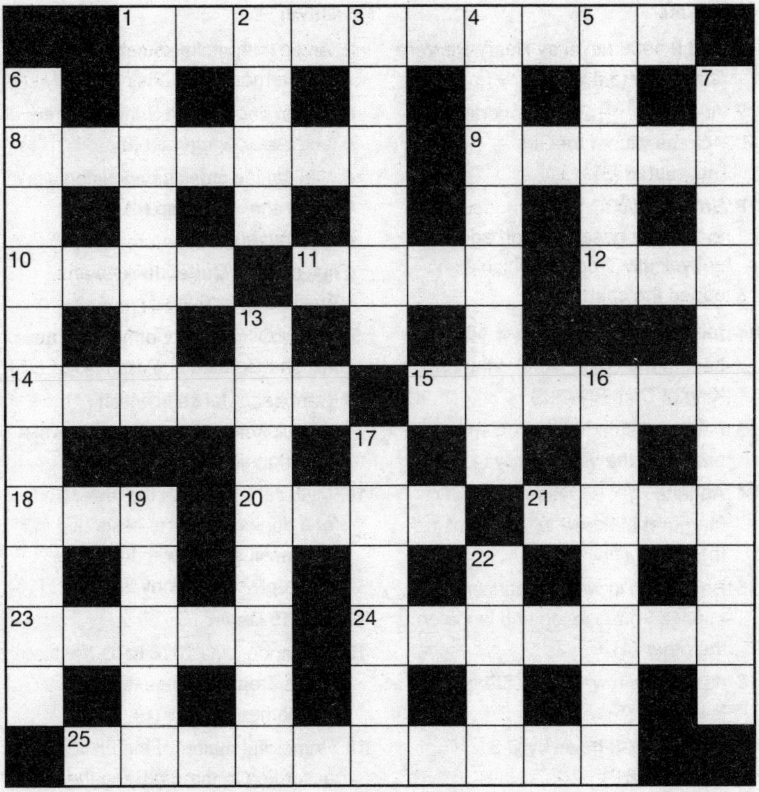

No. 124

Across

1 and 9 1908 novel by Henry De Vere Stacpoole (3,4,6)

7 Angelina ___, Best Supporting Actress winner for Girl, Interrupted (5)

8 Erik ___, WBC Super Bantamweight champion from 1997-2000 (7)

9 See 1 Across

11 and 22 Actor who played Jerry Langford in 1982 film drama The King of Comedy (5,5)

13 Family of stringed instruments that preceded the violin family (4)

14 Annette ___, actress who played Margaret Meldrew in One Foot in the Grave (7)

15 Ballet step in which a dancer springs from one leg and lands on the other (4)

16 Italian city in which the Stadio Friuli is located (5)

17 and 23 1938 novel by C S Forester (6,7)

21 Max ___, England and Manchester City defender; 1920 Olympic men's doubles tennis gold medallist with Noel Turnbull (7)

22 See 11 Across

23 See 17 Across

Down

2 Arctic mammal also called a bladdernose seal (6,4)

3 Eldest daughter of Prince Andrew and Sarah Ferguson (8)

4 ___ Cup, women's badminton world team championship (4)

5 See 6 Down

6 and 5 Composer who shared a Best Music, Original Dramatic Score Oscar with Carmine Coppola for The Godfather, Part II (4,4)

9 Caribbean dance in which participants pass under a bar while leaning backwards (5)

10 Mythical beast with the lower body of a donkey which is described in Athanasius of Alexandria's biography of Anthony the Great (10)

12 See 19 Down

13 Fernando ___, 2016 BRD Nastase Tiriac Trophy singles tennis tournament winner (8)

18 Primordial matter of the universe, according to the Big Bang theory (4)

19 and 12 Oscar-nominated songwriter who starred in, co-wrote and co-directed 1982 comedy Human Highway (4,5)

20 Hideki ___, prime minister of Japan from 1941-44 (4)

No. 124

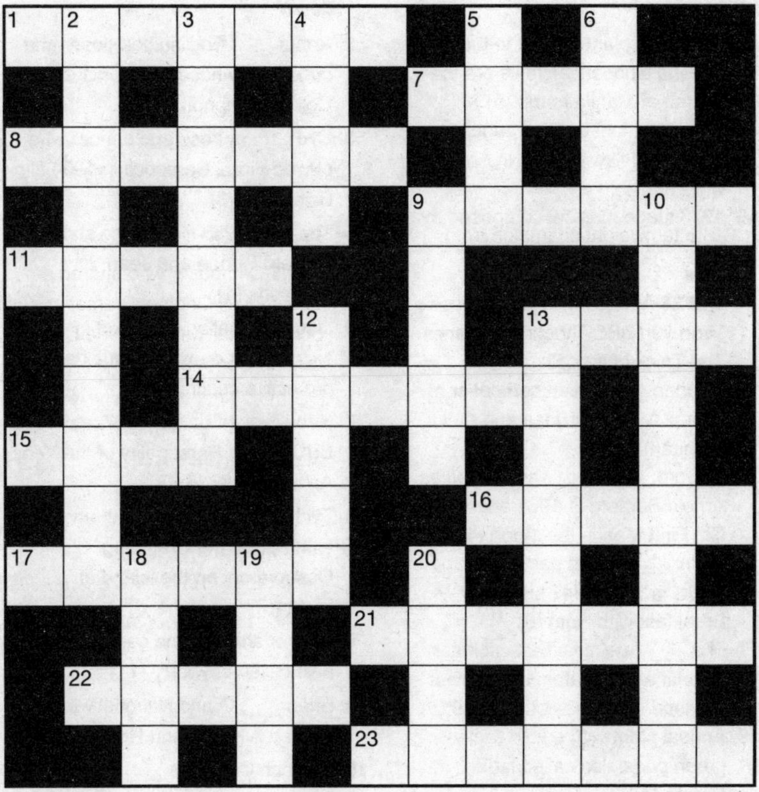

No. 125

Across

1 Philippine plant related to the banana whose leafstalks are the source of Manila hemp (5)

4 Main prey for several penguin, whale and fish species in Antarctic waters (5)

10 1978 stage musical composed by Andrew Lloyd Webber and Tim Rice (5)

11 **and 26** Actress who played Nicola Murray in BBC TV comedy series The Thick of It (7,5)

12 Ottorino ___, Italian composer of operas Maria Egiziaca and Semirâma (8)

13 Edward ___, actor who starred as Arnold Bedford in 1964 adventure film First Men in the Moon (4)

15 Pieter ___, Dutch painter whose works include 1647 still life Breakfast with Ham (6)

17 M J ___, Australia Test cricketer who hit an unbeaten 103 against England at Edgbaston in 2009 (6)

19 Annual plant with edible sticky green pods also called ladies' fingers (4)

20 2002-04 Cheltenham Gold Cup winner ridden by Jim Culloty (4,4)

23 1578 novel by John Lyly subtitled The Anatomy of Wit (7)

24 ___ Castle, Kent home of Anne Boleyn before her marriage to Henry VIII (5)

25 Larry ___, actor who played the title role in 1946 biopic The Jolson Story (5)

26 **See 11 Across**

Down

2 Arthur ___, English composer and conductor whose works include A Colour Symphony (5)

3 Cyd ___, actress and dancer who played Fiona Campbell in 1954 film Brigadoon (8)

5 The ___, 1953 film drama starring Richard Burton and Jean Simmons (4)

6 Liquid of shellac dissolved in alcohol that dries to form a hard protective coating (7)

7 Heavyweight boxer; 1967 and 1970 BBC Sports Personality of the Year Award winner (5,6)

8 Tycho ___, Danish astronomer who established the Uraniborg Observatory on the island of Hven (5)

9 Tree or shrub of the genus Myrica also called bayberry (11)

14 Brian ___, Grand National winner on Red Alligator and Red Rum (8)

16 Heinrich Cornelius ___ von Nettesheim, polymath born in 1486 who authored De Occulta Philosophia (7)

18 Carl ___, optical instruments maker established in Germany in 1846 (5)

21 Patrick ___, New Zealand-born rugby league wing previously with Bradford Bulls (2,3)

22 1996 novel by Melvin Burgess (4)

Across

6 **8 and 21** Long poem by Samuel Taylor Coleridge first published in 1798 volume Lyrical Ballads (3,4,2,3,7,7)

8 **See 6 Across**

9 Motor racing circuit that hosted the F1 San Marino GP between 1981-2006 (5)

10 Mark ___, rugby union fly-half; 1980 Australia Test debutant against New Zealand (4)

12 Port in southwest Morocco almost totally destroyed by an earthquake in 1960 (6)

14 Alloy of copper and zinc containing more than 50 per cent of the former (5)

15 15th-century Hungarian light horseman (6)

16 The ___, 2009 film drama starring Paul Anderson and Calum McNab (4)

19 1976 Alex Haley novel subtitled The Saga of an American Family (5)

21 **See 6 Across**

22 1990 crime drama film starring Sean Penn, Ed Harris and Gary Oldman (5,2,5)

Down

1 2014 action film starring Dwayne Johnson in the title role (8)

2 Jeremy ___, US actor who played the title role in 2013-16 ITV drama series Mr Selfridge (5)

3 **and 4** 2011 novel by Bernard Cornwell (5,2,5)

4 **See 3 Down**

5 US state; capital Columbus (4)

6 1973 adventure film starring Rod Taylor in the title role (6,4)

7 Actor who played Lt Philip Gerard in 1960s US television series The Fugitive (5,5)

11 Bobby ___, ice hockey player; James Norris Memorial Trophy winner from 1968-75 (3)

12 Leslie ___, actress who played Carol Landau in 1985 film comedy Shadey (3)

13 Robert ___, French photographer whose works include 1950's Kiss by the Hôtel de Ville (8)

14 Angela ___, Best Actress in a Leading Role Oscar nominee for What's Love Got to Do With It (7)

17 Island of the Moluccas, Indonesia, on which occurred a 1942 World War II battle between Allied and Japanese forces (5)

18 Melvyn ___, author of novels Crystal Rooms and Now is the Time (5)

20 Meteorological unit of measurement used to calculate cloud cover (4)

No. 127

Across

3 and 22 1984 novel by Frederick Forsyth (3,6,8)

8 Francis Peyton ___, recipient of the 1966 Nobel Prize in Physiology and Medicine (4)

9 In architecture, the near triangular space between the curve of an arch and the framework above (8)

10 1998 mystery film starring Dustin Hoffman and Sharon Stone (6)

13 See 24 Across

14 Ray ___, winner of the 1970 World Snooker Championship (7)

15 In golf, an estimated standard score for a hole that a good player should make (3)

16 Charlotte ___, actress who played Oregon in 2011-16 Channel 4 series Fresh Meat (7)

17 The ___, 2001 novel by Ian Rankin (5)

21 Town in Greater Manchester; birthplace of composer William Walton (6)

22 See 3 Across

23 and 12 Down 2009 novel by William Trevor (4,3,6)

24 and 13 1927 novel by Dorothy L Sayers (9,5)

Down

1 2008 novel by Richard T Kelly (9)

2 Tamzin ___, actress who appeared in TV show The Masked Dancer (9)

4 Jaroslav ___, Czech author of unfinished novel The Good Soldier Švejk (5)

5 Joe ___, World Heavyweight boxing champion from 1970-73 (7)

6 Official language of Pakistan also spoken in India (4)

7 River which rises on the eastern slope of Cross Fell in the North Pennines (4)

11 2008 film drama set in London and featuring Adam Deacon as Jay (9)

12 See 23 Across

14 Jackie ___, Canadian entertainer; first host of ITV game show The Golden Shot (3)

15 Pokemon series character that is yellow-coloured with red cheek pouches (7)

18 19th-century Bohemian dance with three steps and a hop (5)

19 Eleanor ___, actress who played Augusta Colt in 2004 romcom Wimbledon (4)

20 Active volcano in Sicily (4)

No. 128

Across

1 and 25 Comedy actor who played the title role in ITV sitcom Mr Digby Darling (5,5)

7 Chief port and capital of American Samoa (4,4)

8 John ___, 1989 World Indoor Championships 200m gold medallist (5)

10 David ___, 2002 Wimbledon singles tennis championship runner-up (10)

12 Country for which Haile Gebrselassie competed in athletics (8)

14 Ian ___, singer-songwriter portrayed by Andy Serkis in 2010 biopic Sex and Drugs and Rock and Roll (4)

16 African enclosure set up to protect a camp or herd of animals (4)

17 Town in northern Israel; childhood home of Jesus (8)

20 The ___, 1994 adventure film starring Macaulay Culkin and Christopher Lloyd (10)

23 Rugby league team; 1971 Challenge Cup Final winners (5)

24 and 6 Down 1948 novel by Ross Lockridge, Jr (8,6)

25 See 1 Across

Down

1 and 5 2009 novel by Michael Crichton (6,9)

2 Tracey ___, creator of artworks such as Sad Shower in New York and I Promise to Love You (4)

3 Young of a sheep (4)

4 and 13 Mountain in central Crete associated with the worship of Zeus in ancient times (5,3)

5 See 1 Down

6 See 24 Across

9 John ___, actor who played Roper in 1973 action film Enter the Dragon (5)

11 1954 film comedy starring Paul Douglas and Alex Mackenzie (3,6)

13 See 4 Down

15 John ___, 2003 World Championships 200m gold medallist (5)

16 R S ___, England Test cricketer who hit 104 against West Indies in Bridgetown in 2009 (6)

18 John ___, director of films The Breakfast Club and Weird Science (6)

19 Jan ___, prime minister of South Africa from 1939-48 (5)

21 Second-longest river in Scotland (4)

22 Jean ___, Morocco-born actor who played the title role in 1994 crime film Léon (4)

Across

1 English pirate captain born John Rackham executed in Port Royal, Jamaica, in 1720 (6,4)

8 W R ___, England Test cricketer who hit an unbeaten 336 against New Zealand in Auckland in 1933 (7)

9 Joshua ___, founder of the Zimbabwe African People's Union who died in 1999 (5)

10 Fabric made from fine threads produced by certain insect larvae (4)

11 Rottweiler in Australian comedy series Kath and Kim whose name is also the title of a Stephen King novel (4)

12 Currency of Taiwan from 1895 to 1946 (3)

14 Eugene ___, playwright awarded the 1936 Nobel Prize in Literature (6)

15 River that flows through Dublin, Ireland (6)

18 Little Things Mean a ___, Kitty Kallen no 1 hit song in 1954 (3)

20 Ben-ammi's half-brother according to the book of Genesis (4)

21 Terrestrial gastropod mollusc with an absent or reduced shell (4)

23 Insectivorous Old World bird with a bright red breast (5)

24 Tributary of the River Trent upon which Derby stands (7)

25 1937 film comedy starring Stan Laurel and Oliver Hardy (3,3,4)

Down

1 1936 film drama starring Greta Garbo and Robert Taylor (7)

2 Anita ___, author of novels No Mother to Guide Her and Gentlemen Prefer Blondes (4)

3 Brother of Europa and founder of Thebes in Greek mythology (6)

4 Jelena ___, 2007 Wimbledon mixed doubles tennis championship winner with Jamie Murray (8)

5 American golfing family which includes Charles, Kyle, Pierceson and Parker (5)

6 1969 novel by Desmond Bagley (3,8)

7 English poet born circa 1370 whose works include The Floure of Curtesye (4,7)

13 Type of Spanish guitar music accompanied by dancing and singing (8)

16 Another name for a hazelnut (7)

17 Brigitte ___, actress and singer who played the title role in 1959 film comedy Babette Goes to War (6)

19 Ancient Greek double-reeded wind instrument also known as the aulos (5)

22 ___ Larson, winner of the Best Actress Academy Award for Room (4)

Across

1 1980 biopic starring Roger Daltrey in the title role (7)

7 Ken ___, 1962 and 1966 Commonwealth 440yds hurdles gold medallist (5)

8 Tony ___, actor who played Dr Toby Latimer in BBC TV sitcom Don't Wait Up (7)

9 City in California, US, in the centre of the San Joaquin Valley (6)

11 **and 15** Fictional spy created by Ian Fleming (5,4)

13 Rob ___, actor who played Sam Seaborn in US television drama series The West Wing (4)

14 Capital of Kenya (7)

15 **See 11 Across**

16 **and 22** WBC Heavyweight champion from 1995-96 (5,5)

17 1979 film drama starring Dustin Hoffman and Vanessa Redgrave (6)

21 André ___, Minister of War of the French Third Republic from 1931-32 (7)

22 **See 16 Across**

23 Cavity behind the mouth and nose connecting them to the oesophagus (7)

Down

2 1996 Ken Loach film drama starring Robert Carlyle (6,4)

3 **See 6 Down**

4 Tori ___, Cornflake Girl singer (4)

5 River that flows through Leicester (4)

6 **and 3** 2013 film comedy starring James Franco and Jonah Hill (4,2,3,3)

9 2007 action film starring Joanne Whalley and Tom Courtenay (5)

10 Olivia ___, singer and actress who played Sandy in 1978 film musical Grease (6-4)

12 The ___, one of three ships commanded by Christopher Columbus on his first voyage to America (5)

13 1997 film comedy starring Jim Carrey and Maura Tierney (4,4)

18 Yorkshire river starting at Malham Tarn (4)

19 Unit of length equalling four inches used for measuring the height of horses (4)

20 City in Somerset; Latin name Aquae Sulis (4)

Across

1 Andrea ___, 1975 European Indoor Championships 60m gold medallist (5)

4 Ian ___, 1958 Commonwealth 220yds butterfly swimming gold medallist (5)

10 Freddie ___, entrepreneur associated with the Skytrain project who died in 2006 (5)

11 1954 biopic starring Marlon Brando as Napoleon Bonaparte (7)

12 1993 novel by Danielle Steel (8)

13 and 17 Comedian and actor who plays the title role in BBC TV series Jonathan Creek (4,6)

15 Department of France; capital Moulins (6)

17 See 13 Across

19 Peter ___, 17th-century painter whose works include Girl with a Parrot and Two Ladies of the Lake Family (4)

20 High Court judge in the Isle of Man (8)

23 Honey-yielding tree also called the Chilean wine palm (7)

24 Medieval stringed instrument resembling the violin (5)

25 Stacy ___, US actor who played the title role in 1974 film drama Luther (5)

26 Michael ___, Aberdeen-born dancer-choreographer who started his own company in 1984 (5)

Down

2 Territory of northwest Canada; capital Whitehorse (5)

3 Walter ___, US manufacturer who introduced the Plymouth motor car in 1928 (8)

5 Joe ___, violinist and bandleader whose signature tune was In the Mood (4)

6 Arcangelo ___, Italian violinist and composer born in 1653 noted for his Twelve concerti grossi (7)

7 2000 novel by Catherine Alliott (7,4)

8 Alfred ___, Austrian psychiatrist; author of The Neurotic Character and The Practice and Theory of Individual Psychology (5)

9 Actor who played the title role in 1949 film drama The Bad Lord Byron (6,5)

14 Castle and residence of the royal family in southwest Aberdeenshire, Scotland (8)

16 Rene ___, French Art Nouveau designer noted for his frosted glassware (7)

18 Jermain ___, striker who scored for England at the 2010 FIFA World Cup (5)

21 River upon which Rome, Italy, stands (5)

22 ___ blende, yellow to brownish-black mineral also called sphalerite (4)

Across

6 and 8 2009 film comedy starring, co-written and co-directed by Ricky Gervais (3,9,2,5)

8 **See 6 Across**

9 Ed ___, musical collaborator with Spike Milligan whose film scores include 1978 film drama The Thirty Nine Steps (5)

10 Wall or fence set in a ditch so as not to interrupt the landscape (2-2)

12 Des ___, former MP for Kilmarnock and Loudoun; Secretary of State for Defence from 2006-08 (6)

14 Ancient city in central Egypt on the River Nile (5)

15 Asian alcoholic drink made from the sap of the coco palm (6)

16 Acronym for Royal Academy award given to alumni who have distinguished themselves within the music profession (4)

19 Jack ___, actor and director who played Jamie Mitchell in BBC TV soap EastEnders from 1998-2002 (5)

21 James ___, author of novels The Fire Next Time and If Beale Street Could Talk (7)

22 1978 film drama starring Charlton Heston and David Carradine (4,4,4)

Down

1 Byron ___, 1999-2007 New Zealand scrum-half who played club rugby for Stade Francais and Toulouse (8)

2 County town of County Clare, Ireland (5)

3 Golf club with a low angled face (5)

4 Jackie ___, 1969, 1971 and 1973 F1 world drivers' championship winner (7)

5 Helmut ___, Chancellor of West Germany from 1982-90 (4)

6 2010 family film starring Dwayne Johnson and Ashley Judd (5,5)

7 **and 17** 1889 novel by Jerome K Jerome (5,3,2,1,4)

11 River in southeast Wales upon which Newport stands (3)

12 Tributary of the Narew River forming part of Poland's border with Belarus and Ukraine (3)

13 2004 novel by G P Taylor (8)

14 Peter ___, author of novels Chatterton and The Lambs of London (7)

17 **See 7 Down**

18 Raymond ___, US golfer; 1976 Masters Tournament winner (5)

20 Paul Gustave ___, 19th-century French illustrator of works by Rabelais (4)

No. 132

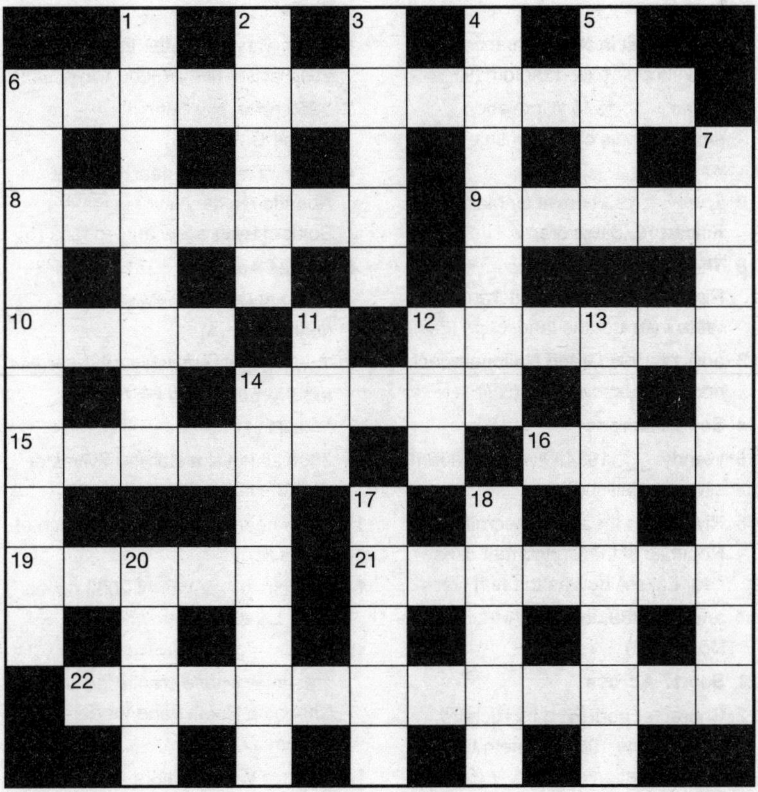

Across

3 Hairy beast in North American folklore also called Bigfoot (9)

8 Arthur ___, 1975 Wimbledon singles tennis championship winner (4)

9 The ___, 1938 novel by Marjorie Kinnan Rawlings (8)

10 The ___, 1970s ITV sitcom starring Richard Beckinsale and Paula Wilcox (6)

13 and 14 1995 Grand National winner ridden by Jason Titley (5,7)

14 See 13 Across

15 Wendy ___, 1984 Olympic 3,000m silver medallist (3)

16 River in northeast Democratic Republic of the Congo that rises near Lake Albert as the Ituri (7)

17 and 21 1889 novel by Arthur Conan Doyle (5,6)

21 See 17 Across

22 Character portrayed by Richard Briers in the 1989 Kenneth Branagh film adaptation of Henry V (8)

23 Goddess of youth and spring in Greek mythology (4)

24 and 5 Down 1962 novel by John le Carré (1,6,2,7)

Down

1 Actor who played the title role in 2012 action film Dredd (4,5)

2 1955 novel by Alain Robbe-Grillet (3,6)

4 Angel of the ___, description of Abaddon in the New Testament Book of Revelation (5)

5 See 24 Across

6 Fruit also known as an Indian gooseberry (4)

7 Town in Galilee where Jesus is said to have performed his first miracle (4)

11 2000 action film starring Sylvester Stallone in the title role (3,6)

12 Town near Jerusalem; birthplace of Jesus (9)

14 Monica ___, author of 2003 novel Brick Lane (3)

15 Carol ___, Scottish television presenter whose credits include Changing Rooms and Wheel of Fortune (7)

18 Town in Vicenza, Italy, east of Lake Garda associated with the wool industry (5)

19 City in North Rhine-Westphalia, Germany, on the River Lippe, severely damaged in the Second World War (4)

20 River which reaches the Baltic Sea via a lagoon north of the Polish city of Szczecin (4)

271

No. 134

Across

1 Town in Thuringia, Germany, west of Erfurt (5)

7 Monster in Greek mythology with the head of a bull and the body of a man (8)

8 Lionel ___, actor and choreographer whose television credits include Give Us a Clue and Name that Tune (5)

10 1959 film musical starring disc jockey Alan Freed as himself (2,6,2)

12 Term originally applied to the Balkan States (4,4)

14 Lake ___, reservoir in Arizona and Nevada formed by the Hoover Dam across the Colorado River (4)

16 Jack ___, 2014 Wimbledon men's doubles tennis championship winner with Vasek Pospisil (4)

17 Erich ___, 1976-89 Chairman of the Council of State in East Germany (8)

20 1890 Anthony Hope novel featuring the Republic of Aureataland (1,3,2,4)

23 Torquato ___, 16th-century Italian author of epic poem Jerusalem Delivered (5)

24 2008 adventure film starring Brendan Fraser and Eliza Hope Bennett (8)

25 See 13 Down

Down

1 Henry ___, comedy actor who played Haven Hamilton in 1975 comedy-drama film Nashville (6)

2 Douglas ___, Field Marshal; Commander-in-Chief of the British Expeditionary Force from 1915-18 (4)

3 Princess of Tyre in classical mythology who founded Carthage (4)

4 Unit of weight equal to 16 ounces (5)

5 Nikolay ___, 2006 and 2007 US Open singles tennis championship semi-finalist defeated by Roger Federer (9)

6 Matthew ___, 19th-century author of poems The Forsaken Merman and Dover Beach (6)

9 **and 19** 1998-2003 BBC TV comedy-drama series starring Robert Daws (5,5)

11 ___ Peninsula, area of Eastern Russia separating the Sea of Okhotsk from the Bering Sea and Pacific Ocean (9)

13 **and 25 Across** City in Brazil housing the Autódromo José Carlos Pace F1 racetrack (3,5)

15 Fred ___, 1968-70 Leader of the House of Commons; 1976-79 Lord Privy Seal (5)

16 Enlargement of the hock of a horse often resulting in lameness (6)

18 18th-century style of music characterised by extreme use of ornamentation (6)

19 See 9 Down

21 Thomas ___, author of 1516 literary work Utopia (4)

22 1978 studio album by Bob Marley and the Wailers (4)

No. 134

273

Across

1 Northern Ireland and Manchester United midfielder; 1968 Ballon d'Or winner (6,4)

8 and 20 2002 film comedy starring Robert De Niro and Billy Crystal (7,4)

9 1963 Derby winner ridden by Yves Saint-Martin (5)

10 Lucien ___, France rugby union lock; 1959 Five Nations Championship-winning captain (4)

11 See 18 Across

12 Arthur ___, journalist born in 1875 best known for The Children's Encyclopaedia (3)

14 Ronald ___, US president from 1981-89 (6)

15 Richard ___, English explorer who, with John Speke, discovered Lake Tanganyika in 1858 (6)

18 and 11 1995 film drama starring Chris O'Donnell and Drew Barrymore (3,4)

20 See 8 Across

21 Tim ___, footballer born in St Louis, Missouri who has played for clubs including Chicago Fire Premier, New York Red Bulls, and Bolton Wanderers (4)

23 Male voice intermediate between baritone and countertenor (5)

24 1922 stage play by John Galsworthy (7)

25 2010 biopic starring Mark Wahlberg as Micky Ward (3,7)

Down

1 City in Andalusia, Spain, housing the Alhambra (7)

2 Genus of large African antelopes that includes the gemsbok (4)

3 Libania ___, 2014 and 2016 European Championships women's 400m gold medallist (6)

4 Port in Gironde, France, on the River Garonne (8)

5 ___ Saberhagen, cat character from the Sabrina the Teenage Witch comic series (5)

6 London Underground station between Barons Court and Ravenscourt Park on the District Line (11)

7 Annual plant of southern Europe with delicate white or blue flowers (4-2-1-4)

13 and 16 1982 novel by Ruth Rendell (6,2,3,4)

16 See 13 Down

17 Smooth elongated insect with leathery forewings (6)

19 Judi ___, Best Actress in a Leading Role Oscar nominee for Mrs Henderson Presents (5)

22 Endless ___, one of the Ashtamangala, or eight auspicious symbols, in Tibetan Buddhism (4)

No. 135

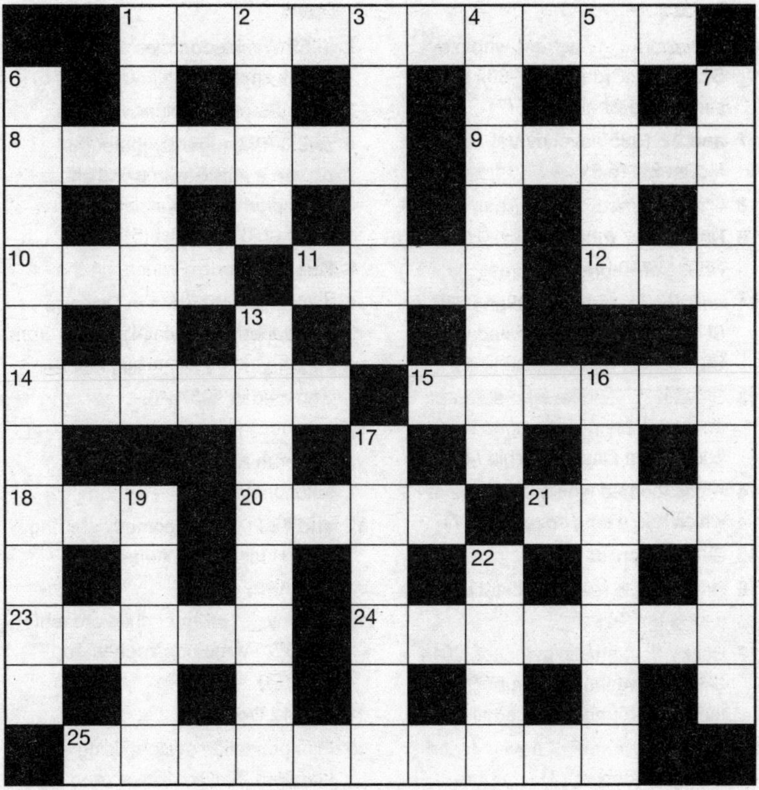

No. 136

Across

1 Alexandra ___, actress who played Sharon McCready in 1960s ITV series The Champions (7)

7 and 22 1995 novel by Val McDermid (5,5)

8 Old Testament wife of Ahab (7)

9 Nancy ___, former Speaker of the US House of Representatives (6)

11 and 15 City in north Indiana, US, on St Joseph River associated with Studebaker automobiles (5,4)

13 Stewart ___, golfer who defeated Tom Watson in a playoff to win the 2009 Open Championship (4)

14 Arctic toothed whale, the male of which has a long spiral tusk (7)

15 See 11 Across

16 Small edible marine crustacean with a long tail (5)

17 Becky ___, artistic gymnast; 2014 Commonwealth uneven bars and team all-around gold medallist (6)

21 Clive ___, author of novels Flood Tide and Iceberg (7)

22 See 7 Across

23 M H ___, England Test cricketer who hit 188 against Australia in Melbourne in 1975 (7)

Down

2 1959 Wimbledon men's singles tennis championship winner (4,6)

3 1978 Stephen King novel (3,5)

4 and 5 IBM supercomputer that played a match with world chess champion Garry Kasparov in 1997 (4,4)

5 See 4 Down

6 Jafar's parrot minion in Disney's 1992 Aladdin movie (4)

9 Charles ___, French film pioneer who died in 1957 (5)

10 The ___, 1960 film drama starring Deborah Kerr and Robert Mitchum (10)

12 and 18 2009 film comedy starring Kate Hudson and Anne Hathaway (5,4)

13 Jeremy ___, former chief presenter of BBC TV motoring series Top Gear (8)

18 See 12 Down

19 Film projection system using a standard 22m by 16m screen (4)

20 Ancient plucked stringed instrument whose body is shaped like a halved pear (4)

No. 136

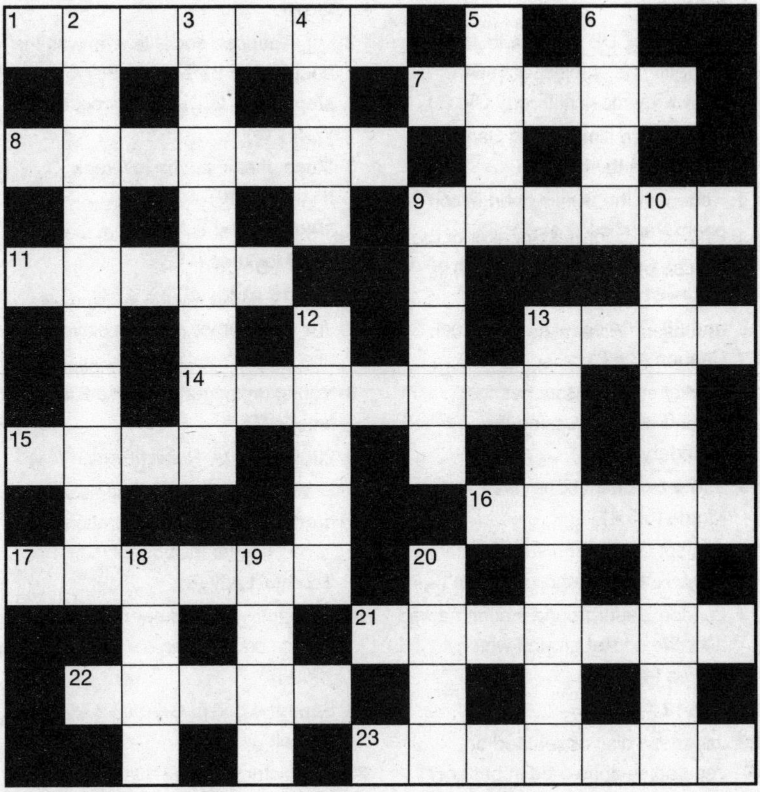

Across

1 Fanny ___, US singer and comedienne; subject of 1964 Broadway musical Funny Girl (5)

4 2000 action film starring Samuel L Jackson in the title role (5)

10 Regent of the Sun in John Milton poem Paradise Lost (5)

11 Don ___, 1976 Olympic 200m gold medallist (7)

12 **and 20** 2004 novella by Michael Chabon (3,5,8)

13 Cricket shot that touches the ground before crossing the boundary (4)

15 **and 6 Down** 2012 novel by Katie Fforde (6,3,4)

17 Ancient Latin hymn sung at matins in the Roman Catholic Church (2,4)

19 London Underground station named after the cricket ground which it serves (4)

20 **See 12 Across**

23 Japanese dish of seafood or vegetables deep-fried in batter (7)

24 Anna Karen's On the Buses character (5)

25 Member of a Germanic people who invaded and settled large parts of England in the 5th and 6th centuries (5)

26 Jule ___, composer of the music for Broadway musicals Gypsy and Hallelujah, Baby! (5)

Down

2 ___ Spencer, socialite who was the daughter of Barbara Cartland and stepmother to Diana, Princess of Wales (5)

3 Muse of epic poetry in Greek mythology (8)

5 1968 musical-comedy film starring The Monkees (4)

6 **See 15 Across**

7 Jez ___, author of stage plays Mojo and Jerusalem (11)

8 Young unfledged bird, especially a pigeon (5)

9 2009 novel by Robert Rankin (11)

14 Francis ___, English Renaissance dramatist whose collaborations with John Fletcher include 1616's The Scornful Lady (8)

16 Graham ___, member of the Monty Python comedy team who died in 1989 (7)

18 Supreme god in Germanic mythology (5)

21 Character in Greek mythology bound to a perpetually turning fiery wheel by Hermes on the orders of Zeus (5)

22 Rod ___, entertainer associated with puppet Emu who died in 1999 (4)

No. 138

Across

6 1997 science fiction and horror film starring Laurence Fishburne and Sam Neill (5,7)

8 and 12 Down Snooker player; 2002 Regal Scottish Open tournament winner (7,3)

9 Host city of the 2014 Winter Olympics (5)

10 and 7 Down US jazz singer who played Maggie Jackson in 1955 film drama Pete Kelly's Blues (4,10)

12 Konrad ___, Austrian psychologist, zoologist and ethologist; joint-winner of the 1973 Nobel Prize in Physiology or Medicine (6)

14 Leonard ___, poet and songwriter whose novels include 1963's The Favourite Game (5)

15 Maurice ___, actor who played George Martin in 1987 film drama 84 Charing Cross Road (6)

16 Member of a Native American people living in central Canada (4)

19 Island in the Baltic Sea separated from mainland Sweden by Kalmar Strait (5)

21 Andrés ___, 2006-18 Spain midfield footballer (7)

22 ___ and Labrador, province of Canada; capital St John's (12)

Down

1 City in northwest Colombia housing the University of Antioquia (8)

2 Daniel ___, 2020 Olympic men's discus gold medallist (5)

3 and 4 1972 biopic starring Simon Ward in the title role (5,7)

4 See 3 Down

5 Thomas ___, top points scorer for France in the 2008 Rugby League World Cup (4)

6 Welsh music, poetry and drama festival (10)

7 See 10 Across

11 Herbert ___, actor who played Chief Inspector Dreyfus in 1975 film comedy The Return of the Pink Panther (3)

12 See 8 Across

13 Catherine ___, character in 1847 Emily Brontë novel Wuthering Heights who weds Edgar Linton (8)

14 Capital of Wales (7)

17 See 20 Down

18 1984 film drama starring Matthew Modine in the title role (5)

20 and 17 2009 and 2011 World Championships men's marathon gold medallist (4,5)

No. 139

Across

3 and 19 Down 2007 comedy-drama film starring Jack Nicholson and Morgan Freeman (3,6,4)

8 and 20 Down 1996-2002 US television sitcom for which Michael J Fox and Charlie Sheen won Golden Globe awards (4,4)

9 and 15 2009 horror film featuring Briana Evigan and Leah Pipes (8,3)

10 1989 comedy-drama film starring Richard Dreyfuss and Holly Hunter (6)

13 See 14 Across

14 and 13 1968 crime film starring Clint Eastwood and Lee J Cobb (7,5)

15 See 9 Across

16 1995 sci-fi film featuring Natasha Henstridge as Sil (7)

17 Georges ___, French composer of 1925 ballet Les Matelots (5)

21 José Clemente ___, Mexican muralist noted for 1930s fresco The Epic of American Civilization (6)

22 The ___, 1987 crime film starring Christopher Lambert and Terence Stamp (8)

23 Muse of history in Greek mythology (4)

24 1977 novel by Paul Scott (7,2)

Down

1 New Zealand-born rugby union scrum-half; 2006-15 Ireland Test player (5,4)

2 Largest city in Wisconsin, US (9)

4 Hermann ___, author of novels The Glass Bead Game and Knulp (5)

5 Stan ___, author of novels A Kind of Loving and The Watchers on the Shore (7)

6 2006 animated film featuring the voice talent of Owen Wilson and Paul Newman (4)

7 Acronym for an economic alliance founded in 1960 and now comprising Iceland, Liechtenstein, Norway and Switzerland (4)

11 1983 World Championships men's 3,000m steeplechase gold medallist (6,3)

12 2009 book by Will Self and Ralph Steadman (6,3)

14 Type of lettuce known as romaine in Canada (3)

15 Overseas region of France in the Indian Ocean; capital Saint-Denis (7)

18 Spiral-horned antelope of central Africa whose coat is bright red-brown with narrow cream stripes (5)

19 See 3 Across

20 See 8 Across

No. 140

Across

1 William ___, 1996-97 WBA Middleweight champion (5)

7 Édouard ___, prime minister of France from 1938-40 (8)

8 Former small coin of France worth three deniers (5)

10 1974 action film starring Charles Bronson in the title role (2,8)

12 and 20 1957 film drama starring Joanne Woodward and David Wayne (3,5,5,2,3)

14 Letitia ___, actress who plays Sharon Watts in BBC TV soap EastEnders (4)

16 Husband of Frigg in Norse mythology (4)

17 Capital of Hungary (8)

20 See 12 Across

23 Department of NE France in the Hauts-de-France region (5)

24 Gaston ___, 1964 Olympic men's 3,000m steeplechase gold medallist (8)

25 Thomas ___, golfer; 2011 Open de France tournament winner (5)

Down

1 and 4 2009 novel by Nick Hornby (6,5)

2 Port in Russia on the Kama River known as Molotov from 1940-57 (4)

3 Port in Japan; largest city on Okinawa Island (4)

4 See 1 Down

5 1871 novel by Louisa M Alcott subtitled Life at Plumfield with Jo's Boys (6,3)

6 The ___, isolated hill in Shropshire west of Telford (6)

9 Shane ___, Australia-born fly-half capped twice by England in 2006 (5)

11 2005 film comedy starring Nicole Kidman and Will Ferrell (9)

13 Large Australian flightless bird (3)

15 City in northeast Estonia near to the Russian border housing 13th-century Hermann Castle (5)

16 City in England at the confluence of the Rivers Thames and Cherwell (6)

18 1978 stage play by Victoria Wood (6)

19 ___ Karatsev, 2021 Australian Open men's singles semi-finalist (5)

21 Gerry ___, co-founder and first leader of the SDLP in Northern Ireland in 1970 (4)

22 Irish Gaelic name for Ireland (4)

No. 140

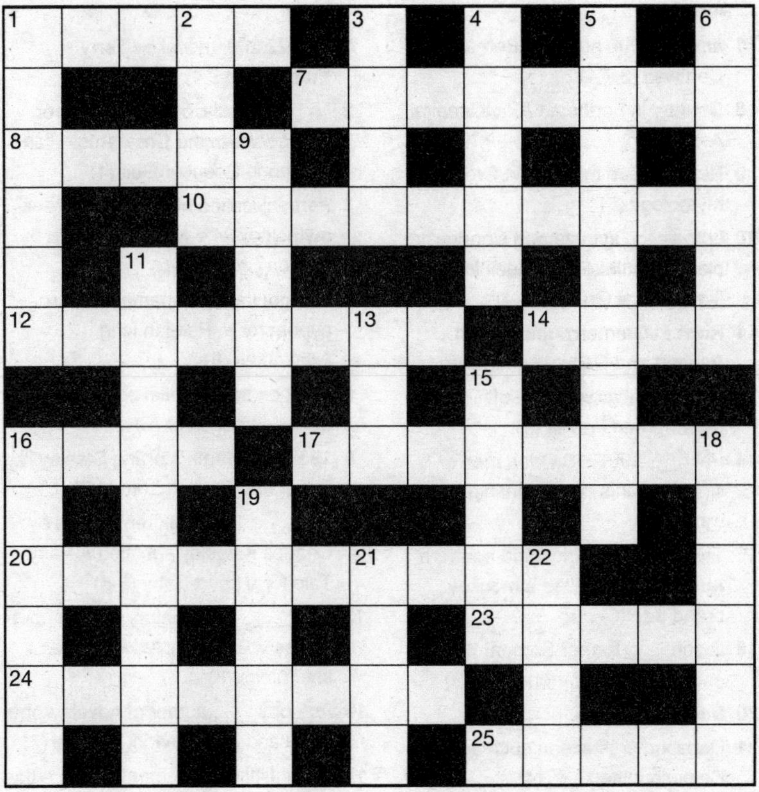

Across

1 **and 20** 2009 novel by Bernard Cornwell (3,7,4)

8 Country in northeast Africa; capital Asmara (7)

9 Nine-headed monster in Greek mythology (5)

10 Lorna ___, actress and singer who played Paulette Rebchuck in 1982 film musical Grease 2 (4)

11 River in Germany upon which Aachen and Geilenkirchen stand (4)

12 Tall annual grass with soft bluish-green leaves (3)

14 Pat ___, 1997 US Open men's singles tennis championship winner (6)

15 Tree native to Africa and northern Australia also called a monkey bread tree (6)

18 Justin ___, former Samoa, Wasps and Glasgow Warriors prop (3)

20 **See 1 Across**

21 Decapod crustacean such as the Chinese mitten ___ (4)

23 Valentino ___, 2002-05, 2008 and 2009 winner of the MotoGP World Championship (5)

24 Ancient Greek galley with three banks of oars on each side (7)

25 1994 romcom starring Michael Keaton and Geena Davis (10)

Down

1 **and 22** 2001 novel by Terry Pratchett (5,2,4)

2 ___ Peninsula, triangular area of land between the Great Australian Bight and Spencer Gulf (4)

3 Personification of the sky in Greek mythology who was overthrown by his son Cronus (6)

4 Book of the Bible named after a cupbearer to Persian king Artaxerxes (8)

5 Point on the celestial sphere directly below an observer (5)

6 1957 film drama starring Stanley Baker and Herbert Lom (4,7)

7 The ___, 1863 children's novel by Charles Kingsley subtitled A Fairy Tale for a Land-Baby (5-6)

13 Paul ___, 19th-century French poet whose volumes include Poèmes saturniens (8)

16 Anthony ___, author of novels Abba Abba and A Clockwork Orange (7)

17 Weightlifting movement in which the weight is raised in one quick motion from the floor to an overhead position (6)

19 Ancient Greek storyteller whose name is also the title of a comedy play by John Vanbrugh (5)

22 **See 1 Down**

No. 141

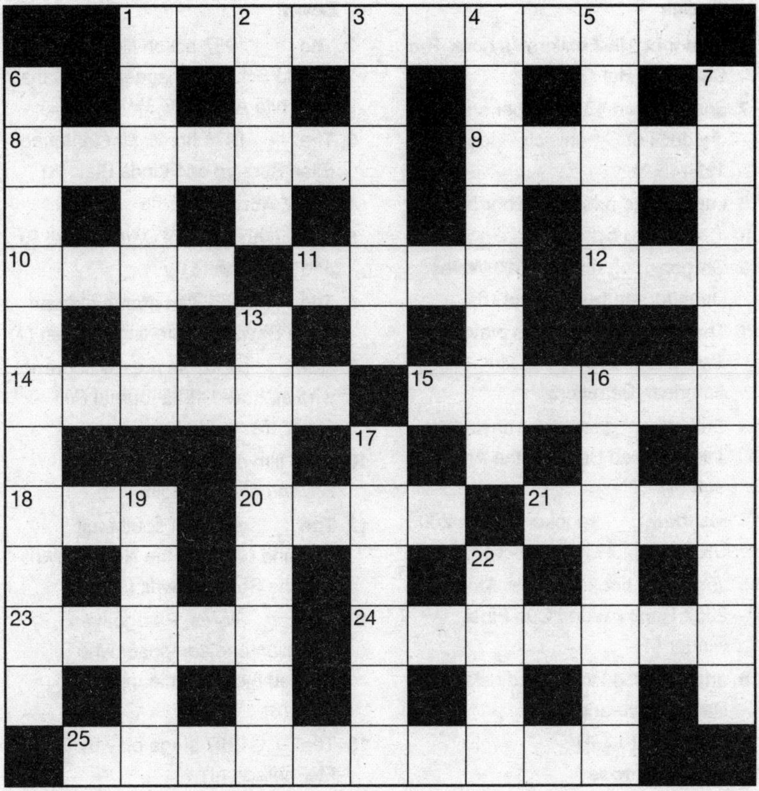

Across

1 Author of 1957 children's book The Cat in the Hat (2,5)

7 and 4 Down 1869 clipper ship in dry dock at Greenwich since 1954 (5,4)

8 Landlocked principality bordered by France and Spain (7)

9 Grégory ___, golfer; 2013 Wales Open tournament winner (6)

11 Thora ___, actress who played Jane Burnham in 1999 film American Beauty (5)

13 Gulf of ___, deepwater basin that links the Red Sea and the Arabian Sea (4)

14 Matthew ___, snooker player; 2003 UK Championship winner (7)

15 John ___, hooker; South Africa 2007 Rugby World Cup Final winner (4)

16 and 17 1954 film comedy starring Danny Kaye and Mai Zetterling (5,2,4)

17 See 16 Across

21 Dara ___, host of BBC TV panel game Mock the Week (1,6)

22 and 23 British violinist whose London debut was in 1977 (5,7)

23 See 22 Across

Down

2 The ___, 1987 action film starring Arnold Schwarzenegger and Maria Conchita Alonso (7,3)

3 The ___; 1974 horror film featuring Ellen Burstyn and Linda Blair (8)

4 See 7 Across

5 Roman goddess of womanhood and childbirth (4)

6 The ___, 1952 film drama starring Bette Davis and Sterling Hayden (4)

9 Janet ___, English mezzo-soprano who authored 1982 journal Full Circle (5)

10 1985 film drama starring Coral Browne and Ian Holm (10)

12 The ___, region of southeast England between the North Downs and the South Downs (5)

13 José ___ Flores, Paraguayan musician and composer who created the guarania musical style (8)

18 The ___, 1997 stage play by Conor McPherson (4)

19 Bill ___, actor who played Compo in BBC TV sitcom Last of the Summer Wine (4)

20 Ernst ___, German physicist and inventor noted for his work in optics (4)

No. 142

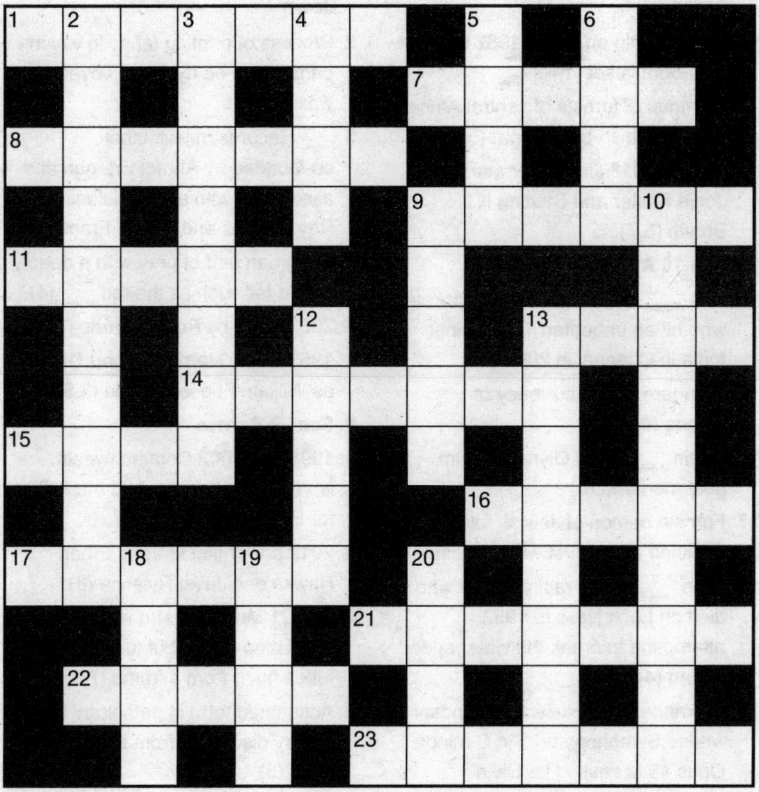

Across

1 Type of ship on which 1982 war film Das Boot is set (1-4)

4 Mammal of forests of central Africa with a reddish-brown coat (5)

10 **and 11** 2018 film thriller starring Jodie Foster and Sterling K Brown (5,7)

11 See 10 Across

12 N D ___, South Africa Test cricketer who hit an unbeaten 155 against India in Chennai in 2008 (8)

13 Standard unit of currency of Ghana (4)

15 Justin ___, 2004 Olympic 100m gold medallist (6)

17 Female demon of Jewish folklore depicted as the first wife of Adam (6)

19 John ___, motor racing driver who died on Loch Ness in 1952 attempting to break the water speed record (4)

20 Alexander ___, Russian composer whose Symphony no 3 in C minor, Opus 43 is entitled Le Divin Poème (8)

23 **and 8 Down** US sports team; 2009 NBA Finals runners-up to Los Angeles Lakers (7,5)

24 Fine net fabric of silk or rayon used as a trimming for hats (5)

25 Airy spirit in William Shakespeare play The Tempest (5)

26 Port in Finistère, France; a major naval station of the country (5)

Down

2 Process of printing fabric in which parts not to be dyed are covered by wax (5)

3 ___ Records, music label co-founded by Ahmet Ertegun and associated with artists including Ray Charles and Aretha Franklin (8)

5 European bird of prey with a deeply forked tail such as the red ___ (4)

6 2003 novel by Robert Harris (7)

7 1951 biopic starring Robert Donat as William Friese-Greene (3,5,3)

8 See 23 Across

9 1998 and 2002 Commonwealth women's triple jump gold medallist for England (5,6)

14 2012 horror film starring Ethan Hawke and Juliet Rylance (8)

16 **and 21** Musical instrument consisting of a set of tuned metal tubes hung from a frame (7,5)

18 Antiquated term in pathology for a watery discharge from a wound or ulcer (5)

21 See 16 Down

22 William ___, winner of the 1953 Pulitzer Prize for Drama for play Picnic (4)

No. 143

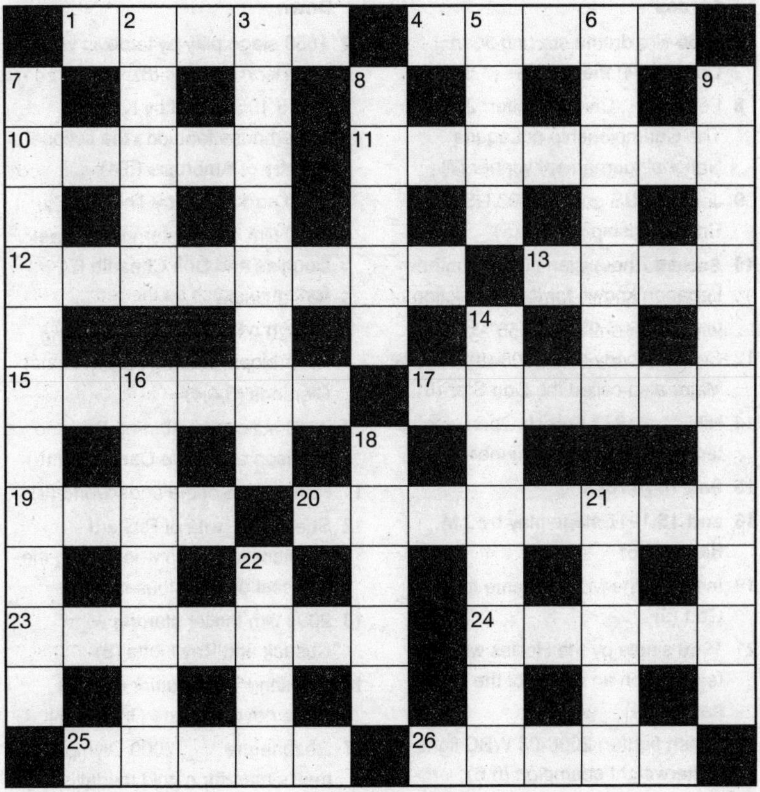

No. 144

Across

6 1950 film drama starring Joan Crawford in the title role (7,5)

8 Felipe ___, Chilean golfer; 2014 The Championship at Laguna National tournament winner (7)

9 Jim ___, US golfer; 2003 US Open Championship winner (5)

10 Ancient Phoenician port in southern Lebanon known for the production of a rare sort of purple dye (4)

12 Celestial body in constellation Canis Major also called the Dog Star (6)

14 Niki ___, 1973 French Open singles tennis championship runner-up (5)

15 See 16 Across

16 **and 15** 1917 stage play by J M Barrie (4,6)

19 In Islam, the Muslim name for God (5)

21 1966 single by the Hollies which featured on an album of the same name (3,4)

22 British fighter; 2006-08 WBC light welterweight champion (6,6)

Down

1 1869 stage play by Ludovic Halévy and Henri Meilhac (8)

2 **and 5** 1959 novel by Keith Waterhouse featuring the fictional country of Ambrosia (5,4)

3 1980 no 1 single by The Jam (5)

4 2000 film drama starring Michael Douglas and Don Cheadle (7)

5 **See 2 Down**

6 **and 20** 2018 film drama starring Nick Offerman and Kiersey Clemons (6,4,4)

7 2018 action film starring Dwayne Johnson and Neve Campbell (10)

11 Roman god of the underworld (3)

12 Sheila ___, wife of Richard Attenborough who was among the first cast of The Mousetrap (3)

13 2003 film thriller starring John Cusack and Ray Liotta (8)

14 Aleksandr ___, author of 1833 verse novel Eugene Onegin (7)

17 Gezahegne ___, 2000 Olympic men's marathon gold medallist (5)

18 John ___, actor who played Gomez Addams in 1960s US sitcom The Addams Family (5)

20 **See 6 Down**

293

No. 145

Across

3 and 21 2009 novel by Kate Mosse (3,6,6)

8 John ___, British mathematician who conceived a diagram using circles to represent sets and their relationships (4)

9 ___ Sea, body of water between the Gulf of Genoa and Corsica (8)

10 Elongated marine fish such as the common ___ with a sucking disc on the top of its head (6)

13 ___ Sea, body of water between Sulawesi and New Guinea (5)

14 Giovanni Battista ___, Italian painter whose works include The Chariot of Aurora and The Banquet of Cleopatra (7)

15 ___ Ben Haim, Israeli footballer who has played for clubs including Bolton Wanderers, Portsmouth and Charlton Athletic (3)

16 Brian ___, US actor who played Ted Montague in 1996 film drama Romeo + Juliet (7)

17 See 18 Down

21 See 3 Across

22 Lake ___, body of water on the Peru-Bolivia border (8)

23 Richard ___, actor who portrayed George Putnam in 2009 biopic Amelia (4)

24 Market town in Powys, Wales, on the River Severn north of Powis Castle (9)

Down

1 and 20 1990 film drama starring Debra Winger and Nick Nolte (9,4)

2 and 15 2018 action film starring Paul Rudd and Evangeline Lilly (3-3,3,3,4)

4 John ___, Hungary-born co-director of 1954 animated film Animal Farm (5)

5 Any of various small long-tailed birds such as the pied ___ or yellow ___ (7)

6 1941 Agatha Christie novel featuring Tommy and Tuppence Beresford (1,2,1)

7 Airline; flag carrier of Israel (2,2)

11 Neil ___, actor who played Rocky Cassidy in ITV comedy-drama series Boon (9)

12 Town in northern Kent housing both a castle and cathedral (9)

14 Longest river in Scotland (3)

15 See 2 Down

18 and 17 Across New Zealand author; creator of detective Inspector Roderick Alleyn (5,5)

19 Mr ___, 2010 crime film based on the autobiography of Howard Marks (4)

20 See 1 Down

Across

1 French river flowing generally northwest to the Seine at Montereau (5)

7 Vegetable also called a turnip cabbage (8)

8 Title character in 1826 J F Cooper novel The Last of the Mohicans (5)

10 and 12 2009 novel by Audrey Niffenegger (3,7,8)

12 See 10 Across

14 Second ___ War, 1899-1902 conflict in South Africa (4)

16 Dave ___, US winner of the 1965 PGA Championship (4)

17 Plant with bell-shaped flowers known in Scotland as the bluebell (8)

20 English singer and songwriter who recorded 1987 no 1 debut album Whenever You Need Somebody (4,6)

23 and 11 Down 1975 studio album by David Bowie (5,9)

24 ___ melon, round fruit with a greenish-white rind and sweet flesh (8)

25 and 1 Down Pakistan Test cricketer who took 5-52 against England at the Oval in 1992 (5,6)

Down

1 See 25 Across

2 ___ Wyle, actor who appeared in more episodes of the medical series ER than any other (5)

3 See 21 Down

4 Edward ___, composer who wrote Salut d'Amour as an engagement present for his fiancee in 1888 (5)

5 Ship that carried the Pilgrims from England to North America in 1620 (9)

6 Henry ___, author of novels Tropic of Cancer and Black Spring (6)

9 Monica ___, 1992 US Open singles tennis championship winner (5)

11 See 23 Across

13 Chris ___, rugby union centre; 1968 Scotland Test debutant against Australia (3)

15 Melvil ___, US inventor of a system for the classification of library books (5)

16 Cillian ___, actor who plays Thomas Shelby in BBC TV drama series Peaky Blinders (6)

18 Bernhard ___, golfer; 1985 and 1993 Masters Tournament winner (6)

19 Collective name for the sepals of a flower (5)

21 and 3 1985 film comedy starring Michael J Fox and James Hampton (4,4)

22 Hindu system of meditation and asceticism (4)

No. 146

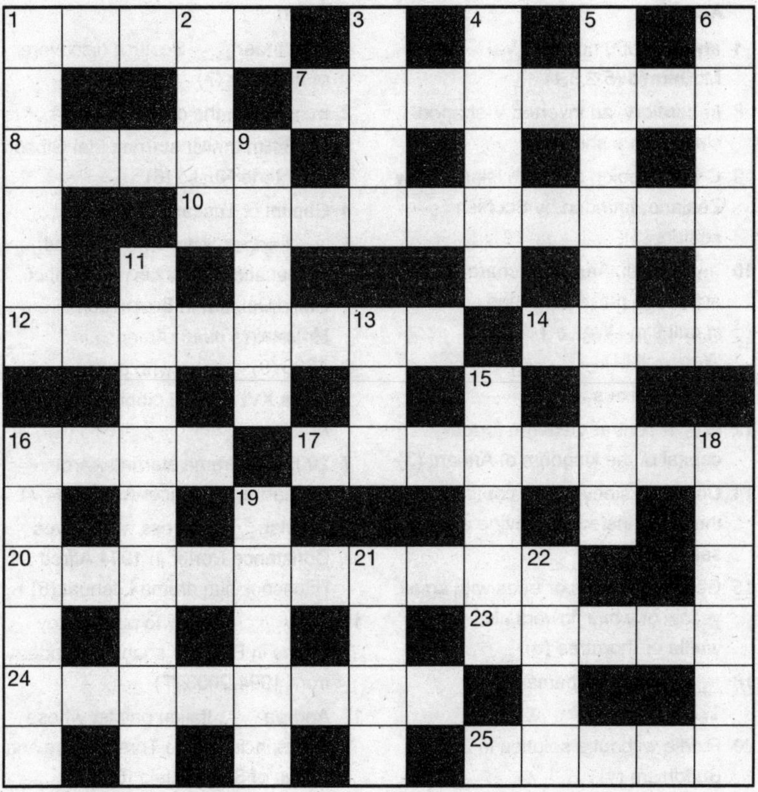

Across

1 **and 11** 2009 novel by Val McDermid (5,2,3,4)

8 In heraldry, an inverted V-shaped charge on a shield (7)

9 Council region of South Island, New Zealand, founded by Scottish settlers (5)

10 ___ Bissell, American character actor who played the mad scientist in cult film I Was a Teenage Werewolf (4)

11 **See 1 Across**

12 Port in central Vietnam; former capital of the kingdom of Annam (3)

14 Coat with sleeves that continue to the collar instead of having armhole seams (6)

15 Genus of shrubs or trees with small yellow or white flowers also called wattle or thorntree (6)

18 ___ I, King of Albania from 1928-39 (3)

20 Riddle without a solution in Zen Buddhism (4)

21 ___ Heynckes, fourth-highest goal scorer in the history of the Bundesliga (4)

23 A Town Like ___, 1950 novel by Nevil Shute (5)

24 Hillary ___, 2009-13 US Secretary of State (7)

25 1959 novel by Ian Fleming (10)

Down

1 Alexander ___, Scottish discoverer of penicillin (7)

2 In heraldry, the colour green (4)

3 1996 film thriller starring Mel Gibson and Rene Russo (6)

4 Capital of Tuscany, Italy (8)

5 ___ Ledger, actor who received critical acclaim for his portrayal of Ennis Del Mar in Brokeback Mountain (5)

6 Jason ___, actor who portrayed Louis XVI in 2006 biopic Marie Antoinette (11)

7 2009 film drama starring Aaron Eckhart and Jennifer Aniston (4,7)

13 Tallulah ___, actress who played Constance Porter in 1944 Alfred Hitchcock film drama Lifeboat (8)

16 Tony ___, actor who played Roy Evans in BBC TV soap EastEnders from 1994-2003 (7)

17 Andrea ___, Italian painter whose works include The Three Marys and Vision of St Romuald (6)

19 Percussion instrument made from a hollow gourd commonly used in Latin American music (5)

22 Imperial dynasty of China from 1368 to 1644 (4)

Across

1 and 23 2009 film comedy starring Vince Vaughn and Jason Bateman (7,7)

7 and 14 2005-16 leader of the Conservative Party (5,7)

8 Alan ___, Home Secretary from 2009-10 (7)

9 Emanuel ___, painter of 1851 oil Washington Crossing the Delaware (6)

11 Brother of Eadwig; king of England from 959-975 (5)

13 Arrochar ___, group of Scottish mountains on the Cowal Peninsula (4)

14 See 7 Across

15 Capital of Italy (4)

16 Charles ___, actor who played Tywin Lannister in US television series Game of Thrones (5)

17 Trademark of a synthetic resin used to coat non-stick cooking utensils (6)

21 City and port of Kenya served by the Moi International Airport (7)

22 Tom ___, US singer and actor who starred as Silva in 1989 film drama Bearskin (5)

23 See 1 Across

Down

2 Double reed woodwind instrument popular during the baroque era (4,6)

3 Ferry port in Cornwall on Mount's Bay (8)

4 Ancient Greek philosophical concept referring to sensual or passionate love (4)

5 and 18 1962 thriller starring Gregory Peck and Robert Mitchum (4,4)

6 Unit of liquid measure of capacity equal to one eighth of a gallon (4)

9 Seventh sign of the zodiac (5)

10 Davide ___, Italy defender signed by Atalanta BC from Chelsea FC in 2021 (10)

12 Port in northwest Germany at the mouth of the River Ems (5)

13 Seat of the University of Michigan, US (3,5)

18 See 5 Down

19 Hippocratic ___, ethical commitment made by doctors of medicine (4)

20 Former gold rush town in west Alaska; finishing point of the Iditarod trail sled dog race (4)

Across

1 Wading bird with the scientific name Gallinago gallinago (5)

4 Gabriel ___, French composer of 1913 opera Pénélope (5)

10 The ___, 2006 novel by Danielle Steel (5)

11 Guy ___, founder of a French fashion house who apprenticed under couturier Jean Dessès (7)

12 A ___, England Test cricketer who took 5-92 against Australia at Lord's in 2009 (8)

13 Jim ___, Scottish fighter; 1979-81 WBC Lightweight champion (4)

15 Island in the Tyrrhenian Sea at the entrance to the Bay of Naples (6)

17 Gastón ___, 2004 French Open singles tennis championship winner (6)

19 City and tourist centre in Lombardy, Italy, housing the Villa Olmo (4)

20 José Maria ___, golfer; 1999 Masters Tournament winner (8)

23 Laurence ___, Best Actor in a Leading Role Oscar nominee for The Boys from Brazil (7)

24 See 7 Down

25 Scottish singer born Mary Sandeman who recorded 1981 no 1 single Japanese Boy (5)

26 Light fabric with a fine ridged or crinkled surface (5)

Down

2 John ___, 1988 Olympic 5,000m gold medallist (5)

3 and 22 1986 romantic drama film starring Molly Ringwald and Harry Dean Stanton (6,2,4)

5 Unit of area equal to 4840 square yards (4)

6 See 8 Down

7 and 24 Across 1854 novel by W H Ainsworth subtitled The Custom of Dunmow (3,6,2,5)

8 and 6 Singer and actor born Harry Webb in British India in 1940 (5,7)

9 Former county of England; administrative centre Kendal (11)

14 Island in the Indian Ocean off the coast of Tanzania (8)

16 Flowering plant of the genus Silene such as the red ___ or white ___ (7)

18 Sandstone formation in Northern Territory, Australia, also known as Ayers Rock (5)

21 Lancashire town whose Britannia Coconut Dancers perform annually on Easter Saturday (5)

22 See 3 Down

Across

6 and 12 Across 1907 children's book by Beatrix Potter (3,4,2,3,6)

8 Brightly-coloured Old World finch such as the black-rumped ___ or swee ___ (7)

9 Pescennius ___, claimant to the title of Roman emperor during the Year of the Five Emperors in 193 AD (5)

10 Currency of the Republic of Yemen (4)

12 See 6 Across

14 1983 film comedy directed by and starring Woody Allen (5)

15 Joseph ___, British surgeon who introduced the use of antiseptics (6)

16 Denis ___, footballer born in 1988 who has represented Belgium and Ghana at international level (4)

19 Fermín ___, men's 1,500m gold medallist at the 1994 European Championships (5)

21 Woodland animal of Europe and Asia with small antlers and a reddish-brown summer coat (3,4)

22 1998 film comedy starring Oliver Platt and Stanley Tucci (3,9)

Down

1 and 7 European television game show launched in 1965 whose judges included Gennaro Olivieri (4,4,10)

2 and 3 US actress who played Sally Lamonsoff in 2010 film comedy Grown Ups (5,5)

3 See 2 Down

4 In Germany, one-hundredth of a Deutschmark until the introduction of the euro (7)

5 Peter ___, Scottish painter whose works include White Canoe and Orange Sunshine (4)

6 Type of building in which J G Ballard's novel High-Rise is set (5,5)

7 See 1 Down

11 2013 sci-fi film drama starring Joaquin Phoenix written and directed by Spike Jonze (3)

12 Rudyard Kipling novel first published in book form in 1901 (3)

13 1995 film comedy starring Nicole Kidman and Matt Dillon (2,3,3)

14 1939 film comedy starring Oliver Hardy and Harry Langdon (7)

17 Gene ___, jazz drummer portrayed by Sal Mineo in a 1959 biopic (5)

18 Rachel ___, Best Actress in a Supporting Role Oscar winner for The Constant Gardener (5)

20 Sammy ___, lyricist who won a Best Music, Original Song Oscar for Three Coins in a Fountain (4)

No. 150

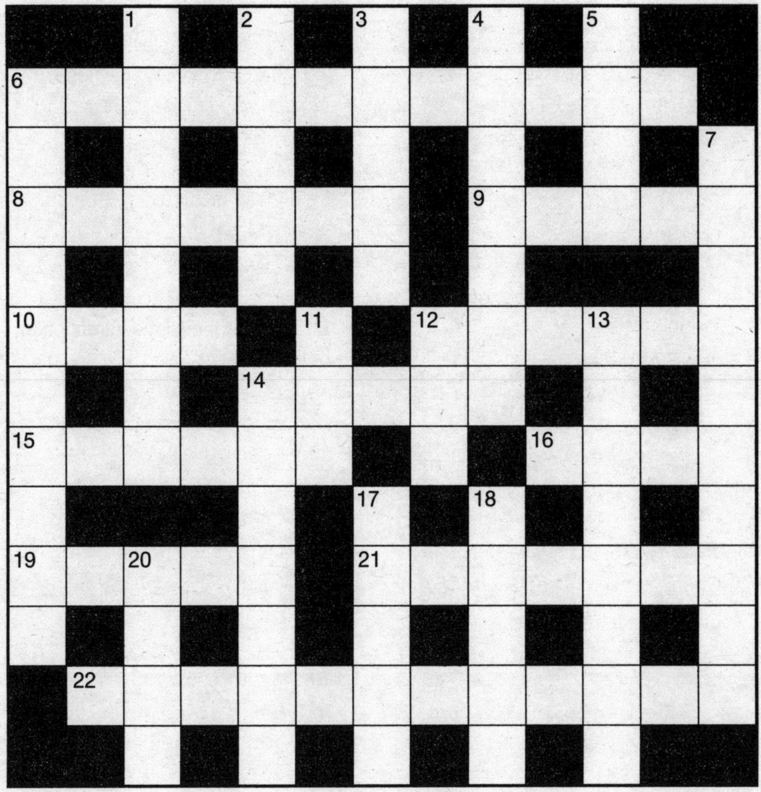

Solutions

No. 1

Across

3 MCDORMAND, 8 INDA,
9 OUTBREAK, 10 OXNARD,
13 EVANS, 14 SEX TAPE, 15 PER,
16 TALARIA, 17 ANGLO, 21 EKLUND,
22 GOLGOTHA, 23 SETH,
24 TETE-BECHE

Down

1 RIGOLETTO, 2 A DENIABLE,
4 COODY, 5 OCTOBER, 6 MARY,
7 NOAH, 11 MACGRUBER,
12 BEYOND THE, 14 SEA,
15 PIASTRE, 18 DEATH, 19 ROSE,
20 AGEE

No. 2

Across

1 JOLLY, 7 GALLIANO, 8 ROGER,
10 SURROGATES, 12 WHISTLER,
14 RYAN, 16 DUFF, 17 ADJUTANT,
20 MONKEY KING, 23 NICAM,
24 GREGORY'S, 25 BLISS

Down

1 JARROW, 2 LEES, 3 TARR,
4 BLIGH, 5 BANTRY BAY, 6 HOBSON,
9 RUTTO, 11 ZINFANDEL, 13 END,
15 QUINN, 16 DAMAGE, 18 THOMAS,
19 DEFOE, 21 KEYS, 22 GIRL

No. 3

Across

1 CARNOUSTIE, 8 ICELAND,
9 PUNCH, 10 NOSE, 11 FOUR,
12 SUK, 14 ASYLUM, 15 DALTON,
18 ORB, 20 KEAN, 21 TARA,
23 IMOLA, 24 EL OBEID,
25 GONDOLIERS

Down

1 CREASEY, 2 ROAD, 3 ODDJOB,
4 SUPERMAN, 5 INNES,
6 MINNEAPOLIS, 7 THE KING AND I,
13 AUCKLAND, 16 TRAVERS,
17 CADELL, 19 BIOKO, 22 CONE

No. 4

Across

1 MONTAND, 7 ROYAL, 8 LOVE YOU,
9 LEGATO, 11 VEGAS, 13 WEEK,
14 THE BLUE, 15 BABY, 16 EDDIE,
17 HRBATY, 21 WITNESS, 22 ROSSO,
23 LESSING

Down

2 ONOCENTAUR, 3 THE PARTY,
4 NOOL, 5 MORE, 6 MAMA, 9 LOLLO,
10 THE WHITSUN, 12 JELLY,
13 WEDDINGS, 18 BOOK, 19 TOSA,
20 HIDE

No. 5

Across

1 ICHOR, 4 A TALE, 10 FRIML,
11 REDRUTH, 12 WOODVINE,
13 HERB, 15 COWANS, 17 MILANO,
19 TERN, 20 BACKLASH, 23 ELLIOTT,
24 JOKER, 25 HYENA, 26 CURRY

Down

2 CAIRO, 3 OLLIVANT, 5 TODD,
6 LOU BEGA, 7 OF TWO CITIES,
8 CRANE, 9 THE BROTHERS,
14 KINKAJOU, 16 WORSLEY,
18 CARTY, 21 ACKER, 22 JOHN

No. 6

Across

6 JIM BROADBENT, 8 THE WIND,
9 RUPEE, 10 RYLE, 12 RUBRIC,
14 TIROP, 15 TAYLOR, 16 OGEE,
19 LANAI, 21 RAPHAEL, 22 IN THE
WILLOWS

Down

1 AMBERLEY, 2 ORRIS, 3 KANDY,
4 UBER CUP, 5 SNAP, 6 JETHRO
TULL, 7 SEYCHELLES, 11 MIR,
12 ROD, 13 RAGNAROK,
14 TONIGHT, 17 CRAWL, 18 SPALL,
20 NINA

No. 7

Across

3 THE WICKED, 8 EPEE, 9 NICE WORK, 10 RUNYON, 13 CATES, 14 SABRINA, 15 RAM, 16 IRIDIUM, 17 KEINO, 21 ENIGMA, 22 PAPHITIS, 23 MOOR, 24 GYROSCOPE

Down

1 PETRUCHIO, 2 BERNSTEIN, 4 HANNA, 5 WICKHAM, 6 COWS, 7 EZRA, 11 RIMINGTON, 12 LAPOTAIRE, 14 SAM, 15 RUBSTIC, 18 AESOP, 19 LADY, 20 THEO

No. 8

Across

1 DODGE, 7 BEAUFORT, 8 MAFIA, 10 PROSCIUTTO, 12 MY COUSIN, 14 SMOG, 16 ROOK, 17 GONZALEZ, 20 CHIMBORAZO, 23 URIAH, 24 EGLAMOUR, 25 HEWER

Down

1 DIM SUM, 2 GRIP, 3 ZEUS, 4 CUPID, 5 ZOETEMELK, 6 STRONG, 9 ARGUS, 11 SCHOFIELD, 13 IBO, 15 MZUZU, 16 RACHEL, 18 ZITHER, 19 OBAMA, 21 ROUS, 22 ORFE

No. 9

Across

1 PUERTO RICO, 8 MADEIRA, 9 BARNA, 10 ROOM, 11 BEAN, 12 AUK, 14 APOLLO, 15 COMINO, 18 BOA, 20 SEAN, 21 IVAN, 23 ROSTI, 24 ARIOSTO, 25 VENGSARKAR

Down

1 PEDROSO, 2 EPIC, 3 TRALEE, 4 ROBINSON, 5 CORIA, 6 SMORGASBORD, 7 JACK JOHNSON, 13 FLUSHING, 16 INVASOR, 17 SAHARA, 19 AISNE, 22 WICK

No. 10

Across

1 ANTYUKH, 7 KUMAR, 8 HOPKINS, 9 WHISKY, 11 LIGHT, 13 HART, 14 MATILDA, 15 BALA, 16 BAIZE, 17 GALORE, 21 RICKETS, 22 ASHES, 23 KICKING

Down

2 NAOMI OSAKA, 3 YOKOHAMA, 4 KING, 5 RUSH, 6 MAYS, 9 WHELK, 10 KYRGYZSTAN, 12 STOWE, 13 HABAKKUK, 18 LOST, 19 RIEL, 20 RIGI

No. 11

Across

1 SPLIT, 4 THYME, 10 RODIN, 11 COLENSO, 12 DEAD CALM, 13 KIND, 15 IRVINE, 17 ARNICA, 19 GNAT, 20 KEESHOND, 23 OF CRUEL, 24 MASER, 25 SCOTT, 26 UDINE

Down

2 PADUA, 3 INNOCENT, 5 HOLT, 6 MANCINI, 7 BRIDLINGTON, 8 SCULL, 9 WOODLANDERS, 14 PRESUMED, 16 VRANCIC, 18 KELLY, 21 OLSEN, 22 HUNT

No. 12

Across

6 BLOEMFONTEIN, 8 LEHMANN, 9 OTARU, 10 IOTA, 12 SAM PIG, 14 NIXON, 15 GORDON, 16 PULI, 19 AIOLI, 21 HAWKINS, 22 PEASEBLOSSOM

Down

1 COP HATER, 2 AMMAN, 3 BOUND, 4 OTTOMAN, 5 AIDA, 6 BILLINGHAM, 7 GUS GRISSOM, 11 GIN, 12 SOW, 13 PLUVIOSE, 14 NORILSK, 17 SHEBA, 18 EWLOE, 20 OPEC

No. 13

Across

3 IBUPROFEN, **8** THUN, **9** BIDEFORD, **10** VIENNA, **13** NIGER, **14** ENGLISH, **15** ILG, **16** GANGULY, **17** BAHA'I, **21** HOBART, **22** VUVUZELA, **23** EDDA, **24** ZOOKEEPER

Down

1 STEVENAGE, **2** AUBERGINE, **4** BABAR, **5** PUDDING, **6** ORFF, **7** EBRO, **11** HIGHLANDS, **12** CHRISTMAS, **14** ELY, **15** ILE DE RE, **18** SHANE, **19** CUJO, **20** DUCK

No. 14

Across

1 TOSCA, **7** M C HAMMER, **8** IDEAL, **10** RUNNER BEAN, **12** NELL GWYN, **14** AGAL, **16** MOXA, **17** POORWILL, **20** NINETY-FOUR, **23** DEVON, **24** CHENILLE, **25** HOBBY

Down

1 TAIWAN, **2** CHAR, **3** ICON, **4** LAURA, **5** AMBERGRIS, **6** BRUNEL, **9** LUNGE, **11** ALEXANDER, **13** YEO, **15** FREUD, **16** MONACO, **18** LINNEY, **19** STEIN, **21** FILO, **22** RENO

No. 15

Across

1 THE HISTORY, **8** FORMICA, **9** APPLE, **10** EDEN, **11** LAKE, **12** NEL, **14** DESSAU, **15** ANDREW, **18** NUT, **20** KEIR, **21** SPIN, **23** ICENI, **24** TEARS OF, **25** THE GIRAFFE

Down

1 TARGETS, **2** ERIE, **3** IBADAN, **4** TRAHERNE, **5** RIPON, **6** OF PENDENNIS, **7** YELLOWKNIFE, **13** MARK KING, **16** RIPOSTE, **17** WINTER, **19** TEETH, **22** TAFF

No. 16

Across

1 SCHMIDT, **7** GHOST, **8** GNOCCHI, **9** HAVE IT, **11** SALLY, **13** BATT, **14** ADELPHI, **15** LUNN, **16** STASI, **17** LET HIM, **21** GARDNER, **22** ABOUT, **23** BICYCLE

Down

2 CANTALOUPE, **3** MCCOLGAN, **4** DOHA, **5** SHEA, **6** ESTE, **9** HAPPY, **10** IN THE SHELL, **12** BELEM, **13** BIRTHDAY, **18** TOBY, **19** INUI, **20** BAYI

No. 17

Across

1 OSUNA, **4** BRAVE, **10** ELBOW, **11** OPHELIA, **12** ETHIOPIA, **13** WITT, **15** GENTLY, **17** DOES IT, **19** BEVY, **20** STARDUST, **23** CARROLL, **24** VIRGO, **25** ANNIE, **26** LARCH

Down

2 SABAH, **3** NEW WORLD, **5** RAHM, **6** VILNIUS, **7** NEVER GO BACK, **8** BOSIE, **9** LAST STATION, **14** MONROVIA, **16** NAVARIN, **18** ITALY, **21** ULRIC, **22** LOKI

No. 18

Across

6 PAUL NICHOLAS, **8** CABARET, **9** PRIDE, **10** ANNE, **12** JERBOA, **14** IDRIS, **15** INSOLE, **16** RICE, **19** LLAMA, **21** HORATIO, **22** AND PREJUDICE

Down

1 HUSBANDS, **2** ANDRE, **3** ACUTE, **4** COUPLES, **5** TAXI, **6** PICCADILLY, **7** SEA ANEMONE, **11** IDE, **12** JIM, **13** BRITTAIN, **14** ILLAMPU, **17** SHREW, **18** TROUT, **20** ARNO

No. 19

Across

3 THE MARK OF, 8 HAAS,
9 BROADWAY, 10 WINKLE,
13 ZORRO, 14 BELLINI, 15 FEN,
16 RUSSELL, 17 GRANT,
21 HAROLD, 22 DOMINICA, 23 YETI,
24 FAIRBANKS

Down

1 THE WIZARD, 2 DANNY ROSE,
4 HABER, 5 MOORHEN, 6 RUDD,
7 OVAL, 11 PICAMOLES,
12 PITTODRIE, 14 BEL, 15 FLORIDA,
18 CHALK, 19 BOMA, 20 BIRR

No. 20

Across

1 NKOSI, 7 MULLINER, 8 VIDAL,
10 WONDERLAND, 12 ATALANTA,
14 JOHN, 16 BEEM, 17 TITANIUM,
20 RAFSANJANI, 23 SAINT,
24 EUROPEAN, 25 LOVER

Down

1 NEVADA, 2 SHAW, 3 QUAD,
4 CLARE, 5 ANNAPOLIS, 6 BRADEN,
9 LOMAX, 11 WATERFORD, 13 TUI,
15 RAINS, 16 BARNES, 18 MEET MR,
19 HARPY, 21 JOAN, 22 IAGO

No. 21

Across

1 EGDON HEATH, 8 EZEKIEL,
9 WHIST, 10 EFTA, 11 DIOR, 12 FAH,
14 OXALIS, 15 THE GUM, 18 ELM,
20 ERIN, 21 IDAS, 23 NIGHT,
24 LUAMANU, 25 AIR MARSHAL

Down

1 ELEKTRA, 2 DRIN, 3 NELLIE,
4 ELWORTHY, 5 THIEF, 6 PENELOPE
ANN, 7 AT THE MUSEUM, 13 TIGER
TIM, 16 GADWALL, 17 MILLER,
19 MAGRI, 22 OATH

No. 22

Across

1 LAPWING, 7 SQUAW, 8 WARNOCK,
9 RADISH, 11 BORIS, 13 CUBE,
14 EBONITE, 15 KING, 16 BARAK,
17 VALLEY, 21 QUETZAL, 22 JESUS,
23 SPASSKY

Down

2 ASAFOETIDA, 3 WINNIPEG,
4 NICE, 5 AQUA, 6 WAMI, 9 REGIA,
10 SABINA PARK, 12 BOOBY,
13 CERASTES, 18 LEEK, 19 EHUD,
20 PULP

No. 23

Across

1 CATCH, 4 HARRY, 10 ELIAS,
11 ARIZONA, 12 ROSEANNA,
13 HOUR, 15 MORGAN, 17 MY SOUL,
19 RUSH, 20 CRICHTON,
23 AALBORG, 24 NETTO, 25 RANGI,
26 CHASE

Down

2 ARIES, 3 CAST AWAY, 5 AMIS,
6 RIO LOBO, 7 GEBREMARIAM,
8 RAINE, 9 BARRY LYNDON,
14 HYACINTH, 16 ROSELLA,
18 FROGS, 21 TITUS, 22 MOOG

No. 24

Across

6 KLIPSPRINGER, 8 LEAWERE,
9 AZOTH, 10 IOLE, 12 CURCIC,
14 TAGUS, 15 GENIUS, 16 SCUM,
19 OSRIC, 21 OSTRAVA,
22 MORNING GLORY

Down

1 TIM ALLEN, 2 ASHER, 3 GREEN,
4 ANTAEUS, 5 LENO, 6 KILLING FOR,
7 THE COMPANY, 11 WAS, 12 CUE,
13 COCKATOO, 14 TUSCANY,
17 YONNE, 18 OTAGO, 20 ROOM

No. 25

Across
3 HAPPY DAYS, 8 HEEL,
9 ARMAGNAC, 10 POISON,
13 AGONY, 14 PIONEER, 15 REN,
16 UIHLEIN, 17 KYOTO, 21 ASLEEP,
22 PENGUINS, 23 THOR,
24 HEYERDAHL

Down
1 THE PLAGUE, 2 VERISOPHT,
4 AGANA, 5 PUMPKIN, 6 DOGS,
7 YUAN, 11 BEFORE THE, 12 MR
POPPER'S, 14 PEN, 15 RIFKIND,
18 FASTH, 19 CETE, 20 OGLE

No. 26

Across
1 STEVE, 7 BEAULIEU, 8 HERAS,
10 SOLHEIM CUP, 12 TRANMERE,
14 SPEY, 16 SUMO, 17 ARPEGGIO,
20 AILSA CRAIG, 23 SIMON,
24 OVERLOAD, 25 HENTY

Down
1 SCHIST, 2 VAAS, 3 LEAH,
4 AUDIE, 5 DISCO PIGS, 6 MURPHY,
9 SOMME, 11 MAX MILLER,
13 R.U.R., 15 LEWIS, 16 SHADOW,
18 O HENRY, 19 TABLA, 21 RIAL,
22 GIDE

No. 27

Across
1 BASUTOLAND, 8 EVESHAM,
9 NIMMO, 10 RAKI, 11 KAYE, 12 YEN,
14 BARRAS, 15 CONWAY, 18 TOM,
20 TRON, 21 KLEE, 23 OH GOD,
24 ATOM ANT, 25 SONNY TERRY

Down
1 BREAKER, 2 SOHO, 3 TAMMAR,
4 LANCELOT, 5 NIMOY,
6 RETRIBUTION, 7 JOHNNY LEOTA,
13 MASTODON, 16 WALLABY,
17 MORANT, 19 MIGNO, 22 BOAR

No. 28

Across
1 THE DEBT, 7 CANIS, 8 OGILVIE,
9 TAOISM, 11 ISERE, 13 AVRO,
14 MORANIS, 15 IRIS, 16 THREE,
17 PATTEN, 21 COMPTON,
22 MINOR, 23 WINGATE

Down
2 HIGH SIERRA, 3 DOLDRUMS,
4 BRIE, 5 NANA, 6 DILI, 9 TURNS,
10 SHREVEPORT, 12 BRIAN, 13 AS
THE PIG, 18 TAIT, 19 EDOM, 20 ROTI

No. 29

Across
1 FOSSE, 4 ALULA, 10 ACCRA,
11 ARCADIA, 12 BIRDSONG,
13 PECK, 15 THALIA, 17 BROLIN,
19 ERIC, 20 LIAONING,
23 UMBERTO, 24 ERODE, 25 JAMES,
26 ASTON

Down
2 OSCAR, 3 STARSHIP, 5 LACE,
6 LIDDELL, 7 RABBIT REDUX,
8 CARNE, 9 WATKINS GLEN,
14 TROOPERS, 16 AKII-BUA,
18 DIXON, 21 IROKO, 22 CREE

No. 30

Across
6 PUBERTY BLUES, 8 ISOBATH,
9 ANZIO, 10 KISS, 12 HAMMAM,
14 LAVER, 15 NANSEN, 16 STAN,
19 ORLOP, 21 KIPRUTO,
22 COLLEY CIBBER

Down
1 ABHORSON, 2 PRIAM, 3 BY THE,
4 ALCAZAR, 5 GETZ, 6 PRICKING OF,
7 BODMIN MOOR, 11 HAN, 12 HEN,
13 MY THUMBS, 14 LEOPOLD,
17 OKAYO, 18 OPHIR, 20 LOOP

No. 31

Across

3 GLASSWORT, **8** NARA,
9 CALABASH, **10** WINDLE,
13 ROWAN, **14** TORTUGA,
15 NEW, **16** PUCKOON, **17** MALLE,
21 HYSSOP, **22** THE HAGUE,
23 BURR, **24** MANGANITE

Down

1 SNOWDROPS, **2** BRUNSWICK,
4 LACEY, **5** SALCHOW, **6** WEBB,
7 ROSS, **11** BURLESQUE,
12 DAVENPORT, **14** TEN,
15 NONAGON, **18** GHENT,
19 RHEA, **20** SHAG

No. 32

Across

1 IRISH, **7** HIGHMORE, **8** LUMET,
10 WICKED THIS, **12** DIOGENES,
14 ODIN, **16** ADEN, **17** WAY COMES,
20 SCHEINMANN, **23** EIGHT, **24** SAN
PEDRO, **25** PAPER

Down

1 ISLAND, **2** SMEW, **3** DICK,
4 RHODE, **5** JOSH ADAMS,
6 BENSON, **9** TIGER,
11 SOMETHING, **13** ETA, **15** SCONE,
16 ASSISI, **18** SETTER, **19** NIMES,
21 MARY, **22** NIPA

No. 33

Across

1 THE SISTERS, **8** EVEREST,
9 REITH, **10** YARD, **11** FINN, **12** ELI,
14 AMPERE, **15** HORNET, **18** SOB,
20 TOLE, **21** OWEN, **23** VOILE,
24 GUAYULE, **25** TOPSY-TURVY

Down

1 THE DROP, **2** EDEN, **3** ISTRIA,
4 TURANDOT, **5** RHINE, **6** NEW
YEAR'S EVE, **7** CHRISTENSEN,
13 BROTHERS, **16** NEWBURY,
17 FLIGHT, **19** BOITO, **22** MARR

No. 34

Across

1 CATALPA, **7** ROYAL, **8** BABASSU,
9 FAMILY, **11** ADERE, **13** AIRE,
14 OPOSSUM, **15** PLOT, **16** BIRDS,
17 OFFICE, **21** BUS STOP, **22** ANGRY,
23 STARKEY

Down

2 A HANDFUL OF, **3** A PATRIOT,
4 POST, **5** COVA, **6** MAXI, **9** FLASH,
10 LORNA DOONE, **12** FOR ME,
13 AMRITSAR, **18** FUNK, **19** CORK,
20 DUST

No. 35

Across

1 CHAPE, **4** FORTH, **10** LIBRE,
11 LIAM FOX, **12** CORBIERE,
13 NERO, **15** DAY OUT, **17** A GRAND,
19 HARD, **20** SQUIRREL, **23** ILLYRIA,
24 OSAGE, **25** LYDON, **26** NACHO

Down

2 HUBER, **3** PRECIOUS, **5** OBAN,
6 TAFFETA, **7** BLACK DAHLIA,
8 CLARE, **9** OXFORD BLUES,
14 AGRICOLA, **16** YARDLEY,
18 SQUAB, **21** ROACH, **22** TRIO

No. 36

Across

6 THE FAITHLESS, **8** ENGLISH,
9 MYALL, **10** URAL, **12** ANGELO,
14 ADAMS, **15** SETTLE, **16** WHIT,
19 EGYPT, **21** UDAIPUR,
22 WRECKING CREW

Down

1 SERGEANT, **2** MAXIE, **3** STAHL,
4 CLEMENS, **5** OSSA, **6** THE
PURSUED, **7** E L DOCTOROW,
11 EDE, **12** AMY, **13** ECHO PARK,
14 ALETSCH, **17** MUSIC, **18** FARGO,
20 YORK

No. 37

Across

3 BLACKBALL, **8** ARAD, **9** NEW HAVEN, **10** ANKARA, **13** HANDL, **14** DETTORI, **15** KAY, **16** THE LAND, **17** GIRLS, **21** ADRIAN, **22** SHANGHAI, **23** KNEE, **24** SIXTH SEAL

Down

1 YAMASHITA, **2** FALKENDER, **4** LYNAM, **5** COWDREY, **6** BAAL, **7** LOEB, **11** FOUR LIONS, **12** KIESINGER, **14** DAD, **15** KNIGHTS, **18** NAIRA, **19** THAI, **20** KNOT

No. 38

Across

1 APPLE, **7** BROUGHAM, **8** THUMB, **10** BLACKTHORN, **12** FRANKLIN, **14** ITMA, **16** DOOM, **17** NEYAGAWA, **20** JOSEY WALES, **23** STONE, **24** VIOLENCE, **25** FROME

Down

1 ACTS OF, **2** LAMB, **3** ERIC, **4** QUITO, **5** THE OUTLAW, **6** AMANDA, **9** BLAKE, **11** AARON'S ROD, **13** ICE, **15** JAMES, **16** DEJA VU, **18** ARIEGE, **19** SYKES, **21** ARCE, **22** STAR

No. 39

Across

1 SARAH LUCAS, **8** ORESTES, **9** DOLLY, **10** KING, **11** DIER, **12** NET, **14** OSMIUM, **15** CHIRAC, **18** LUR, **20** DOTT, **21** ODOI, **23** EMMEN, **24** ROANOKE, **25** AND MAXWELL

Down

1 STERNUM, **2** RUTH, **3** HESTIA, **4** UNDER THE, **5** ALLEN, **6** ROCK FOLLIES, **7** MYSTIC RIVER, **13** DUODENUM, **16** REDPOLL, **17** STYRAX, **19** ROMAN, **22** LANE

No. 40

Across

1 MATTHEW, **7** DAVID, **8** ADMETUS, **9** SKEPTA, **11** DRAHM, **13** HOW I, **14** SINATRA, **15** LUNT, **16** SKIBO, **17** ARNOLD, **21** LIVE NOW, **22** FLUDD, **23** NETSUKE

Down

2 AND MRS MUIR, **3** THE GHOST, **4** ELUL, **5** PARK, **6** DIOP, **9** SOUTH, **10** TOWER BLOCK, **12** SNEAD, **13** HARKNESS, **18** NILE, **19** LUDD, **20** VINE

No. 41

Across

1 MARSH, **4** DRAKE, **10** HOGAN, **11** HIBACHI, **12** MAN OF WAR, **13** WOLF, **15** NEOSHO, **17** TERFEL, **19** NEEL, **20** AL PACINO, **23** HAMMOND, **24** ERNIE, **25** ANAND, **26** STARK

Down

2 ARGON, **3** SON OF THE, **5** ROBA, **6** KICK-OFF, **7** THE MAN ON THE, **8** UHLAN, **9** EIFFEL TOWER, **14** DEMAREST, **16** OBERMAN, **18** SLADE, **21** ISNER, **22** JOAN

No. 42

Across

6 THE COMEDIANS, **8** MASSINE, **9** COPRA, **10** LENA, **12** REDCAR, **14** DINAR, **15** DRIVER, **16** DICK, **19** WIGHT, **21** WHITTLE, **22** DARREN CLARKE

Down

1 HELSINKI, **2** LOUIS, **3** LEGER, **4** FINCHER, **5** SNAP, **6** TUMBLEDOWN, **7** LAURA KEENE, **11** FIR, **12** RAM, **13** CHILTERN, **14** DETTORI, **17** SWANK, **18** HILLS, **20** GUAM

No. 43

Across

3 HAMSTRING, 8 AYIA, 9 ROAD HOME, 10 ROTHKO, 13 JARRY, 14 CADFAEL, 15 POD, 16 HAUNTED, 17 PABLO, 21 NERUDA, 22 QUEEQUEG, 23 ICON, 24 RETRIEVER

Down

1 BARRY JOHN, 2 JITTERBUG, 4 AARON, 5 SHAHZAD, 6 ROHM, 7 NOME, 11 LAMBRUSCO, 12 CLEO LAINE, 14 COD, 15 PERFUME, 18 ANGLE, 19 AUDE, 20 HERR

No. 44

Across

1 PURGE, 7 VICTORIA, 8 LILAC, 10 FER-DE-LANCE, 12 STAUNTON, 14 YIPS, 16 BASS, 17 MEL BLANC, 20 NOTTINGHAM, 23 SALOP, 24 THE MUMMY, 25 VENUS

Down

1 PELVIS, 2 GRAF, 3 BIRD, 4 STILL, 5 PRINCIPAL, 6 HABEAS, 9 CERNE, 11 SAPS AT SEA, 13 ONE, 15 ABBAS, 16 BONITO, 18 CORPUS, 19 PIQUE, 21 GAME, 22 MACE

No. 45

Across

1 SCHUMACHER, 8 KLAMMER, 9 TAIGA, 10 SIDE, 11 TARO, 12 ASO, 14 ROKEBY, 15 MOSSAD, 18 LOB, 20 WEKA, 21 RALF, 23 OUIJA, 24 ABILENE, 25 THE EMERALD

Down

1 SHARDIK, 2 HUME, 3 MORGAN, 4 CITY OF OZ, 5 ERICA, 6 A KESTREL FOR, 7 JASON DUFNER, 13 EBBW VALE, 16 SEAWEED, 17 A KNAVE, 19 BEITH, 22 PISA

No. 46

Across

1 MCADAMS, 7 LEWIS, 8 VICIOUS, 9 CIRCLE, 11 MCKAY, 13 BLUE, 14 IVANHOE, 15 ULNA, 16 GULES, 17 HAWAII, 21 GIBLETS, 22 PEASE, 23 PUDDING

Down

2 CHINCHILLA, 3 DEIDAMIA, 4 MAUI, 5 LEVI, 6 ZINC, 9 CACHO, 10 LAUNCESTON, 12 CAPRI, 13 BEGUILED, 18 WREN, 19 IASI, 20 AINU

No. 47

Across

1 MOUSE, 4 WHITE, 10 OTTEY, 11 HAWKEYE, 12 DEFOREST, 13 BAHT, 15 KELLEY, 17 MAI TAI, 19 LEEK, 20 DAMASCUS, 23 COSTARD, 24 OLIVE, 25 GRASS, 26 SNAKE

Down

2 OUT OF, 3 SEYFRIED, 5 HOWE, 6 THE PAST, 7 KOHDE-KILSCH, 8 CHESS, 9 WESTMINSTER, 14 MACAROON, 16 LOESSER, 18 BANDA, 21 CLICK, 22 LAOS

No. 48

Across

6 THE LAST MOVIE, 8 ESTORIL, 9 QUEEN, 10 TROY, 12 GAMBIA, 14 GOGOL, 15 RIDERS, 16 FREE, 19 WILLY, 21 THE ROSE, 22 OF SEBASTOPOL

Down

1 WESTWOOD, 2 LAWRY, 3 STILL, 4 RORQUAL, 5 NINE, 6 THE IT CROWD, 7 ANNA SEWELL, 11 COS, 12 GOA, 13 BARDOLPH, 14 GREYHEN, 17 STRAW, 18 YENTL, 20 LIFE

No. 49

Across

3 HIGHSMITH, **8** ODIN, **9** MISSOURI, **10** DORATI, **13** ROOPE, **14** KIPYEGO, **15** DAN, **16** SHIRLEY, **17** LUCIC, **21** PEORIA, **22** LOK SABHA, **23** RENE, **24** BAD SISTER

Down

1 GOLDCREST, **2** CIRRHOSIS, **4** IZMIR, **5** HUSSAIN, **6** MOON, **7** TURK, **11** DESCARTES, **12** LON CHANEY, **14** KAY, **15** DELIBES, **18** SPADE, **19** BOMA, **20** ISIS

No. 50

Across

1 VASCO, **7** KEY LARGO, **8** NIORT, **10** RAMPRAKASH, **12** EXISTENZ, **14** STAR, **16** DULL, **17** STILWELL, **20** GARY OLDMAN, **23** DAVID, **24** MUZOREWA, **25** NIXON

Down

1 VENICE, **2** CARR, **3** DEEP, **4** ELWAY, **5** GREAT TREK, **6** MOTHER, **9** TARTU, **11** GIRL CRAZY, **13** NET, **15** ILIAD, **16** DA GAMA, **18** LONDON, **19** CORRI, **21** DOWN, **22** NABI

No. 51

Across

1 NIGHT SHIFT, **8** HARTMAN, **9** BRUNI, **10** KAYE, **11** TEES, **12** TEA, **14** SEVERN, **15** DURAND, **18** EAT, **20** YANG, **21** WALL, **23** ROMEO, **24** ORIGAMI, **25** GRAEME DOTT

Down

1 NUREYEV, **2** GAME, **3** TANNER, **4** HIBISCUS, **5** FAUST, **6** SHAKESPEARE, **7** PINAR DEL RIO, **13** PRAY LOVE, **16** ADAM ANT, **17** IN LOVE, **19** TAMAR, **22** TITO

No. 52

Across

1 ISOTOPE, **7** CLOUD, **8** EMBUREY, **9** SARONG, **11** CROWN, **13** IOWA, **14** NIOBIUM, **15** BLUE, **16** HERGE, **17** VELVET, **21** PELICAN, **22** ATLAS, **23** ROULADE

Down

2 SOMERVILLE, **3** THUGWANE, **4** PREY, **5** ELBA, **6** SUMO, **9** SATIN, **10** NEW ENGLAND, **12** MOUNT, **13** IMPERIAL, **18** LYTE, **19** EGAN, **20** REGO

No. 53

Across

1 JOPPY, **4** U-BOAT, **10** ASTON, **11** OBADIAH, **12** CRAWFORD, **13** ZULU, **15** HENDRY, **17** FATHOM, **19** GOBI, **20** INTAGLIO, **23** LAIDLAW, **24** ELVER, **25** SKARA, **26** STONE

Down

2 OSTIA, **3** PONSFORD, **5** BRAE, **6** AZIMUTH, **7** MARC CHAGALL, **8** CORRY, **9** CHAULMOOGRA, **14** PARAKEET, **16** NIBLICK, **18** SNOWY, **21** LEVEN, **22** SLUR

No. 54

Across

6 BLACKCURRANT, **8** NUMBERS, **9** TOSCA, **10** EAST, **12** VERVET, **14** JASON, **15** HANDEL, **16** ONAN, **19** LYNNE, **21** SEAGULL, **22** ASPERN PAPERS

Down

1 HARMISON, **2** SKEET, **3** RUSSO, **4** BRITTEN, **5** ENOS, **6** BUNKER HILL, **7** CANTINFLAS, **11** TAL, **12** VOL, **13** VAN OUTEN, **14** JEZEBEL, **17** OSUNA, **18** QATAR, **20** NASH

No. 55

Across

3 BOOMERANG, **8** AZOV, **9** LION KING, **10** TUKALO, **13** MAPLE, **14** SEQUOIA, **15** WAN, **16** MAUGHAM, **17** OCTET, **21** MALAWI, **22** COMANECI, **23** JUPP, **24** CASSOULET

Down

1 PANTOMIME, **2** YOM KIPPUR, **4** ORLOP, **5** MOORHEN, **6** RAKI, **7** NONO, **11** PORT SALUT, **12** XANTHIPPE, **14** SAM, **15** WATTEAU, **18** SMIKE, **19** SOYA, **20** JAWS

No. 56

Across

1 CIRCE, **7** SULAWESI, **8** ISAAC, **10** THE MAN WITH, **12** SEWELLEL, **14** CROP, **16** BABE, **17** AMY ADAMS, **20** CHATTERTON, **23** REDON, **24** LANDRACE, **25** ETUDE

Down

1 CRIPPS, **2** CHAT, **3** GUAM, **4** PAINE, **5** DESI ARNAZ, **6** BISHOP, **9** CHILE, **11** TWO BRAINS, **13** ELM, **15** GABOR, **16** BACALL, **18** SPENCE, **19** STERN, **21** ROCK, **22** NEWT

No. 57

Across

1 SALMANAZAR, **8** OF HUMAN, **9** LOEWE, **10** DART, **11** BAIN, **12** TOG, **14** NOONAN, **15** VISHNU, **18** RUN, **20** AMIS, **21** KYAT, **23** WRACK, **24** BONDAGE, **25** BARRINGTON

Down

1 SUHARTO, **2** LOME, **3** AENEAS, **4** ATLANTIS, **5** AMENT, **6** GORDON BROWN, **7** REDGAUNTLET, **13** GAVASKAR, **16** HAY WAIN, **17** GIBBON, **19** NYASA, **22** KNOT

No. 58

Across

1 MINTOFF, **7** OUT OF, **8** CHEETAH, **9** BEGLEY, **11** SPATS, **13** TAPE, **14** NABUCCO, **15** ANTE, **16** ROBIN, **17** EDFORS, **21** DAI REES, **22** SIGHT, **23** ASKWITH

Down

2 IT HAPPENED, **3** THE STONE, **4** FRAM, **5** LUTE, **6** JOEL, **9** BEECH, **10** EXPERIMENT, **12** ABYSS, **13** TOMORROW, **18** FOIL, **19** RUHR, **20** MARS

No. 59

Across

1 KYOTO, **4** THETA, **10** AZURE, **11** MACBETH, **12** NAGASAKI, **13** LEAD, **15** SEWARD, **17** YARROW, **19** FAME, **20** TRIMURTI, **23** HANCOCK, **24** ANGEL, **25** OF THE, **26** NORTH

Down

2 YOUNG, **3** TREASURY, **5** HOCK, **6** THE YEAR, **7** SAINTS OF THE, **8** UMEKI, **9** SHADOW BIBLE, **14** NAUM GABO, **16** WOMAN OF, **18** IROKO, **21** ROGET, **22** MOTH

No. 60

Across

6 JEEVES AND THE, **8** RIGATTI, **9** MONET, **10** MOSS, **12** SOCCER, **14** NOYON, **15** KINSEY, **16** IAIN, **19** RIGEL, **21** AGRIPPA, **22** WEDDING BELLS

Down

1 FERGUSON, **2** DELTA, **3** DAVIS, **4** ADAMSON, **5** SHIN, **6** JEROME KERN, **7** ST TRINIANS, **11** JOY, **12** SOU, **13** CHAPPELL, **14** NED LUDD, **17** HANNA, **18** GREBE, **20** GLEN

No. 61

Across

3 FOOL'S GOLD, 8 OBAN,
9 AGRIMONY, 10 GUITAR, 13 HOFFA,
14 KING AND, 15 BEE, 16 MAXWELL,
17 HENRY, 21 ARDANT, 22 FIELDING,
23 SKIN, 24 ROUNDTREE

Down

1 LONGCHAMP, 2 JAMIE FOXX,
4 O'HARE, 5 LARAMIE, 6 GAME,
7 LENA, 11 IAIN BANKS,
12 EDDYSTONE, 14 KEL,
15 BLERIOT, 18 NAGLE, 19 LIMO,
20 OLIN

No. 62

Across

1 BRYAN, 7 ALASTAIR, 8 OWENS,
10 ANDY SERKIS, 12 ELIZONDO,
14 ONLY, 16 JUTE, 17 ADELAIDE,
20 SUNDERLAND, 23 NURMI,
24 PHILLIPS, 25 STONE

Down

1 BROOME, 2 ANNA, 3 CLAY,
4 ASKEY, 5 MACKENZIE, 6 CROSBY,
9 SNOOD, 11 RIN TIN TIN, 13 DAD,
15 FLYNN, 16 JOSEPH, 18 EMPIRE,
19 SELLA, 21 LAPP, 22 DUST

No. 63

Across

1 SAINT-SAENS, 8 O'HANLON,
9 EDGAR, 10 TYUS, 11 VEAL,
12 ROD, 14 URANUS, 15 ROUBLE,
18 SPA, 20 AYIA, 21 NAPA,
23 REARD, 24 CHARLIE,
25 MONTGOMERY

Down

1 SCAPULA, 2 IDLE, 3 TUNNEY,
4 A BELL FOR, 5 NIGER, 6 SOUTH
UTSIRE, 7 BRIDGEWATER,
13 TURANDOT, 16 BRADLEY,
17 JIPCHO, 19 ADANO, 22 KALE

No. 64

Across

1 THE GODS, 7 ABDUL, 8 ANDRIES,
9 ROBERT, 11 TIBIA, 13 SAVA,
14 OF GUILT, 15 ETON, 16 OPIUM,
17 HOBART, 21 MOSES IN,
22 QADIR, 23 MESSINA

Down

2 HENNIE OTTO, 3 GARRISON,
4 DREY, 5 EBRO, 6 EURE, 9 ROBIN,
10 REVOLUTION, 12 EGYPT,
13 STEPHENS, 18 BEAN, 19 REID,
20 ROSE

No. 65

Across

1 ASCOT, 4 SWEDE, 10 ISERE,
11 MO FARAH, 12 HONOLULU,
13 X-MEN, 15 COGGAN, 17 A MAN
OF, 19 MOTO, 20 NIARCHOS,
23 ROWLING, 24 SALEM, 25 NYLON,
26 PARTS

Down

2 STEIN, 3 OVERLOAD, 5 WEFT,
6 DARKMAN, 7 NIGHTCOMERS,
8 SMALL, 9 THINK FAST MR,
14 AMBROSIA, 16 GETAWAY,
18 WINGS, 21 HOLST, 22 FILO

No. 66

Across

6 TRIGONOMETRY, 8 JARHEAD,
9 BUZZI, 10 KEEP, 12 BLITHE,
14 TOPOL, 15 SPIRIT, 16 TOJO,
19 ACCRA, 21 BELUSHI, 22 THE
INNOCENTS

Down

1 DISRAELI, 2 TOWER, 3 GOUDA,
4 NETBALL, 5 CRUZ, 6 TAJIKISTAN,
7 VILE BODIES, 11 LOT, 12 BOW,
13 THOUSAND, 14 TITANIA,
17 EBONY, 18 BLACK, 20 COHN

No. 67

Across

3 GREENWICH, 8 AMOS,
9 FALMOUTH, 10 EAST OF,
13 ALL IS, 14 STRANGE, 15 SET,
16 ETRURIA, 17 OMEGA, 21 EUCLID,
22 CAROUSEL, 23 EDEN,
24 L'ESTRANGE

Down

1 SAFE HAVEN, 2 ROESELARE,
4 RUFFE, 5 ELLIOTT, 6 WOOD,
7 CATT, 11 INTERLUDE,
12 GERALDINE, 14 SEA, 15 SILESIA,
18 ZELIG, 19 PAGE, 20 LOST

No. 68

Across

1 MOORE, 7 ROSE BOWL, 8 DURAN,
10 MAURITANIA, 12 EXORCIST,
14 EDGE, 16 BEEF, 17 OR SALMON,
20 VERSAILLES, 23 SCOTT,
24 RANDOLPH, 25 IMRIE

Down

1 MADAME, 2 REAM, 3 BOHR,
4 HEATH, 5 JOHN ADAMS, 6 PLEASE,
9 NANCY, 11 HOMEFRONT, 13 SIR,
15 CAPES, 16 BOVARY, 18 NETTLE,
19 CAPON, 21 LUPU, 22 SCUM

No. 69

Across

1 THE TITANIC, 8 AIRDRIE,
9 CURSE, 10 DAIN, 11 BORS, 12 NIN,
14 CAGNEY, 15 HERMES, 18 PIP,
20 NEON, 21 AYER, 23 RAISE,
24 ASHANTI, 25 STONEHENGE

Down

1 TURNING, 2 EZRA, 3 IRETON,
4 ALCESTER, 5 IMRAN, 6 HAYDOCK
PARK, 7 DENNIS BRAIN,
13 HEINLEIN, 16 MAYENNE,
17 POTASH, 19 POINT, 22 KHAN

No. 70

Across

1 KRISTEN, 7 MOVIE, 8 PUSHKIN,
9 BRATBY, 11 SHEBA, 13 NOOL,
14 REBECCA, 15 WEST, 16 RIPON,
17 OTTAWA, 21 NAMIBIA, 22 MOVIE,
23 CORYPHA

Down

2 ROUGH QUEST, 3 SCHUBERT,
4 ERIN, 5 HOUR, 6 MINT, 9 BLACK,
10 BROCKOVICH, 12 MBIRA,
13 NATIVITY, 18 TRON, 19 WIIG,
20 FARO

No. 71

Across

1 RUMER, 4 ADIGE, 10 LOUSE,
11 SHALLOT, 12 SEALYHAM,
13 RHYL, 15 GROGAN, 17 GODDEN,
19 ROPE, 20 TERIYAKI, 23 OREILLY,
24 EWING, 25 OSAGE, 26 SOUSA

Down

2 UVULA, 3 EVERYMAN, 5 DRAM,
6 GALAHAD, 7 FLASH GORDON,
8 ASLAN, 9 AT BLANDINGS,
14 SOLIMENO, 16 ORPHEUS,
18 BEUYS, 21 ARIES, 22 CLOG

No. 72

Across

6 THOMAS DEKKER, 8 ELECTRA,
9 NEMEA, 10 APIA, 12 PISCES,
14 NOLAN, 15 LUMLEY, 16 FINN,
19 AWDRY, 21 HOLIDAY, 22 GEORGE
ORWELL

Down

1 NOBELIUM, 2 WAITZ, 3 ADDAX,
4 A KING IN, 5 BEEM, 6 THE
RAILWAY, 7 RASSENDYLL, 11 HOY,
12 PAN, 13 CHILDREN, 14 NEW
YORK, 17 SHREW, 18 CLARK,
20 DIER

No. 73

Across

3 THE FAMILY, 8 ILES, 9 CLARENCE,
10 KATICH, 13 NGENY, 14 BEZIQUE,
15 BEL, 16 OCTAGON, 17 EMILY,
21 AEGEAN, 22 SAUNDERS,
23 MUNI, 24 HYPERLINK

Down

1 DICKINSON, 2 WESTMEATH,
4 HECHT, 5 FRANKEL, 6 MEEK,
7 LACY, 11 EQUISETUM, 12 VERY
ANNIE, 14 BEN, 15 BOSWELL,
18 MASON, 19 MARY, 20 KNEE

No. 74

Across

1 SZABO, 7 CHARCOAL, 8 UNCAS,
10 GARY PLAYER, 12 STAKEOUT,
14 HUON, 16 SIRK, 17 BARNABAS,
20 LEDERHOSEN, 23 SITKA, 24 SINN
FEIN, 25 PEACH

Down

1 STUBBS, 2 BRAG, 3 WHEY,
4 KRILL, 5 TONY TUBBS, 6 FLORIN,
9 SAVED, 11 CARRADINE, 13 UNA,
15 ANDES, 16 SPLASH, 18 SQUASH,
19 CROFT, 21 OTIS, 22 NIKE

No. 75

Across

1 CIRCUMFLEX, 8 CHAMOIS,
9 RAMBO, 10 DEEP, 11 PERU,
12 SIM, 14 MILTON, 15 WALKER,
18 COP, 20 NEAL, 21 UTAH,
23 LOTTO, 24 SCANDAL,
25 ZOMBIELAND

Down

1 CLAVELL, 2 RIOS, 3 UNSEEN,
4 FARQUHAR, 5 EAMES,
6 ACADEMICALS, 7 ROSMERSHOLM,
13 JOHN COBB, 16 KATYDID,
17 MASSIE, 19 POTTO, 22 BALA

No. 76

Across

1 THE TIME, 7 DEFOE, 8 JAMESON,
9 BLADES, 11 AMIES, 13 HAIR,
14 OF GLORY, 15 STEN, 16 SCORE,
17 ARGENT, 21 GUNNELL, 22 PLATH,
23 MACHINE

Down

2 HEADMASTER, 3 THE DEMON,
4 MOOG, 5 HEEL, 6 HOAD, 9 BORON,
10 ELINOR GLYN, 12 EGRET,
13 HYACINTH, 18 GILL, 19 NUTS,
20 JURA

No. 77

Across

1 PERTH, 4 CLOSE, 10 EAGLE,
11 AFGHANI, 12 SORCERER,
13 OPIK, 15 NIMBUS, 17 PERSIA,
19 HARE, 20 MICHENER,
23 GRENADA, 24 RELIC, 25 GLENN,
26 JEANE

Down

2 ELGAR, 3 THE SET-UP, 5 LUGE,
6 SHARPES, 7 WESSINGHAGE,
8 CAREY, 9 KIRKPATRICK,
14 SEAHORSE, 16 MARVELL,
18 MIDAS, 21 NOLAN, 22 MANN

No. 78

Across

6 MAUREEN O'HARA, 8 LOVE AND,
9 SHOYU, 10 WADE, 12 LIZARD,
14 MELUN, 15 SUSMAN, 16 YETI,
19 ARBUS, 21 ORANTES, 22 SKULL
BENEATH

Down

1 QUO VADIS, 2 DEGAS, 3 ANODE,
4 THE SKIN, 5 ARGO,
6 MR LEWISHAM, 7 JUDD HIRSCH,
11 SEN, 12 LUX, 13 ALEUTIAN,
14 MANSELL, 17 ZOMBA, 18 MAINE,
20 BAKU

No. 79

Across

3 TARRAGONA, 8 DEAD, 9 ROCK
DOVE, 10 ENIGMA, 13 DUBAI,
14 PONTIAC, 15 MAN, 16 MEASLES,
17 LANGE, 21 RANSOM,
22 HIBERNIA, 23 GUNN,
24 ROSEMARIE

Down

1 EDIE ADAMS, 2 CARIBBEAN,
4 ARRAN, 5 RACCOON, 6 GIDE,
7 NAVE, 11 DIONYSIUS,
12 ACKERMANN, 14 PAS,
15 MENINGA, 18 CRAXI, 19 BIKO,
20 BEDE

No. 80

Across

1 RILKE, 7 TIRAMISU, 8 THUMB,
10 PADEREWSKI, 12 FREEJACK,
14 YUAN, 16 RAPE, 17 REMEDIES,
20 HERMAN WOUK, 23 RICCI,
24 ALTAMIRA, 25 CLEGG

Down

1 RITE OF, 2 KEMP, 3 NICE,
4 CAMEL, 5 MISS JULIE, 6 DURIAN,
9 BANJO, 11 DESPERATE, 13 CUE,
15 FEMUR, 16 RAHMAN, 18 SPRING,
19 PARMA, 21 WORK, 22 KIEL

No. 81

Across

1 DEAD-NETTLE, 8 OWN GOAL,
9 SOLTI, 10 OPIE, 11 MOYA, 12 EBB,
14 ROGERS, 15 GINGER, 18 VAN,
20 TRIM, 21 OSLO, 23 RIOJA,
24 LEBLANC, 25 LAWN TENNIS

Down

1 DENNING, 2 AVON, 3 NELSON,
4 TASMANIA, 5 LILLE,
6 ROTOGRAVURE, 7 WILBERFORCE,
13 BRITTAIN, 16 GASBAGS,
17 WILLIE, 19 NDOLA, 22 OBAN

No. 82

Across

1 MCLAREN, 7 PEPYS, 8 VENISON,
9 GRAEME, 11 ESSEX, 13 MUCK,
14 TITANIC, 15 OBOE, 16 JOYCE,
17 ANGOLA, 21 MOSELLE,
22 GLASS, 23 GARLAND

Down

2 CHELSEA BUN, 3 ANISETTE,
4 EROS, 5 PEAR, 6 KYLE, 9 GRANT,
10 MACLACHLAN, 12 STUKA,
13 MCDOWELL, 18 GOLD, 19 LISA,
20 MONA

No. 83

Across

1 SWORD, 4 BEVAN, 10 CATES,
11 APOSTLE, 12 EURYDICE,
13 SONG, 15 DOLENZ, 17 UTOPIA,
19 ITMA, 20 BERT LAHR,
23 ESTEVEZ, 24 NATAL, 25 UDALL,
26 BAIRD

Down

2 WATER, 3 RESIDENT, 5 ETON,
6 ALTHORP, 7 SCREWDRIVER,
8 NANCY, 9 LEO G CARROLL,
14 STOTINKA, 16 LIMITED,
18 HENZE, 21 ASTOR, 22 EVIL

No. 84

Across

6 PLAYBOY OF THE, 8 LUALABA,
9 SMASH, 10 IRAQ, 12 ZAHEER,
14 COLES, 15 TRIPOS, 16 OPAL,
19 RIFLE, 21 EURASIA, 22 WESTERN
WORLD

Down

1 KALAHARI, 2 ABBAS, 3 WYMAN,
4 FFOS LAS, 5 RHEA, 6 PALMINTERI,
7 CHERYL LADD, 11 SOS, 12 ZEN,
13 EXPOSURE, 14 COLETTE,
17 HENRY, 18 CREWE, 20 FLEA

No. 85

Across

3 ULLSWATER, 8 ADEN,
9 O'HERLIHY, 10 BOURDY,
13 ASSEN, 14 LEPANTO, 15 CIA,
16 TROUBLE, 17 LIEGE, 21 IN MIND,
22 MUSIC MAN, 23 DILL,
24 BERKELIUM

Down

1 GALBRAITH, 2 REPULSION,
4 LLOYD, 5 SWEE'PEA, 6 AMLA,
7 ECHO, 11 ENTERITIS,
12 COVERDALE, 14 LIE,
15 CLONMEL, 18 XINGU, 19 BUTE,
20 CINK

No. 86

Across

1 DRACO, 7 BORACHIO, 8 KORAN,
10 MANDLIKOVA, 12 FARTHING,
14 IGOR, 16 SAUL, 17 SEMOLINA,
20 A RIVER RUNS, 23 ONEGA,
24 CHARTISM, 25 UPNEY

Down

1 DUKE OF, 2 CRAM, 3 GOLD,
4 FAGIN, 5 THROUGH IT, 6 MOHAIR,
9 NACHO, 11 BRAUTIGAN, 13 NYE,
15 PORNO, 16 SNATCH, 18 ALBANY,
19 PESTO, 21 RUSH, 22 SNAP

No. 87

Across

1 HOMECOMING, 8 LAROCHE,
9 CABER, 10 EMIN, 11 WEAR,
12 ANN, 14 BAGLEY, 15 CHEERS,
18 ROP, 20 GALT, 21 LYRA, 23 IBIZA,
24 MAURIAC, 25 CEREBELLUM

Down

1 HARDING, 2 MACH, 3 CHENEY,
4 MCCARTHY, 5 NUBIA, 6 ELLEN
BARKIN, 7 BRANDS HATCH,
13 BELGRADE, 16 ELYSIUM,
17 KLIMKE, 19 PRICE, 22 MULL

No. 88

Across

1 AMHARIC, 7 ANWAR, 8 TOM KING,
9 DAKOTA, 11 IFANS, 13 ODER,
14 O'CONNOR, 15 SWAN, 16 FARNE,
17 ARMAGH, 21 BALDWIN, 22 SADAT,
23 SLEEPER

Down

2 MOONFLOWER, 3 ATKINSON,
4 IONA, 5 ANOA, 6 FADO, 9 DRONE,
10 THE TONTINE, 12 NORTH,
13 ORGANDIE, 18 MOAB, 19 GOAT,
20 MARL

No. 89

Across

1 SPODE, 4 AGAMA, 10 OHNET,
11 EURYALE, 12 THE WELSH,
13 SMEW, 15 FROZEN, 17 SECRET,
19 PHIZ, 20 TREE FROG, 23 ITALIAN,
24 ALIEN, 25 RIVER, 26 WATER

Down

2 PENCE, 3 DOTTEREL, 5 GIRL,
6 MYANMAR, 7 PORT OF SPAIN,
8 KELSO, 9 MEN WITH GUNS,
14 DEMERARA, 16 ORIGAMI,
18 PRUNE, 21 RAINE, 22 VIRE

No. 90

Across

6 THE MILL ON THE, 8 ALI BABA,
9 INDRI, 10 IPOH, 12 AND THE,
14 FLOSS, 15 MUMBAI, 16 PEAT,
19 SUMAC, 21 DAWN RUN,
22 FORTY THIEVES

Down

1 BENIDORM, 2 MILAN, 3 ULSAN,
4 INDIANS, 5 CHAD, 6 TRAGIC
MUSE, 7 LIFE STINKS, 11 ELI,
12 ASS, 13 THE BRAVE, 14 FAT CITY,
17 ODETS, 18 SWAIL, 20 MOOG

No. 91

Across

3 THREE TALL, 8 LEAN, 9 SCHILLER, 10 CAROLE, 13 WOMEN, 14 LOMBARD, 15 RAY, 16 SORGHUM, 17 SEBUM, 21 MILLER, 22 CAGLIARI, 23 BOND, 24 TENNESSEE

Down

1 CLOCKWISE, 2 BARRYMORE, 4 HOSEA, 5 ECHO BOY, 6 TALC, 7 LEES, 11 CAT BALLOU, 12 ADAM BRODY, 14 LAM, 15 RUGRATS, 18 SMIKE, 19 BALE, 20 ALAN

No. 92

Across

1 GLESS, 7 LOMBARDO, 8 YOUNG, 10 GETTYSBURG, 12 AL MURRAY, 14 WHIT, 16 CORK, 17 TYMPANUM, 20 ANGRY HILLS, 23 LAVER, 24 KEIGHLEY, 25 SUSIE

Down

1 GUYANA, 2 SING, 3 COOT, 4 ABYSS, 5 CROUCH END, 6 NOUGAT, 9 GEHRY, 11 IMBRUGLIA, 13 AMY, 15 SPALL, 16 CLARKE, 18 MONROE, 19 HYTHE, 21 IDEA, 22 SABU

No. 93

Across

1 WORST WITCH, 8 OBERMAN, 9 VERDI, 10 TUTU, 11 ALPS, 12 LEL, 14 ONE DAY, 15 RIYADH, 18 EFT, 20 FORT, 21 TAMM, 23 ISERE, 24 PROVINE, 25 LAUDERDALE

Down

1 WHEN THE, 2 RIMU, 3 TENALI, 4 IZVESTIA, 5 CAROL, 6 BOAT COMES IN, 7 LILLEHAMMER, 13 GARFIELD, 16 AT A TIME, 17 DRAPER, 19 THETA, 22 COMA

No. 94

Across

1 STYRENE, 7 HOUSE, 8 WENDERS, 9 PEARCE, 11 PEARL, 13 TAEL, 14 GOULASH, 15 CHOO, 16 STASI, 17 OF KEYS, 21 KINGDOM, 22 SNIPE, 23 FLORIDA

Down

2 THE TEETH OF, 3 RODERIGO, 4 NORD, 5 LOVE, 6 YSER, 9 PRIAM, 10 CHELMSFORD, 12 HURTS, 13 THE TIGER, 18 KING, 19 YIPS, 20 DILL

No. 95

Across

1 IDOWU, 4 HEART, 10 DURAN, 11 MORAVIA, 12 MARRINER, 13 TOFU, 15 DUFNER, 17 SHRIMP, 19 MARK, 20 CIPRIANI, 23 NEVILLE, 24 MUNGO, 25 BROWN, 26 ANGEL

Down

2 DURER, 3 WINNIPEG, 5 EZRA, 6 RAVIOLI, 7 ADAM ADAMANT, 8 AMBER, 9 KABUMPO IN OZ, 14 THEREMIN, 16 FOREVER, 18 LIVES!, 21 ANNIE, 22 BLOW

No. 96

Across

6 THE MYSTERY OF, 8 ESCOLAR, 9 GABOR, 10 NAVE, 12 RAMEAU, 14 PAVEY, 15 LILLAK, 16 ELBA, 19 SUSHI, 21 TIPURIC, 22 GUINEA-BISSAU

Down

1 PERCEVAL, 2 MYALL, 3 STARK, 4 URUGUAY, 5 COBB, 6 THE ENGLISH, 7 DR FU MANCHU, 11 OAK, 12 REA, 13 EELGRASS, 14 PATIENT, 17 ATLAS, 18 SPLIT, 20 SAUL

No. 97

Across

3 SHADOW OF A, 8 REUS,
9 HAMILTON, 10 MORGAN,
13 DOUBT, 14 CENTAVO, 15 EID,
16 RIHANNA, 17 GREEN,
21 ARTHUR, 22 HOROWITZ, 23 PALK,
24 FAIRCHILD

Down

1 DROMEDARY, 2 BURROUGHS,
4 HUHNE, 5 DAMAGED, 6 WILT,
7 FOOT, 11 GATESHEAD,
12 CORNCRAKE, 14 CIA,
15 ENGLISH, 18 HAZEL, 19 ZOLA,
20 HOUR

No. 98

Across

1 GULES, 7 MCINTYRE, 8 ORLOP,
10 REPENTANCE, 12 ROAD KILL,
14 COOL, 16 WADE, 17 HELM WIND,
20 DAN MASKELL, 23 LUCAS,
24 ED KALMAN, 25 BENIN

Down

1 GLOVER, 2 EBOR, 3 OCHE,
4 ANITA, 5 MY ANTONIA, 6 LE VELL,
9 PERKY, 11 KANDINSKY, 13 LIE,
15 SMALL, 16 WADDEN, 18 DOBSON,
19 WALL-E, 21 KEAN, 22 LUGE

No. 99

Across

1 SAMOTHRACE, 8 RAISING,
9 PINGU, 10 NOTT, 11 AINU, 12 CUT,
14 GRUDGE, 15 DOUALA, 18 RIB,
20 RAPE, 21 BEDE, 23 RIOJA,
24 ARIZONA, 25 NOLAN HENKE

Down

1 SHIATSU, 2 MUIR, 3 TIGRIS,
4 RAPE UPON, 5 CYNIC, 6 BRUNO
GIRARD, 7 PUNTA ARENAS,
13 AGARTALA, 16 ADEFOPE,
17 SPLASH, 19 BUONO, 22 FIEN

No. 100

Across

1 BARRATT, 7 MARTY, 8 FELDMAN,
9 KUNG FU, 11 LARRY, 13 DEAD,
14 SEATTLE, 15 KRIS, 16 GALLE,
17 FAMOUS, 21 VAN OOST,
22 DAVID, 23 JARRETT

Down

2 ALEXANDRIA, 3 RED CROSS,
4 TEAK, 5 BAKU, 6 STAG, 9 KEITH,
10 FRANZ LISZT, 12 MARKS,
13 DE LA TOUR, 18 MEAD, 19 UGIE,
20 MARA

No. 101

Across

1 ELGIN, 4 PARMA, 10 PORNO,
11 LAUTNER, 12 ROADSIDE,
13 AGES, 15 SACRED, 17 HEARTS,
19 FOOL, 20 THE NIGHT, 23 LES
PAUL, 24 LILLE, 25 OSAKA,
26 OXEYE

Down

2 LORCA, 3 I MOBSTER, 5 ARUM,
6 MANAGER, 7 IPCRESS FILE,
8 BLADE, 9 IRISH SETTER, 14 AEON
FLUX, 16 CROSSES, 18 CHILE,
21 GULLY, 22 DARK

No. 102

Across

6 MUST LOVE DOGS, 8 TENNANT,
9 IMRIE, 10 EDIE, 12 ANG LEE,
14 FALCO, 15 RENFRO, 16 GNAT,
19 NAGLE, 21 GAMBOGE,
22 QUADRAGESIMA

Down

1 ASUNCION, 2 ELWAY, 3 OVETT,
4 ADRIANO, 5 AGAR,
6 MITTERRAND, 7 DEMENTIEVA,
11 LAO, 12 ACE, 13 LENA OLIN,
14 FRIENDS, 17 OGHAM, 18 EMMEN,
20 GLUE

No. 103

Across

3 MY SISTER'S, **8** EBRO, **9** ACCIDENT, **10** KEEPER, **13** BARON, **14** SOPRANO, **15** EAR, **16** RECORDS, **17** COHEN, **21** LIOTTA, **22** CADILLAC, **23** DAVE, **24** SUNNYSIDE

Down

1 TEWKSBURY, **2** FRIEDRICH, **4** YEARS, **5** INCISOR, **6** TIDY, **7** RING, **11** MANHATTAN, **12** MOONRAKER, **14** SAS, **15** ED BALLS, **18** EL CID, **19** OAHU, **20** FINN

No. 104

Across

1 WHORL, **7** BARATHEA, **8** GOGOL, **10** KOOKABURRA, **12** ROAD TO OZ, **14** SOSA, **16** WICK, **17** ATLANTIC, **20** EGDON HEATH, **23** HEROD, **24** EYE LEVEL, **25** CANDY

Down

1 WAGNER, **2** ROOK, **3** WARK, **4** DARBY, **5** CHARLOTTE, **6** PARANA, **9** LOTTO, **11** NANCY DREW, **13** OAT, **15** EARTH, **16** WEEKES, **18** CORDAY, **19** UNGER, **21** EDEN, **22** HERA

No. 105

Across

1 JOHN BRAINE, **8** ALCAZAR, **9** EDDIE, **10** ELSA, **11** WEBB, **12** LOE, **14** MANTLE, **15** SCHALK, **18** RUE, **20** EARL, **21** PAUL, **23** AWDRY, **24** IVY TREE, **25** BRASSED OFF

Down

1 JACKSON, **2** HEZE, **3** BURGER, **4** AUERBACH, **5** NADAL, **6** JANET MORGAN, **7** HELEN KELLER, **13** BLUE EYES, **16** A PAIR OF, **17** IRVINE, **19** ELDER, **22** NYRO

No. 106

Across

1 PHYSICS, **7** NIGHT, **8** BLONDIN, **9** PANAMA, **11** SOFIA, **13** WATT, **14** GIRL ON A, **15** ALTO, **16** BLACK, **17** CYGNET, **21** REBECCA, **22** IVORY, **23** CHAGAEV

Down

2 HELLO DOLLY!, **3** SAN DIEGO, **4** CHIP, **5** LIRA, **6** RHEA, **9** PHLOX, **10** MOTORCYCLE, **12** FROST, **13** WAHLBERG, **18** GOVE, **19** EYRE, **20** SETH

No. 107

Across

1 O'SHEA, **4** MAYBE, **10** AIOLI, **11** MOSELLE, **12** NORQUIST, **13** WEFT, **15** CERIUM, **17** RANKIN, **19** BABY, **20** FLORIZEL, **23** REREDOS, **24** SKINK, **25** ASARI, **26** ENCKE

Down

2 STOUR, **3** EPICURUS, **5** APSE, **6** BELLEEK, **7** BANNOCKBURN, **8** SMASH, **9** SEXTON BLAKE, **14** HARRISON, **16** ROBERTS, **18** FLUSH, **21** ZWICK, **22** EDER

No. 108

Across

6 ONE TRUE THING, **8** SWORD OF, **9** ADAMS, **10** EDIE, **12** OLATHE, **14** JOULE, **15** HONOUR, **16** BEEM, **19** IZMIT, **21** ANTHONY, **22** SIX FEET UNDER

Down

1 DEVOTION, **2** PRIDE, **3** DELFT, **4** CHEADLE, **5** INCA, **6** OOSTERHUIS, **7** OSTERMEYER, **11** DOR, **12** OLD, **13** THE WOODS, **14** JUSTIFY, **17** CAPER, **18** STOUT, **20** MAID

No. 109

Across

3 THE ROSE OF, 8 AVRO,
9 ANDERSON, 10 SUMMER,
13 JONES, 14 GONZALO, 15 WAX,
16 HOLIDAY, 17 LENIN, 21 PERSIA,
22 CAROTENE, 23 JUHA,
24 KANKKUNEN

Down

1 IAN ST JOHN, 2 FREMANTLE,
4 HEARD, 5 RUDEBOX, 6 SARK,
7 OMOO, 11 MAGNESIUM,
12 YOUNG ADAM, 14 GAY,
15 WATTEAU, 18 SPEKE, 19 TARA,
20 PORK

No. 110

Across

1 HITCH, 7 VOLUMNIA, 8 GIANT,
10 THE NIGHT OF, 12 SCHNAPPS,
14 LEVY, 16 HAIR, 17 HEREWARD,
20 MAURITANIA, 23 AHMED,
24 LONG JUMP, 25 IBSEN

Down

1 HAGGIS, 2 CANT, 3 JOHN,
4 PURGE, 5 AND THE MAN,
6 BARFLY, 9 THIAM, 11 THE IGUANA,
13 POE, 15 SEPIA, 16 HAMILL,
18 DRYDEN, 19 NINJA, 21 ARMS,
22 AHAB

No. 111

Across

1 MACPHERSON, 8 HEIRESS,
9 HAITI, 10 MARR, 11 BEBB, 12 RAT,
14 DUTTON, 15 ZANDER, 18 IFE,
20 DEAL, 21 BAUM, 23 HERNE,
24 ATOM ANT, 25 SEERSUCKER

Down

1 MAIGRET, 2 CLEA, 3 HOSTEL,
4 REHOBOAM, 5 OSIER, 6 THE
MIDNIGHT, 7 WINTERSMITH,
13 GOODYEAR, 16 DEAD AIR,
17 XANADU, 19 EARLE, 22 FOLK

No. 112

Across

1 CRICKET, 7 AT THE, 8 SNOOKER,
9 A NIGHT, 11 ALESI, 13 BYNG,
14 NEPTUNE, 15 SWAG, 16 ELGAR,
17 MYOPIA, 21 WALCOTT, 22 CEJKA,
23 SAVIANO

Down

2 RONALDSWAY, 3 CROSSING,
4 EPEE, 5 ETON, 6 WHIG, 9 ADOUR,
10 HUNSTANTON, 12 OPERA,
13 BELLUCCI, 18 OVER, 19 ICKX,
20 RATA

No. 113

Across

1 SPARK, 4 BECKY, 10 HAPPY,
11 BRAILLE, 12 KEY LARGO,
13 CYAN, 15 SEDDON, 17 RETURN,
19 EHLE, 20 PHILLIPS, 23 RAINIER,
24 OKAYO, 25 MAINZ, 26 UTZON

Down

2 POPPY, 3 ROY MASON, 5 EDAM,
6 KELLY HU, 7 SHAKESPEARE,
8 UBOGU, 9 HENNINGSSON,
14 BELLWORT, 16 DULCIMA,
18 SHARP, 21 IDAHO, 22 SIAN

No. 114

Across

6 PAUL WHITEMAN, 8 ORLANDO,
9 O'HARA, 10 SHAG, 12 DOMBEY,
14 RODIN, 15 AND SON, 16 KALI,
19 KOALA, 21 ARUNDEL, 22 PAULA
SPENCER

Down

1 VUILLARD, 2 SWANN, 3 DIJON,
4 PELOTON, 5 PAPA, 6 POOL
SHARKS, 7 LADY KILLER, 11 TON,
12 DIX, 13 BRADDOCK, 14 ROUAULT,
17 MARSH, 18 LUMEN, 20 AJAX

No. 115

Across

3 FULLALOVE, **8** HAKE, **9** BISCAYNE,
10 GAGGLE, **13** LA RUE, **14** TRIPOLI,
15 BAY, **16** URANIUM, **17** BUENO,
21 FORMIC, **22** PUTUMAYO,
23 POLK, **24** AXMINSTER

Down

1 BHAGALPUR, **2** SKAGERRAK,
4 UMBER, **5** LA STORY, **6** LEAD,
7 VINE, **11** HONEYMOON,
12 NINOTCHKA, **14** TAM,
15 BUSMAN'S, **18** AFOBE,
19 QUAX, **20** PULI

No. 116

Across

1 AXTON, **7** RUSH HOUR, **8** ROCCA,
10 A GOOD MAN IN, **12** ASHENDEN,
14 HOWE, **16** BOSS, **17** DEPARTED,
20 EUCALYPTUS, **23** SLATE,
24 MENANDER, **25** BETEL

Down

1 AFRICA, **2** ORCA, **3** SUMO,
4 THYME, **5** GOIN' SOUTH,
6 ORANGE, **9** AGENT, **11** THE
SECOND, **13** EVE, **15** TAGUS,
16 BREHME, **18** DOWELL,
19 PLANE, **21** PUEL, **22** SLOE

No. 117

Across

1 FAR AND AWAY, **8** HOWLING,
9 LYNCH, **10** ABEL, **11** ANOA,
12 SOH, **14** EXTRAS, **15** CLOSER,
18 ICC, **20** TRIM, **21** ONCE, **23** ARIES,
24 BRENTON, **25** SPENNYMOOR

Down

1 FAWCETT, **2** RIIS, **3** NAGANO,
4 'ALLO 'ALLO, **5** ANNUS, **6** THE
AMERICAN, **7** THE HORSE AND,
13 MATTESON, **16** SENATOR,
17 HIS BOY, **19** CRISP, **22** PETO

No. 118

Across

1 ZWILICH, **7** SAROS, **8** FITZROY,
9 FERRIC, **11** SELMA, **13** DOTT,
14 THE WIRE, **15** LEAH, **16** BIXBY,
17 IN TIME, **21** JOHNSON, **22** OXIDE,
23 ALLENDE

Down

2 WHITE QUEEN, **3** LIZ SMITH,
4 COOK, **5** ZALE, **6** BOAR, **9** FAGIN,
10 IN THE BLOOD, **12** KEBLE,
13 DEFIANCE, **18** TAXI, **19** MIDI,
20 BOLL

No. 119

Across

3 DELFTWARE, **8** DOHA, **9** HOLLIDAY,
10 IAN URE, **13** GIRLS, **14** BASENJI,
15 BEN, **16** ONLY DAD, **17** MAGOG,
21 ANSTEY, **22** CATALANI, **23** HEEL,
24 CANDLEMAS

Down

1 ADDINGTON, **2** SHANGRI-LA,
4 ETHER, **5** FELDMAN, **6** WIIG,
7 RYAN, **11** KNIGHTLEY, **12** RING
CYCLE, **14** BED, **15** BABBAGE,
18 NAIRA, **19** JAVA, **20** HARD

No. 120

Across

6 THE UNNAMABLE, **8** ECKHART,
9 PUNCH, **10** HOAD, **12** LILLEE,
14 BOWEN, **15** NANSEN, **16** RAAB,
19 NOLAN, **21** MACCHIO, **22** MEET
JOE BLACK

Down

1 BECKMANN, **2** SNEAD, **3** WALTZ,
4 DAUPHIN, **5** ALAN, **6** THE SHINING,
7 UHLENBROEK, **11** DON, **12** LEW,
13 LEACHMAN, **14** BENNETT,
17 AMMON, **18** SCUBA, **20** LEEK

No. 121

Across

3 BLEASDALE, 8 OBOE, 9 ATLANTIS,
10 ECCLES, 13 RUSSO,
14 RAMAALA, 15 JAY,
16 CAESIUM, 17 MCKAY,
21 LUGOSI, 22 CORALINE, 23 BELL,
24 DEGENERES

Down

1 BONECRACK, 2 DONCASTER,
4 LHASA, 5 ALLOWAY, 6 DINE, 7 LOIT,
11 RAIKKONEN, 12 BABYVILLE,
14 RAM, 15 JUSTINE, 18 GLEBE,
19 FOXE, 20 CAKE

No. 122

Across

1 ISLAY, 7 LOVELACE, 8 LUMET,
10 RUBINSTEIN, 12 DEAD CALM,
14 LIES, 16 EIGG, 17 WILL SELF,
20 PARMENTIER, 23 SALOP,
24 ROUGH CUT, 25 SANDY

Down

1 INLAND, 2 AYER, 3 GOBI, 4 YEAST,
5 PALE RIDER, 6 DENNIS, 9 TUCCI,
11 DANGEROUS, 13 LEI, 15 FLIES,
16 EMPIRE, 18 FURPHY, 19 LETHE,
21 TRUE, 22 RAGA

No. 123

Across

1 MENECRATES, 8 OUR TOWN,
9 IBIZA, 10 ERIE, 11 LION, 12 TUI,
14 LUNGHI, 15 LIEBIG, 18 NAP,
20 ARAL, 21 ANNA, 23 EGRET,
24 CROATIA, 25 NANCY LOPEZ

Down

1 MARTIAN, 2 NEON, 3 CON AIR,
4 ALIENS IN, 5 ELIOT,
6 HOHENLINDEN, 7 DAVID GRAHAM,
13 THE ATTIC, 16 BENITEZ,
17 PASCAL, 19 PARRA, 22 SOAP

No. 124

Across

1 THE BLUE, 7 JOLIE, 8 MORALES,
9 LAGOON, 11 JERRY, 13 VIOL,
14 CROSBIE, 15 JETE, 16 UDINE,
17 FLYING, 21 WOOSNAM, 22 LEWIS,
23 COLOURS

Down

2 HOODED SEAL, 3 BEATRICE,
4 UBER, 5 ROTA, 6 NINO, 9 LIMBO,
10 ONOCENTAUR, 12 YOUNG,
13 VERDASCO, 18 YLEM, 19 NEIL,
20 TOJO

No. 125

Across

1 ABACA, 4 KRILL, 10 EVITA,
11 REBECCA, 12 RESPIGHI,
13 JUDD, 15 CLAESZ, 17 CLARKE,
19 OKRA, 20 BEST MATE,
23 EUPHUES, 24 HEVER, 25 PARKS,
26 FRONT

Down

2 BLISS, 3 CHARISSE, 5 ROBE,
6 LACQUER, 7 HENRY COOPER,
8 BRAHE, 9 CANDLEBERRY,
14 FLETCHER, 16 AGRIPPA,
18 ZEISS, 21 AH VAN, 22 JUNK

No. 126

Across

6 THE RIME OF THE, 8 ANCIENT,
9 IMOLA, 10 ELLA, 12 AGADIR,
14 BRASS, 15 HUSSAR, 16 FIRM,
19 ROOTS, 21 MARINER, 22 STATE
OF GRACE

Down

1 HERCULES, 2 PIVEN, 3 DEATH,
4 OF KINGS, 5 OHIO, 6 TRADER
HORN, 7 BARRY MORSE, 11 ORR,
12 ASH, 13 DOISNEAU, 14 BASSETT,
17 AMBON, 18 BRAGG, 20 OKTA

No. 127

Across

3 THE FOURTH, 8 ROUS,
9 SPANDREL, 10 SPHERE,
13 DEATH, 14 REARDON, 15 PAR,
16 RITCHIE, 17 FALLS, 21 OLDHAM,
22 PROTOCOL, 23 LOVE,
24 UNNATURAL

Down

1 CRUSADERS, 2 OUTHWAITE,
4 HASEK, 5 FRAZIER, 6 URDU,
7 TEES, 11 ADULTHOOD, 12 AND
SUMMER, 14 RAE, 15 PIKACHU,
18 POLKA, 19 BRON, 20 ETNA

No. 128

Across

1 PETER, 7 PAGO PAGO, 8 REGIS,
10 NALBANDIAN, 12 ETHIOPIA,
14 DURY, 16 BOMA, 17 NAZARETH,
20 PAGEMASTER, 23 LEIGH,
24 RAINTREE, 25 JONES

Down

1 PIRATE, 2 EMIN, 3 LAMB, 4 MOUNT,
5 LATITUDES, 6 COUNTY, 9 SAXON,
11 THE MAGGIE, 13 IDA, 15 CAPEL,
16 BOPARA, 18 HUGHES, 19 SMUTS,
21 SPEY, 22 RENO

No. 129

Across

1 CALICO JACK, 8 HAMMOND,
9 NKOMO, 10 SILK, 11 CUJO,
12 YEN, 14 O'NEILL, 15 LIFFEY,
18 LOT, 20 MOAB, 21 SLUG,
23 ROBIN, 24 DERWENT, 25 WAY
OUT WEST

Down

1 CAMILLE, 2 LOOS, 3 CADMUS,
4 JANKOVIC, 5 COODY, 6 THE
SPOILERS, 7 JOHN LYDGATE,
13 FLAMENCO, 16 FILBERT,
17 BARDOT, 19 TIBIA, 22 BRIE

No. 130

Across

1 MCVICAR, 7 ROCHE, 8 BRITTON,
9 FRESNO, 11 JAMES, 13 LOWE,
14 NAIROBI, 15 BOND, 16 FRANK,
17 AGATHA, 21 MAGINOT,
22 BRUNO, 23 PHARYNX

Down

2 CARLA'S SONG, 3 IS THE END,
4 AMOS, 5 SOAR, 6 THIS, 9 FLOOD,
10 NEWTON-JOHN, 12 PINTA,
13 LIAR LIAR, 18 AIRE, 19 HAND,
20 BATH

No. 131

Across

1 LYNCH, 4 BLACK, 10 LAKER,
11 DESIREE, 12 VANISHED, 13 ALAN,
15 ALLIER, 17 DAVIES, 19 LELY,
20 DEEMSTER, 23 COQUITO,
24 REBEC, 25 KEACH, 26 CLARK

Down

2 YUKON, 3 CHRYSLER, 5 LOSS,
6 CORELLI, 7 OLIVIA'S LUCK,
8 ADLER, 9 DENNIS PRICE,
14 BALMORAL, 16 LALIQUE,
18 DEFOE, 21 TIBER, 22 ZINC

No. 132

Across

6 THE INVENTION, 8 OF LYING,
9 WELCH, 10 HA-HA, 12 BROWNE,
14 ASYUT, 15 ARRACK, 16 FRAM,
19 RYDER, 21 BALDWIN, 22 GRAY
LADY DOWN

Down

1 KELLEHER, 2 ENNIS, 3 WEDGE,
4 STEWART, 5 KOHL, 6 TOOTH
FAIRY, 7 THREE MEN IN, 11 USK,
12 BUG, 13 WORMWOOD,
14 ACKROYD, 17 A BOAT, 18 FLOYD,
20 DORE

No. 133

Across

3 SASQUATCH, 8 ASHE,
9 YEARLING, 10 LOVERS, 13 ROYAL,
14 ATHLETE, 15 SLY, 16 ARUWIMI,
17 MICAH, 21 CLARKE,
22 BARDOLPH, 23 HEBE,
24 A MURDER OF

Down

1 KARL URBAN, 2 THE VOYEUR,
4 ABYSS, 5 QUALITY, 6 AMLA,
7 CANA, 11 GET CARTER,
12 BETHLEHEM, 14 ALI, 15 SMILLIE,
18 SCHIO, 19 HAMM, 20 ODER

No. 134

Across

1 GOTHA, 7 MINOTAUR, 8 BLAIR,
10 GO, JOHNNY, GO!, 12 NEAR
EAST, 14 MEAD, 16 SOCK,
17 HONECKER, 20 A MAN OF MARK,
23 TASSO, 24 INKHEART, 25 PAULO

Down

1 GIBSON, 2 HAIG, 3 DIDO,
4 POUND, 5 DAVYDENKO,
6 ARNOLD, 9 ROGER,
11 KAMCHATKA, 13 SAO, 15 PEART,
16 SPAVIN, 18 ROCOCO, 19 ROGER,
21 MORE, 22 KAYA

No. 135

Across

1 GEORGE BEST, 8 ANALYZE,
9 RELKO, 10 MIAS, 11 LOVE, 12 MEE,
14 REAGAN, 15 BURTON, 18 MAD,
20 THAT, 21 REAM, 23 TENOR,
24 WINDOWS, 25 THE FIGHTER

Down

1 GRANADA, 2 ORYX, 3 GRENOT,
4 BORDEAUX, 5 SALEM,
6 HAMMERSMITH, 7 LOVE-IN-A-MIST,
13 MASTER OF, 16 THE MOOR,
17 EARWIG, 19 DENCH, 22 KNOT

No. 136

Across

1 BASTEDO, 7 CLEAN, 8 JEZEBEL,
9 PELOSI, 11 SOUTH, 13 CINK,
14 NARWHAL, 15 BEND, 16 PRAWN,
17 DOWNIE, 21 CUSSLER,
22 BREAK, 23 DENNESS

Down

2 ALEX OLMEDO, 3 THE STAND,
4 DEEP, 5 BLUE, 6 IAGO, 9 PATHE,
10 SUNDOWNERS, 12 BRIDE,
13 CLARKSON, 18 WARS, 19 IMAX,
20 LUTE

No. 137

Across

1 BRICE, 4 SHAFT, 10 URIEL,
11 QUARRIE, 12 THE FINAL,
13 FOUR, 15 RECIPE, 17 TE DEUM,
19 OVAL, 20 SOLUTION,
23 TEMPURA, 24 OLIVE, 25 ANGLE,
26 STYNE

Down

2 RAINE, 3 CALLIOPE, 5 HEAD,
6 FOR LOVE, 7 BUTTERWORTH,
8 SQUAB, 9 RETROMANCER,
14 BEAUMONT, 16 CHAPMAN,
18 WOTAN, 21 IXION, 22 HULL

No. 138

Across

6 EVENT HORIZON, 8 STEPHEN,
9 SOCHI, 10 ELLA, 12 LORENZ,
14 COHEN, 15 DENHAM,
16 CREE, 19 OLAND, 21 INIESTA,
22 NEWFOUNDLAND

Down

1 MEDELLIN, 2 STAHL, 3 YOUNG,
4 WINSTON, 5 BOSC,
6 EISTEDDFOD, 7 FITZGERALD,
11 LOM, 12 LEE, 13 EARNSHAW,
14 CARDIFF, 17 KIRUI, 18 BIRDY,
20 ABEL

No. 139

Across

3 THE BUCKET, **8** SPIN, **9** SORORITY, **10** ALWAYS, **13** BLUFF, **14** COOGAN'S, **15** ROW, **16** SPECIES, **17** AURIC, **21** OROZCO, **22** SICILIAN, **23** CLIO, **24** STAYING ON

Down

1 ISAAC BOSS, **2** MILWAUKEE, **4** HESSE, **5** BARSTOW, **6** CARS, **7** EFTA, **11** PATRIZ ILG, **12** PSYCHO TOO, **14** COS, **15** REUNION, **18** BONGO, **19** LIST, **20** CITY

No. 140

Across

1 JOPPY, **7** DALADIER, **8** LIARD, **10** MR MAJESTYK, **12** THE THREE, **14** DEAN, **16** ODIN, **17** BUDAPEST, **20** FACES OF EVE, **23** AISNE, **24** ROELANTS, **25** LEVET

Down

1 JULIET, **2** PERM, **3** NAHA, **4** NAKED, **5** LITTLE MEN, **6** WREKIN, **9** DRAHM, **11** BEWITCHED, **13** EMU, **15** NARVA, **16** OXFORD, **18** TALENT, **19** ASLAN, **21** FITT, **22** EIRE

No. 141

Across

1 THE BURNING, **8** ERITREA, **9** HYDRA, **10** LUFT, **11** WURM, **12** RYE, **14** RAFTER, **15** BAOBAB, **18** VA'A, **20** LAND, **21** CRAB, **23** ROSSI, **24** TRIREME, **25** SPEECHLESS

Down

1 THIEF OF, **2** EYRE, **3** URANUS, **4** NEHEMIAH, **5** NADIR, **6** HELL DRIVERS, **7** WATER-BABIES, **13** VERLAINE, **16** BURGESS, **17** SNATCH, **19** AESOP, **22** TIME

No. 142

Across

1 DR SEUSS, **7** CUTTY, **8** ANDORRA, **9** BOURDY, **11** BIRCH, **13** ADEN, **14** STEVENS, **15** SMIT, **16** KNOCK, **17** ON WOOD, **21** O BRIAIN, **22** NIGEL, **23** KENNEDY

Down

2 RUNNING MAN, **3** EXORCIST, **4** SARK, **5** JUNO, **6** STAR, **9** BAKER, **10** DREAMCHILD, **12** WEALD, **13** ASUNCION, **18** WEIR, **19** OWEN, **20** ABBE

No. 143

Across

1 U-BOAT, **4** OKAPI, **10** HOTEL, **11** ARTEMIS, **12** MCKENZIE, **13** CEDI, **15** GATLIN, **17** LILITH, **19** COBB, **20** SCRIABIN, **23** ORLANDO, **24** TULLE, **25** ARIEL, **26** BREST

Down

2 BATIK, **3** ATLANTIC, **5** KITE, **6** POMPEII, **7** THE MAGIC BOX, **8** MAGIC, **9** ASHIA HANSEN, **14** SINISTER, **16** TUBULAR, **18** ICHOR, **21** BELLS, **22** INGE

No. 144

Across

6 HARRIET CRAIG, **8** AGUILAR, **9** FURYK, **10** TYRE, **12** SIRIUS, **14** PILIC, **15** BRUTUS, **16** DEAR, **19** ALLAH, **21** BUS STOP, **22** JUNIOR WITTER

Down

1 FROUFROU, **2** BILLY, **3** START!, **4** TRAFFIC, **5** LIAR, **6** HEARTS BEAT, **7** SKYSCRAPER, **11** DIS, **12** SIM, **13** IDENTITY, **14** PUSHKIN, **17** ABERA, **18** ASTIN, **20** LOUD

No. 145

Across

3 THE WINTER, 8 VENN, 9 LIGURIAN,
10 REMORA, 13 BANDA,
14 TIEPOLO, 15 TAL, 16 DENNEHY,
17 MARSH, 21 GHOSTS,
22 TITICACA, 23 GERE,
24 WELSHPOOL

Down

1 EVERYBODY, 2 ANT-MAN AND,
4 HALAS, 5 WAGTAIL, 6 N OR M?,
7 EL AL, 11 MORRISSEY,
12 ROCHESTER, 14 TAY, 15 THE
WASP, 18 NGAIO, 19 NICE, 20 WINS

No. 146

Across

1 YONNE, 7 KOHLRABI, 8 UNCAS,
10 HER FEARFUL, 12 SYMMETRY,
14 BOER, 16 MARR, 17 HAREBELL,
20 RICK ASTLEY, 23 YOUNG,
24 HONEYDEW, 25 WAQAR

Down

1 YOUNIS, 2 NOAH, 3 WOLF,
4 ELGAR, 5 MAYFLOWER, 6 MILLER,
9 SELES, 11 AMERICANS, 13 REA,
15 DEWEY, 16 MURPHY, 18 LANGER,
19 CALYX, 21 TEEN, 22 YOGA

No. 147

Across

1 FEVER OF THE, 8 CHEVRON,
9 OTAGO, 10 WHIT, 11 BONE,
12 HUE, 14 RAGLAN, 15 ACACIA,
18 ZOG, 20 KOAN, 21 JUPP,
23 ALICE, 24 CLINTON,
25 GOLDFINGER

Down

1 FLEMING, 2 VERT, 3 RANSOM,
4 FLORENCE, 5 HEATH,
6 SCHWARTZMAN, 7 LOVE
HAPPENS, 13 BANKHEAD,
16 CAUNTER, 17 SACCHI, 19 GUIRO,
22 MING

No. 148

Across

1 COUPLES, 7 DAVID, 8 JOHNSON,
9 LEUTZE, 11 EDGAR, 13 ALPS,
14 CAMERON, 15 ROME, 16 DANCE,
17 TEFLON, 21 MOMBASA,
22 WAITS, 23 RETREAT

Down

2 OBOE D'AMORE, 3 PENZANCE,
4 EROS, 5 CAPE, 6 PINT, 9 LIBRA,
10 ZAPPACOSTA, 12 EMDEN,
13 ANN ARBOR, 18 FEAR, 19 OATH,
20 NOME

No. 149

Across

1 SNIPE, 4 FAURE, 10 HOUSE,
11 LAROCHE, 12 FLINTOFF, 13 WATT,
15 ISCHIA, 17 GAUDIO, 19 COMO,
20 OLAZABAL, 23 OLIVIER,
24 BACON, 25 ANEKA, 26 CREPE

Down

2 NGUGI, 3 PRETTY IN, 5 ACRE,
6 RICHARD, 7 THE FLITCH OF,
8 CLIFF, 9 WESTMORLAND,
14 ZANZIBAR, 16 CAMPION,
18 ULURU, 21 BACUP, 22 PINK

No. 150

Across

6 THE TALE OF TOM, 8 WAXBILL,
9 NIGER, 10 RIAL, 12 KITTEN,
14 ZELIG, 15 LISTER, 16 ODOI,
19 CACHO, 21 ROE DEER,
22 THE IMPOSTERS

Down

1 JEUX SANS, 2 MARIA, 3 BELLO,
4 PFENNIG, 5 DOIG, 6 TOWER
BLOCK, 7 FRONTIERES, 11 HER,
12 KIM, 13 TO DIE FOR, 14 ZENOBIA,
17 KRUPA, 18 WEISZ, 20 CAHN

Notes

Notes

Notes

Notes